Radicalisation and Med

C000144844

This book examines the circulation and effects of radical discourse by analysing the role of mass media coverage in promoting or hindering radicalisation and acts of political violence.

There is a new environment of conflict in the post-9/11 age, in which there appears to be emerging threats to security and stability in the shape of individuals and groups holding or espousing radical views about religion, ideology, often represented in the media as oppositional to Western values. This book asks what, if anything, is new about these radicalising discourses, how and why they relate to political acts of violence and terror, and what the role of the mass media is in promoting or hindering them.

This includes exploring how the acts themselves and explanations for them on the web are picked up and represented in mainstream television news media or Big Media, through the journalistic and editorial uses of words, phrases, graphics, images and videos. It analyses how interpretations of the term 'radicalisation' are shaped by news representations through investigating audience responses, understandings and misunderstandings. Transnational in scope, this book seeks to contribute to an understanding of the connectivity and relationships that make up the new media ecology, especially those that appear to transcend the local and the global, accelerate the dissemination of radicalising discourses and amplify media/public fears of political violence.

This book will be of interest to students of security studies, media studies, terrorism studies, political science and sociology.

Akil N. Awan is a Lecturer in Contemporary Islam and the current RCUK Fellow in the 'Contemporary History of Faith, Power and Terror' in the Department of History at Royal Holloway, University of London. **Andrew Hoskins** is Interdisciplinary Research Professor of Global Security in the College of Social Sciences at the University of Glasgow. **Ben O'Loughlin** is Reader in International Relations at Royal Holloway University of London and Associate Director of the New Political Communication Unit.

Media, War and Security
Series Editors: Andrew Hoskins
University of Glasgow
and
Oliver Boyd-Barrett
Bowling Green State University

This series interrogates and illuminates the mutually shaping relationship between war and media as transformative of contemporary society, politics and culture.

Global Terrorism and New Media
The post al-Qaeda generation
Philip Seib and Dana M. Janabek

Radicalisation and Media
Connectivity and terrorism in the new media ecology
Akil N. Awan, Andrew Hoskins and Ben O'Loughlin

Radicalisation and Media
Connectivity and terrorism in the new
media ecology

Akil N. Awan, Andrew Hoskins and
Ben O'Loughlin

Millennium: Journal of International Studies
The London School of Economics
and Political Science
Houghton Street
London   WC2A 2AE
E-mail: millennium@lse.ac.uk
Web site: http://www.e-millennium.ac

Routledge
Taylor & Francis Group
LONDON AND NEW YORK

First published 2011
by Routledge
2 Park Square, Milton Park, Abingdon, Oxon OX14 4RN

Simultaneously published in the USA and Canada
by Routledge
711 Third Avenue, New York, NY 10017

Routledge is an imprint of the Taylor & Francis Group, an informa business

First issued in paperback 2012

Typeset in Times by Wearset Ltd, Boldon, Tyne and Wear

British Library Cataloguing in Publication Data
A catalogue record for this book is available from the British Library

Library of Congress Cataloging-in-Publication Data
A catalog record has been requested for this book

ISBN13: 978-0-415-64199-9 (pbk)
ISBN13: 978-0-415-55035-2 (hbk)
ISBN13: 978-0-203-82967-7 (ebk)

Contents

Illustrations

Figures

Tables

Boxes

Acknowledgements

This book is a direct outcome of an empirical research project undertaken between 2007 and 2009 led by the authors, entitled 'Legitimising the discourses of radicalisation: political violence in the new media ecology'. We are grateful to the Economic and Social Research Council (ESRC) Programme 'New Security Challenges: "Radicalisation" and Violence – A Critical Reassessment', which funded this project (award number: RES-181-25-0042). We are also very grateful to Stuart Croft, Director of ESRC New Security Challenges for his considerable support and excellent leadership.

We acknowledge the following who have all contributed importantly to the research outlined herein: Mina Al-Lami, Carole Boudeau, Dahlia Al-Lami, Ryan Al-Natour, Pierrick Bonno, Michael Dunning, Janroj Keles, Yannis Pappas, Catherine Somi, and Lene Mosegaard Søbjerg.

In addition we wish to thank: Olivia Allison, Lawrence Ampofo, Matilda Andersson, Cristina Archetti, Oliver Boyd-Barrett, Steven D. Brown, Andrew Chadwick, Maura Conway, Nat Dawbarn, Bill Durodie, Paul Eedle, Amy Ekins at Wearset, Marie Gillespie, Jonathan Githens-Mazer, James Gow, Ramaswami Harindranath, Rachel Hendrick, Christina Hughes, Athina Karatzogianni, Nuria Lorenzo-Dus, Lisa McInerney, Sue Littleford at Apt Words, Georgie McLean, Ces Moore, Greg Noble, Shawn Powers, Sheryl Prentice, Kumar Ramakrishna, Paul Rayson, Barry Richards, Johnny Ryan, Philip Seib, Caroline Soper, Tim Stevens, Paul J. Taylor, Jean-Louis Tiernan, Nur Azlin Mohamed Yasin, and Gillian Youngs.

Finally, for their professionalism and support, we are indebted to Andrew Humphrys and Rebecca Brennan at Routledge.

1 Media and radicalisation

Grappling uncertainties in the new media ecology – radicalisation gone wild

As part of her evidence to the UK government appointed Iraq Inquiry,[1] Baroness Eliza Manningham-Buller, Director General of MI5, 2002–2007, directly connected the UK's role in the US-led invasion and occupation of Iraq in 2003 to an increased threat of radicalisation in Britain. She stated:

> Our involvement in Iraq radicalised, for want of a better word, a whole generation of young people – not a whole generation, a few among a generation – who saw our involvement in Iraq and Afghanistan as being an attack on Islam.

This quote from Baroness Manningham-Buller's recorded evidence was one of a number that soon appeared on news websites, and in the national UK press the following day. For instance, the above quote was exactly how it appeared (in inverted commas) contained within a story on page 7 of *The Guardian* of the 21 July 2010, under the title: 'Iraq invasion radicalised British Muslims and raised terror threat, says ex-MI5 chief' (*Guardian* 2010). However, applying a modified form of conversation analysis to the video recording of this extract from the Iraq Inquiry (Box 1.1, below) the emphases and texture of Baroness Manningham-Buller's words and expressions can be illuminated:

Box 1.1 Modified conversation analysis transcript of the television recording of a short segment of Baroness Manningham-Buller's evidence to the Iraq Inquiry (*BBC News Channel*, 20 July 2010)

Our involvement (0.5) in Iraq (1.0) erm (0.5) radicalised er for want of a better word
[part laughs]
but [inhales] erm (0.5) a whole generation (0.5) of young people (0.5) some of them
[sits back in seat]
British Citizens–not-a-whole-generation (0.3) a *few*
among a generation (0.5) e- who
[gesticulates with hands held outward]
were erm saw our involvement in (0.5) Iraq on top of our involvement in Afghanistan as being an attack on Islam.

The timed (approximate) pauses (indicated with the timing in brackets) show the highly reflective pace of Baroness Manningham-Buller's talk. So, she can clearly be heard (and seen – she looked down for most of this part of her evidence rather than looking at the committee members arranged in a semi-circle before her) to be choosing her words very carefully. Her nervous-sounding qualification of her use of the term 'radicalisation' thus seems out-of-synch with her very purposefully chosen phrases, suggesting perhaps that this was a rehearsed ambiguity. In other words, the qualification of the term 'radicalisation' here is indicative of the term's wider ambiguous or controversial status.

The slipperiness of the application of the term radicalisation and the scaling of the threat it posed is also indicated by what appears at least to be a genuine (or that might even have been a rehearsed) slip (indicated by the Baroness sitting back in her seat and gesticulating as she tries to find the right qualification to her words). The correction of 'a *few* among a generation' after the suggestion that 'a whole generation of young people' had been radicalised by the UK's military involvement in Iraq, is indicative of the paradox at the heart of the UK media-political-security service inception of the term radicalisation in the 2000s. This is their characterisation of a terrorist threat from young Muslim men as potential terrorists that is ubiquitous, i.e. any one person could potentially be radicalised and thus pertains to a 'whole generation', and yet only 'a few among a generation' have been found to commit or plot to commit violent acts (in this context routinely described by the same media-political-security services as 'terrorist').

In this way, the use of the term radicalisation is an ideal extension of the media, political and security services discourses of the incalculable scale and other parameters of the threat posed by twenty-first century terrorism. Furthermore, this points to the minimal prospects for ever attaining precision in terms of the proportionality of response to or pre-emption of a threat conceived in such an imprecise and non-scalable term.

And what the extract above reveals is that the term 'radicalisation' no longer serves those who one would think were (at least initially) its very purveyors. And so, the former Director of MI5, who was absolutely pivotal to the former government's counter-terrorist strategy in which the countering of 'radicalisation' was a central plank, shows unease even in using the term.

Here then we can talk not just of the slippage of radicalisation in terms of its meaning and usage, but of its slippage from the hands of its former would-be masters. Radicalisation has been unleashed, it has, so to speak, 'gone wild'. And it is the 'going wild' of the central UK counter-terrorist agenda constructed around radicalisation, that this book takes as its problematic. This is not just a matter of the exploration of a set of somehow detached media and government discourses speculating and attempting to pre-empt the nature and varying degrees of the threat posed by terrorism and other twenty-first century risk. Rather, the emergence of radicalisation is a sign of a new pervasive mediatised condition of 'hypersecurity' (Masco 2006; Hoskins and O'Loughlin 2010a).

This condition marks a shift from a relatively institutionalised (i.e. via mainstream broadcast media) and ordered discursive regime of terror threats to one characterised by an emergent 'contingent openness' (Urry 2005: 3). And yet, at the same time, seemingly paradoxically, there occurs a reflexive institutionalisation of this very contingent openness of terror in and of the contemporary era through attempts to demarcate and control perceived and potential security threats by those charged with the protection of the many. It is these attempts to 'make terror at least governable' according to Michael Dillon, that spawns a 'radical ambiguity': 'western societies themselves governed by terror in the process of trying to bring terror within the orbit of their political rationalities and governmental technologies' (2007: 8).

Radicalisation, we are suggesting here, is both symptom and cause of the state of hypersecurity, which is an optimum candidate for what Dillon (ibid.) proposes, namely a 'double-reading' of terror. And so it is with the intangibility of 'radicalisation': it feeds a state of hypersecurity through the term's glossing over of any coherent and generalisable explanation in terms of why, when and how individuals become 'radicalised'. There is no reliable prescription that can account for the so-called 'journey' of stereotypically disenfranchised and disaffected young British Muslim men (or anyone else for that matter) from citizen to terrorist.

Moreover, the traditional targeting of an 'enemy' as previously understood as a meaningful requirement for the constitution of a threat is divested under the conditions of hypersecurity. Rather, it is more the case that the notion of 'enemy' has been replaced with the threat itself, something that Frank Furedi, for example, considers is 'a threat beyond meaning (2007: 77). Radicalisation in the UK but also elsewhere across Europe, has quickly emerged as a tangible, intangible threat, feeding into the radical ambiguity of the construction of and responses to 'terrorism' and particularly in the UK following the 2005 London bombings.

In what follows we interrogate the emergence and the mediatisation of radicalisation, as a discursive frame that has 'gone wild' in escaping the very parameters its deployment was intended to control, or at least be seen to control.

Box 1.2 Defining radicalisation

The OED defines 'radicalisation' as: 'The action or process of making or becoming radical, esp. in political outlook'[2] and 'radical' as: '*Polit.* Advocating thorough or far-reaching political or social reform; representing or supporting an extreme section of a party.'[3] In fact to trace a genealogy of the term is to reveal its application to having a certain strength of character, in espousing radical principles in UK and US eighteenth and nineteenth century politics, for example. Yet, it is in the twenty-first century that radicalisation has suddenly emerged in its least-benign form as a key concern of policymakers, security services, and journalists, notably as a threat to the stability and security of countries around the world. Radicalisation, to these groups, is often constructed as a *process* which a person (or persons) undergoes that *may* result in their committing violent, and moreover, 'terrorist' acts. Put another way: radicalisation today is seen as: 'The phenomenon of people embracing opinions, views and ideas which *could* lead to acts of terrorism' (emphasis added).[4]

To provide another example, this time taken from the Netherlands 'National Coordinator for Counterterrorism' (2007: 91):

> Radicalization is seen primarily as a process with some sort of start, and can end in the worst cases with a transition to terrorism. Indicating where radicalization starts and ends is not an exact science, however, and there are also a range of determinative positions.
>
> Again, the criticality of the 'end point' of radicalisation is in its resulting in a violent act. Given it is very difficult to attribute beginning and ending points and any other generalisable characteristics and effects to the process of radicalisation, its identification and pursuit as a security threat for government, directly feeds hypersecurity, as we have already set out.
>
> From the above definitions, the heavy qualifications are immediately apparent, and are indicative of the highly speculative nature of the discourses on security threats in the opening decade of a century already marked with what is often presumed to be a 'series' of terrorist attacks which have been intensely and extensively reported. To give just one example from the UK: Figure 1.1 reveals the sudden engendering of the term 'radicalisation' in the British press in its Islamic context. This followed the 7 July 2005 ('7/7') London bombings in which four suicide bombers killed 52 and injured more than 770 people in co-ordinated attacks in central London, and the attempted bombings again in London two weeks later. Yet radicalisation as a discernible cause of this or other terrorist atrocities at the same time appears to be tenuous at best, So, as the official House of Commons report into the London Bombings concluded, for at least three of the four 7/7 bombers, 'there is little in their backgrounds which mark them out as particularly vulnerable to radicalisation' (Home Office 2006: 26). The considerable difficulties in both identifying someone who has undergone a process of radicalisation and also those likely to become radicalised does appear to render the term as employed by those charged with counter-terrorist strategies and operations, as not particularly useful. What explanations are there then for the establishment of the term radicalisation in security discourses and what function does it perform and for whom?

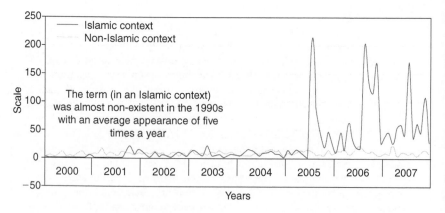

Figure 1.1 The term 'radicalisation' in Islamic and non-Islamic contexts in British papers 2000–2008 (source: al-Lami 2008).

The emergence of radicalisation: the new media ecology

The answers to these questions this book situates in the study of contemporary security in a 'new media ecology' (Hoskins and O'Loughlin 2010a; cf. Cottle 2006; Fuller 2007; Postman 1970). This is the current rapidly shifting media saturated environment characterised by a set of somewhat paradoxical conditions, of, on the one hand, 'effects without causes', in Faisal Devji's terms (2005), yet, on the other, a profound connectivity through which places, events, people and their actions and inactions, seem increasingly connected. So, for example, Hoskins (2011) identifies a 'connective turn', as the 'massively increased abundance, accessibility and searchability of communication networks and nodes, and the seemingly paradoxical status of the ephemera and permanence of digital media content'.

There are a number of cross-cutting and in some ways convergent accounts of the characteristics of the new media ecology across the social sciences and humanities. A resurgent term that is particularly useful in exploring the relationship between media and radicalisation in terms of the mapping out of its presence and influence in security discourses is the idea of 'mediatisation'. Stig Hjarvard is one of the most influential proponents of the term. He writes of the mediatisation of society itself and defines this as:

> the process whereby society to an increasing degree is submitted to, or becomes dependent on, the media and their logic. This process is characterized by a duality in that the media have become *integrated* into the operations of other social institutions, while they also have acquired the status of social institutions *in their own right*. As a consequence, social interaction – within the respective institutions, between institutions, and in society at large – take place via the media.
>
> (2008: 113, original emphasis)

War and conflict, education, business practices, family life and other social realms today, to differing extents, are not simply mediated (relations sustained via media as medium); they are actually dependent upon media and, consequently, have been transformed to increasingly follow media logics; they are mediatised.

Across much of the advanced and developing worlds there are few times and spaces that can be conceived of as existing 'outside' of the new media ecology. But across new media studies there are emergent a range of positions along an axis of mediation – mediatisation with different scholars positioning social, political and cultural phenomena as embedded in or subject to media logics to varying extents (see Couldry 2008; Livingstone 2009). Crucially, this also involves a broadening and a deepening of the definition of 'media' itself to include but go beyond that which was once subsumed under the generic 'mass media'. For instance, in their study of terrorism in the context of a 'new *memory* ecology', Brown and Hoskins (2010: 88) state:

'Media' … refers not only to formal broadcast media but also to the multitude of techniques, technologies and practices through which discourse and
interaction is mediated. In other words something like the entire 'semiotic
environment' in which terrorism is understood and made relevant to a given
community or group of persons.

Across these works we see a sense of a growing entanglement of media with
phenomena to an extent that their separate conceptualisation and study actually
misses the most significant dynamics of their production and impact.

Do these shifts towards an increasingly mediatised society actually represent
an acceleration of existing trends to which long-standing theoretical and methodological tools of analysis can simply be applied and perhaps tweaked? Or do
they represent a paradigmatic shift that requires a much more radical orientation
to a study of media. This is highly contested by some scholars and particularly in
the UK version of 'Media Studies' (see, for example, Barker 2006). The very
paradigm shift in the velocity, accessibility, and connectivity afforded by
advances in digital technologies, facilitates the phenomenon of radicalisation,
both its actuality and its discursive iterations, and of course that which comes
from the co-constitution of the two. Furthermore, where our approach is distinctive is in our demarcation of two 'phases' of mediatisation (following Hoskins
and O'Loughlin 2010a) to help illuminate the nature, extent and timing of the
shift. The first phase of mediatisation involves the forms, practices and experiences associated with the dominant media and institutions of the broadcast era,
and particularly television. The second phase interconnects and overlaps with
elements of the first, but is distinctive in that it requires a shift in how we
approach and formulate the very relationship we have with media. Notably, this
is owing to its much more immediate and extensive interpenetration with the
everyday on an individual, social and continual basis. The formal broadcast and
print news media are so thoroughly penetrated and affected by the digital in
terms of production, dissemination and consumption that they are no longer
separable as institutions of mass media, for they exist and can only exist in the
new media ecology.

The condition of hypersecurity emerges through a sense of connectivity to a
range of threats and risks that is suddenly and continuously available online, but
which is also mediated through and connected by so-called traditional mainstream media, but which also construct a sense of pervasiveness and an unknowable and thus uncontainable arena of all that which is 'out there on the Internet'.
The new media ecology is not a matter of old or new media, but rather it is the
environment through which media content and forms are 'remediated' (Bolter
and Grusin 1999) through both established and emergent media. Put another
way, radicalisation has been incubated in the cracks or fissures that have opened
up through a fundamental miscomprehension of the very nature of mediatisation
and attempts to 'govern' security, as we alluded to above, in the new media
ecology. So, radicalisation and those who radicalise and those who are radicalised constitute 'a threat beyond meaning' in Furedi's terms, above (2007: 77),

partly owing to inculcation and attempted combating through 'media beyond meaning'. Yet, at the same time, a kind of accumulative structural meaning is shaped by the 'non-institutional timeworld' of al-Qaeda members, for example (Knorr Cetina 2005: 222). This is facilitated by the information infrastructure through which 'global microstructures' (Knorr Cetina 2005) take on a particular emergent unity; emergent events can be rapidly assimilated into already-established narratives in a powerfully diffused way through the digital tools (blogs, social networking sites, videos) employed by amateurs as well as by 'official' al-Qaeda media productions. What is key here and significantly over-looked in the field is the relationship between global microstructures and their digital connectivities, and their representation in and relationship to the mainstream media, and this we argue is critical to understanding the dynamic workings of radicalisation in the new media ecology.

This book concerns discourses through which it is presumed people are radicalised: specifically, the arguments disseminated by al-Qaeda and other Jihadists as they wage what is, according to the British government, a 'battle of ideas' to win public support. But we are also concerned with discourse *about* radicalisation: the ways in which media, political institutions and security agencies represent 'radicalisers', 'the radicalised' and 'radicalising websites', how Jihadist media culture is portrayed and its effects conceptualised. It is the discourses about radicalisation, we argue, that are constituted by a consistent set of misunderstandings. Our main argument is: *Uncertainty about how discourses* of *radicalisation operate in the new media ecology is the condition for discourses* about *radicalisation to proliferate.* Discourses of radicalisation do not cause discourses about radicalisation, but media, political institutions and security agencies have responded in ways that encourage, sustain and at times exploit this disjuncture.

To understand how these disjunctures and misconceptions operate, it is useful to examine how 'Global Jihad', media and fear are assumed by academics, policymakers and journalists to be intimately connected.

Global threats: risk, fear and resilience

Modernity is defined by the creation by humans of problems they cannot control, argues Ulrich Beck (2006). Institutions such as science, business, and government may have brought advances in many spheres of life, but simultaneously they have generated new risks. These include 'side effects' of modernity such as climate change and the contagious behaviour of financial markets which can bring economic instability and collapse. But modernity also creates the conditions for intentional, deliberate harm from terrorism and the exploitation of social fears. From the exploitation of industrial logic for mass killing in the Holocaust to the exploitation of modern air transport for mass killing on 11 September 2001, modernity produces risks that can easily be transformed into catastrophes.

The relationship between risk and catastrophe presents a problem of knowledge. Contemporary risks are fiendishly complex, involving chains of causation

that are uncertain but potentially rapid. For instance, new communications technologies enable quicker financial market transactions, making regulation of
markets more difficult, making a crash more likely, which then has knock-on
effects on housing, social welfare, jobs; these in turn affect patterns of travel and
migration, which are a vector for the spread of pandemics. Simple cause-and-
effect models of policy become difficult: based on this chain, are better communications technologies a cause or a way to reduce the risk of pandemics?
Radicalisation looms at the nexus of risk and catastrophe. There appears to be a
risk that 'vulnerable' people could turn to violence under the general cause of
'Jihad', but there is very little grounded knowledge about how this process might
occur. What factors make a person 'at risk', and what conditions or influences
would make them more likely to 'tip over' into acts of violence? For example,
Githens-Mazer and Lambert (2010) analyse the lifecourse of two brothers who
shared the same upbringing, were both 'exposed' to radical materials, but only
one of whom went on to commit terrorist acts. The same explanatory factors
were present (ideology, social networks, political ideology) but the outcomes
differed. In studies of convicted terrorists, such factors are usually considered
causal, but as Githens-Mazer and Lambert suggest, these factors are 'present in a
variety of cases where individuals *don't* become terrorists' (2010: 895). Some
security agencies recognise the impossibility of objective risk measures based on
reliable models, but 'useful fictions' like 'pathways' to radicalisation or stereotyped imaginaries of 'loners in their bedroom' being 'radicalised through the
Internet' continue to circulate in public debate.

The objective degree of risk is in some sense irrelevant in public debates. To
point out that fewer people die from terrorism than from smoking or traffic acci-
dents is to miss the point. The emergent, cross-cutting forces of risk society
could lead to something not only *more* catastrophic but that also could occur
anywhere, at any time, to any society. It is this spectre of unknowability that is
the dilemma for anyone seeking to make sense of terrorism. It is the condition
for hypersecurity.

Beck's global risk thesis originated before the terrorist attacks of 11 September 2001. However, that date has become significant in public debates about
global risks to the extent that the term 'post-9/11' has become a meaningful
marker of a discrete period. We have witnessed the conduct of a 'global war on
terror', and the geographical pattern of Jihadist attacks appears to be reasonably
global in scope, including Bali, Mumbai, Riyadh, Baghdad, Istanbul, Madrid,
London, and New York City and Washington DC (Latin America and China
seem to have escaped). But this does not necessarily imply global fear has been
created. Rachel Pain (2009a) has conducted an overview of academic studies of
global risks and global fear and discovered that these assumed trends are questionable in key respects.

First, treatment of the concept 'fear' is problematic. Academics rarely talk to
the supposedly fearful. Numerous studies show the majority of Western populations suffer elevated levels of fear following terrorist events but these levels soon
decrease (Pain 2009b). However, for marginalised groups in those societies, fear

is felt at higher levels. While Beck (2006), for instance, points to the greater impact of catastrophes on the world's poor, he does not explore how the poor within Western societies feel continual insecurity. As Gillespie has documented through a series of ethnographic studies of insecurity in cities in the UK, fears and insecurities are contextual and localised (Gillespie 2006; Poynting *et al.* 2004). Emphasis on fear of 'global' risks such as terrorism comes at the expense of attention to other issues around which people feel fear. There is also a need to understand the fears of those whom people are afraid of: if media reports on terrorism continually reference 'signs' of radicalisation like growing a beard or attending mosques, how do people with those signs feel, facing the possibility that they make others afraid?

There is a lack of historical awareness in studies of fear. Pain writes,

> we might see emotions not just as blank canvasses, waiting to be affected by wider events and relations, but as … already formed and always changing … It was not dropped onto western countries following the handful of terrorist attacks since 2001.
>
> (Pain 2009a: 478)

Who fears who and what is a question demanding analysis of historical trajectories and relationships. For instance, we might ask whether fear of Muslims among white-majority Western societies in recent years is tied to colonial histories, where migrants are not only a reminder of empires lost, and atrocities committed in the name of empire, but migrants may also be perceived to pose the threat of 'reverse colonisation' (Gilroy 2006). Is fear of radicalisation a proxy for other fears?

The second major problematic aspect of the global risk, global fear thesis is the assumed global dimension or scale of fear. The very idea of 'global fear' posits a unified phenomenon, which may overlook the differentiated degree and experience of fear around the world. Who fears what may depend on gender, ethnicity, class, experiences and media consumption. Nor is it clear exactly *how* fear would become global. Do emotions just 'move' as if across empty space, or rather must we account for emotions being pushed and pulled through complex and uneven webs of social and material relations? How do news media or entertainment genres amplify or contain vectors of fear or sympathy forming around events?

In discourses of global risks and how these discourses travel, we must also ask how and why some processes or threats become understood as risks and some do not. This is not always clear in accounts of global risks. There is a large body of studies in political science demonstrating that certain actors in any society have the capacity to set agendas for what become recognised as public and significant matters-of-concern and what matters remain absent or invisible. But as far as global risks are presented, it appears that 'risks are determined in a level playing field' (Isin 2004: 219). What national and transnational interest groups benefit if we understand the world as constituted by certain risks? Just as we can speak of a Holocaust industry – the various cultural centres and academic institutes that depend upon and actively support the importance of the Holocaust – is there now a radicalisation industry, namely the think tanks, academics, private security firms, religious clerics and various other experts and consultants who provide diagnoses and solutions to the problem of radicalisation? To the extent this is the case, do journalists take this into account when introducing these figures during news reports? If not, journalists reporting on 'global risks' such as radicalisation may be inadvertently functioning in the interests of these groups.

We might also ask what rhetorical work is done by the label 'global', and what assumptions it suggests about how the world is constituted. For Pain, many studies assume an ontology of global and local phenomena, and that fear is part of global events which trickle down and are absorbed in local, everyday relations. To speak of 'global fear' is to assume a level of action and experience that is distinct from the non-global but that is subject to impact from global forces. The past decade has seen a proliferation of studies of 'the everyday', although it is worth noting while some reify this distinction by identifying an everyday level of social life within which 'resistance' to 'global' forces can be found and encouraged, not all make this move (Hobson and Seabrooke 2007; Langley 2008). Nevertheless, if academics fail to disaggregate actual experiences of risks, threats and anxieties then we may not expect journalists, under pressure in breaking news events, to question officials who may refer sweepingly to 'global' risks and threats.

Global risk discourses can also be questioned for assuming that fear and insecurity are bad things in themselves. We examine this critique next.

Is insecurity so bad? Are we not resilient?

The absence of studies of how people live with fear in the context of risks, an absence evident in the work of Isin and Beck, is significant because the resulting analysis or discourse lends support to notions that societies need support in the face of risks; that individuals and societies are *vulnerable* and need to be made *resilient*.

This discourse emerges around Jihadist radicalisation in the UK. Malignant 'radicalisers' prey upon 'vulnerable' individuals who are already Muslim or might convert to Islam; if only the individuals' families, communities or the state had helped them become more resilient and resistant to radicalising influences, for instance by helping them realise that the radicalisers misrepresent Islam or that British values are compatible with and complementary to Islam. But a similar discourse emerges around a society's infrastructure: transport systems, energy supplies, information and communication networks become classified as vulnerable entities which require intervention and management to ensure they are resilient.

The 2007 report of the UK Cabinet Office, *Dealing with Disaster*, claims that the 'central government's approach to civil contingency planning is built around the concept of resilience', though it does not define 'resilience' (Furedi 2008: 645). Is resilience a property of individuals or infrastructures, or is it the external factors that contribute to individuals or infrastructures being resilient? An earlier Cabinet Office report, the *Draft Contingencies Bill* of 2003, defined resilience as the ability 'at every relevant level to detect, prevent, and if necessary, to handle and recover from disruptive challenges' (op. cit.: 646). Here, resilience seem synonymous with emergency planning, conceived as something done by states in association with private, business and voluntary sectors, but not done by communities of their own accord. From this particular understanding follows prescriptions for the form of response – joint public-private expert-led practices – and a temporality of response: such risks are with us for the foreseeable future. They will not be solved, only managed.

Against this, Furedi argues resilience is the default condition. The aftermaths of both 9/11 and 7/7 demonstrate not only that people will cope with disruption, but that the organic ties that develop as people try to solve problems together generate solidarity that enhances resilience – independently of any state or expert intervention. His argument is supported by a review of empirical studies by Shalev and Errera (2008) of civilian responses to terrorist attacks. They note than in many cases, authorities now diagnose resilience in terms of whether populations suffer post-traumatic stress disorder (PTSD) following an attack. But defining resilience as the absence of PTSD is dubious, they suggest, since we all suffer and overcome many risks, dangers and challenges in our lifetimes such that the number of people without PTSD, i.e. people who are resilient, is almost everyone. Rather than conceiving resilience as the negation of something (PTSD), it must be defined as the presence of some capacity, such as the capacity to adapt. It seems Shalev and Errera's findings complement Furedi's warnings against a precautionary cultural milieu. So there seems a dichotomous way we can think about risk suggested by Ulrich Beck: 'The philosophy of laissez-faire – it's safe, as long as it has not been proven to be dangerous; and the philosophy of precaution – nothing is safe, as long as it has not been proven harmless' (2006: 10). For Furedi, the latter results in a diminished conception of humanity: that we cannot act or get on with our lives just in case there is a small risk.

The work of Shalev and Errera is important because much discussion of resilience, like the global fear discourse, remains empirically unsubstantiated. For instance, Furedi's argument about the construction of a 'culture of fear' depends on unsystematic selection of news articles that support his thesis, and use of opinion polls as evidence of the degree to which publics are afraid. As Bleiker and Hutchinson (2008: 19) argue, opinion polls and surveys are evidence of what people *say* about fear, how they represent their emotions. They are not evidence of fear itself, or any other emotion. It may be that fear and trauma cannot easily be put into words. It may be that we need to analyse how people's actions are modified, or not, because of fear. People may tell opinion pollsters they are not afraid, but fear is 'an emotion with embodied sensations and material implications. Fear inhabits people, and they, rather than ethereal, mobile or free-floating discourses, [should be] the subject of empirical and analytical attention' (Pain 2009a: 475). What is reported in news is evidence of a news discourse, which may be part of a culture but is not synonymous with it. Furedi's 'culture' is a series of representations. How might we step beyond the rather generalised claims of Beck and Furedi that propose a dichotomy of paralysing global risks versus resilient humanity?

What is required is a methodology that shows how global 'threats' like Jihadists are represented in media cultures by journalists and understood by ordinary people in different countries. It is the dynamic workings, the translations between and across – the remediations – of extremist 'messages', discourses, events and responses to events by a host of connected actors that require illumination to enable a critical inquiry into the nature of the phenomenon called 'radicalisation', its emergence and its consequences. And this basis for what follows here was developed through our 2007–2009 empirical inquiry 'Legitimising the discourses of radicalisation: political violence in the new media ecology', funded by the Economic and Social Research Council (ESRC) Programme 'New Security Challenges: 'Radicalisation' and Violence – A Critical Reassessment programme.[5] We devote the remainder of this introductory chapter to providing an overview of our empirical project, its objectives, methodology, and findings.

The empirical research project: New Security Challenges

Context

Research completed on phase two of the ESRC New Security Challenges Programme: 'Shifting Securities' by Gillespie, Gow, Hoskins and O'Loughlin (www.mediatingsecurity.com) (hereafter *Shifting*) identified a growing 'securitisation of everyday life' in Britain whereby the ritualised interactions of policymakers, journalists and citizen audiences constitute the 'media-security nexus' as a 'battlespace' of mutual disrespect and suspicion. This contributes to the marginalisation of British Muslims and is one of the many antecedents to potential radicalisation. These developments suggested that policymakers face a range of new and difficult challenges, at the heart of which is the legitimation of security policy to hostile and sceptical national and diasporic media that question key policy assumptions.

Our *Legitimising* project built directly on the *Shifting* research by adopting the issue identified as pivotal in the media-security nexus – that of legitimacy – and exploring its origins, function, impact, significance and, from a counterterrorist strategic perspective, its robustness, in discourses of and about radicalisation.

Legitimacy has repeatedly been perceived as the critical 'measure' of progress in the prosecution of the War on Terror (Kagan 2004; Reid 2006); its absence held to be corrosive of the efficacy of certain policies. Our theorisation of legitimacy in *Shifting* provided the basis of a conceptual framework for an investigation of radicalising discourses. But whereas *Shifting* focused on print and broadcast media in a primarily UK context, this project took the Internet as the centrifugal and transnational dynamic of the legitimising and the contesting of discourses of radicalisation in the new media ecology. In other words, *Legitimising* was not merely an investigation of the content of media and 'representations' of political violence and its antecedents, support and contestations. Rather, this project revealed the tensions and conflicts in the 'mediality' or 'medialogical significance' (Grusin 2010) of 'radicalisation' to an array of actors in an emergent new media ecology. Mediality refers to our relationship to mediation itself, and it is important to analyse not just how actors engage with events and issues reported on, but how they engage with the presence of such reports themselves, particularly given the increased scope for people who are not professional journalists to produce, distribute, annotate and adapt media content.

Legitimising explored 'Web 2.0' (second generation services available on the Web to which users can contribute as easily as they can consume) as the forum of choice for terrorists and for those intent on radicalising and recruiting individuals, groups and organisations to their cause. It is the collaborative and participatory potential of these web tools and environments that make them rich attractors of support, combined with their ease of creation, access and mobility (to other web spaces and at other times). Thus, Web 2.0 facilitates asymmetrical warfare, particularly with regard to a 'war of ideas', by allowing relatively insignificant non-state actors to compete with (and often supersede) state entities, whilst cloaking the personal or organisational security of those non-state voices.

Our work contributes to an understanding of the diffused prolificacy of the Internet which appears in a perpetually '*pre*paradigmatic' state insofar as there is no stable object around which a research paradigm could cohere (Hine 2005, emphasis added). Although we have moved beyond the stage of the treatment of the mass media as separate and separable from the 'negatively globalised' (Bauman 2006) setting in which contemporary terrorism operates, government and academia appear to be increasingly ill-equipped to address the pace and the seeming perpetuity of the technological transformations that have ensured the 'weaponisation' of media. Our aim was to make a significant contribution to an understanding of the connectivities and relationships that make up the new media ecology especially those that appear to transcend the local and the global, accelerate the dissemination of radicalising discourses, and amplify media/public fears of political violence.

Our approach was divided into three interconnecting strands of research undertaken by academic experts in different fields. The first investigated how Web 2.0 blogs, chat rooms, social networking and other forums were being used to spread ideas that might be considered to be radicalising in advocating political or religious acts of violence and terror, particularly against Western cultures and institutions. This work included exploring how these messages and acts published or broadcast on the Web were supported and legitimated. The second strand of research examined how the acts themselves and explanations for them on the Web are 'picked up' and represented in the mainstream television news media, through the journalistic and editorial uses of words, phrases, graphics, images, videos and so on. Finally, the third strand explored how interpretations of the term radicalisation are shaped by news representations through investigating audience responses, understandings and misunderstandings, through audience research in England, France, Denmark and Australia.

Instead of focusing on just one medium or event, we employed the three strand approach as a way of tracking and understanding how support for political or religious violence emerged and shifted over time across different media and in response to events considered as newsworthy in national and global news cultures. It is by integrating these three strands that an analytical grip on the nexus of places, events, people and their actions and inactions. We will now briefly outline the methodology we employed that contributed to this approach.

Methodology

We conducted a multilingual investigation of the discourses of radicalisation: their circulation through Web 2.0 and mainstream media, and their role in legitimating Jihadist actors, acts and ideologies. The new media ecology context for this research is one in which the availability and interactivity of a range of news sources contributes to a proliferation of (online) public–private spheres with loose and problematic engagements with mainstream public institutions and debates. The emergent and amorphous character of these communication networks demands innovative, dynamic research methods and conceptual frameworks, particularly in an investigation of their shaping of a new language of radicalisation including the mediated contestation of the divergent meanings of this term and thus divergent responses to the nature of the 'threat' it describes. We conceptualised these intersecting empirical strands through the 'nexus analysis' framework proposed by Scollon and Scollon (2004), which they define as 'the study of the semiotic cycles of people, objects, and discourses in and through moments of socio-cultural importance'.

We investigated radicalising discourses as dynamically configured through synchronic and diachronic mediated spaces and narratives and took key events as triggers for research across the three methodological strands. For example, the conflict in Gaza in December 2008 and January 2009 between Hamas and Israel triggered claims across all three strands: on Jihadist forums, members called on Muslims to fight for their suffering brothers and sisters; in mainstream media, news reported or speculated upon the potential for the radicalisation of Muslims in Western countries in response to media coverage of the violence in Gaza; audiences too were aware of the conflict, enabling us to evaluate the extent to which they were aware of attempts to radicalise or news media reports about the threat of radicalisation. Across the empirical research period (2007–2009) a number of triggering events enabled us to map how these 'cycles' of meaning around radicalisation were initiated, sustained, and contested, across both languages and geographic and mediated spaces.

The three strand approach

Strand A: Identify, map and evaluate the discursive legitimation of the culture and ideology of Jihadism in Web 2.0 and related emergent Internet forums.

The diffused prolificacy of the Internet poses a challenge for qualitative research, especially given the fluidity and ephemerality of much Internet content. This is particularly the case for Jihadist sites that are either closed down by anti-terrorist agencies or which shift or disguise their URLs to avoid detection. Our awareness of this 'hydraulic effect' whereby Jihadi content moves from site to site, allowed us to tailor our data collection and archiving processes. Our identification and selection of Jihadist websites and other content was initially guided by terrorism-monitoring sites such as Internet Haganah, SITE and MEMRI in addition to snowball and convenience sampling approaches. Other selection factors were influenced by the mainstream media discourses aspects of the project given our aim of tracing intermedial discursive flows. This includes, for instance, references to and listings of 'sister Jihadist sites' found on the ones initially identified, as well as the writings of prominent 'Jihadists' themselves who cited forums (e.g. al-Zawahiri on al-Tawhid wal Jihad site).

Our initial selection process identified a number of Jihadi forums as being relevant to the current study. These were selected on the basis of their popularity, hosting of extremist content, accessibility and credibility within Jihadist circles. These included al-Hesba, al-Ikhlaas, al-Buraq, al-Nusra, al-Firdaws, Shumookh al-Islam, Tawhid and Jihad, At-Tibyan, Islamic Army in Iraq, and Aljazeeratalk forum.

Having established the basic corpus for initial analysis, our researcher then applied for membership of these communities. The membership process is inconsistent across forums, and one that can range from being instantaneous to taking weeks for membership to be bestowed – in some cases, membership was only open for short periods of time or was never granted. After the initial period of registering for membership and cursively scouting forums, a new sample subset was identified based upon accessibility, popularity and relevance to our research questions. The research then focused on this subset and entailed:

- daily observation of forums in order to follow new stories, threads and patterns, etc.;
- mapping of dissemination routes for individual stories across forums;
- analysis of language, mostly Arabic, used: colloquial, standard, dialect, references to religious text, etc. Language is important as it could indicate the region of the author or member if using a regional dialect; the extent of his/her education and finally theological as well as political and historical knowledge. Language is very powerful in lending legitimacy or disqualifying its speaker or author;

- study of members including posting patterns, interactions, online identification markers (such as avatars, etc.);
- examination of archived material, particularly postings contemporaneous to critical security events (e.g. 7/7, etc.);
- observation of responses to ideological tracts and statements;
- analysis of Jihadist video production, with a focus on distinctions between producers, distributors and posters;
- analysis of Nasheeds and devotional music accompanying videos and their emotive impact;
- examination of legitimating tools on online forums, including religious/ theological aspects;
- translation and analysis of key statements and texts from ideologues.

All material was archived by downloading relevant multimodal material (text, videos, audios and images) saving HTML pages as offline content, and printing out (and filing) hard copies of pages and material of vital importance.

In February 2009, a substantial dataset was added to the project corpus of Jihadi propaganda material comprising of more than 50 websites and forums from 2002–2005.[6] This includes much of the original al-Qaeda website 'al-Neda' from 2002, and some of the most prominent sites during the early years of Jihadist media: Azzam.com, Khilafa.com, Jehad.net, al-Farooq, Ansar, Sawt-al-Jihad, Islamic-minbar.com, Mojahedoon.net, Waaqiah.com, Khurassan.com, al-Ikhlaas, Minbar al-Tawhid wal Jihad, al-Ansar News Agency, al-Mohajeroon.net.

Strand B: Identify, map and evaluate mainstream media representations of political violence and the uses of the term 'radicalisation' and its associated terms, contexts and discourses.

We undertook a multimodal content and discourse analysis of international television and online news images and stories recorded, digitised and transcribed, and coded these using *NVivo 8* software. Pivotal events analysed were: the July 2005 London bombings, June 2006 Forest Gate Police Raid, and the August 2006 Airlines Terror Plot. In accordance with the project's 'data-driven' philosophy we identified and analysed a range of news stories that have emerged over the lifetime of the project to date. Prominent amongst these are:

- The turn from Hizb ut-Tahrir to deradicalisation operations by Maajid Nawaz in September 2007.
- The conviction of Mohammed Hamid on 26 February 2008, found guilty of training men in secret camps in the Lake District and New Forest to prepare them to fight overseas.
- The Israeli military offensive in Gaza and the West Bank from late December 2008 to mid-January 2009.

For several of these stories, we undertook analysis of Arabic media and Jihadist media. For example, al-Jazeera and al-Arabia satellite channels on 7/7 and the planes plot and al-Ikhlaas and al-Firdaws Jihadist forums on 7/7, enabled us to follow the story's trajectory across media publics. This allows for a nexus analysis of the contours and content of a story as it moves across cultures.

> **Strand C:**[7] Identify, map and evaluate mainstream news public understandings and interpretations of political violence and the term 'radicalisation' and its associated terms, contexts and discourses.

We developed and extended the methodology of collaborative ethnography integrated with media text analysis and processes of legitimation pioneered by Gillespie (2006) and employed on the *Shifting* project. A total of 67 interviews were conducted by our research team in London, Aarhus (Denmark), Paris and Sydney. The population was broad, with news audiences of different generations, gender and faith. Participants initially recruited were part of the social networks of our team of ethnographic researchers, with further participants recruited through snowballing. In addition to the interviews, two focus groups were carried out, one focused on a specific episode of BBC's *Newsnight* on the Gaza crisis, another on citizens' anxieties around media technologies. The analysis of the interviews was first organised through their coding into *Nvivo 8*. Categories for coding were designed in relation to this strand of the *Legitimising* project and to other strands, to achieve integrated analysis across the project of key themes such as legitimacy, violence and visuality. However, close analysis was then conducted on the transcripts. This was informed by approaches to ordinary language and experience in the social sciences and humanities.

The central idea underpinning our audience research was that the meaning of radicalisation, like the meaning of any other word, is ordinary. Minimally, this means that there is no need for a specialised language, academic or otherwise, for radicalisation to mean anything; it is an expression belonging to the ordinary language and hence that makes sense within this ordinary language. Additionally, this idea suggests that radicalisation is used in practice and bound to its usages; it does not have a meaning outside its practical uses. In order to identify everyday understandings of radicalisation then, our interviews needed to afford opportunities for our respondents to connect this concept of the ordinary language to some people, activities and situations in order to render the concept a witnessable phenomenon (Coulter 1979; Wittgenstein 1967). The interviews were not organised so as to decide what 'radicalisation' ultimately means. This is not to say that all conceptions of 'radicalisation' are equal. Rather, ethnomethodology and the philosophy of ordinary language suggest that understandings and misunderstandings are tied to the circumstances of use of the term. Hence, interviewers did not ask for ostensive definitions and instead focused on identifying what is connected to radicalisation in practical situations of uses of the term.

Concrete examples were mobilised in the interviews in order to elicit reactions as to whether or not they can meaningfully be described as instances of radicalisation. In this approach, what was constituted as *not* being related to radicalisation was as important as what was construed as being related to it. Finding out what is not associated with it enabled us to touch the limits of the practical meaning of radicalisation: the moment when it disappears and when something else becomes relevant; that is, it allowed us to draw the boundaries between this expression and others. The analysis of the interviews was first organised through their coding into *NVivo 8*. Categories were designed in relation to those of Strands A and B in order to achieve the integration of the three strands of the project.

Results

Strand A: Web and Web 2.0 content analysis of Jihadi and related discourses

The ideological conflict that underlies the 'Global War on Terror' is being conducted almost entirely on the Internet's battlefield. Prominent Jihadist ideologues like Ayman al-Zawahiri, aware of their increasingly marginalised status vis-à-vis the mainstream media as a consequence of 'the media war on terrorism' have sought to legitimate their aims, goals, methods and tactics through the virtual realm in this ideological conflict for the 'hearts and minds of fellow Muslims'.

However, Jihadist forums, which are popularly assumed to be the principle vehicles for the propagation of the ideology and culture of Jihadism, do not ostensibly serve to legitimate Jihadist acts and thus their role in radicalising potential supporters or neutral publics is questionable. Instead, these forums are often exclusively closed spaces that seek to reinforce a 'group-think' mentality amongst committed members and thus are often proverbially 'preaching to the converted'. Indeed, key findings are:

1   They are hierarchically organised, with a highly controlled dissemination process that adopts a systematic, centralised, and controlled top-down approach in production and distribution.
2   This control over media has made Jihadi forums less interactive and made members mere recipients, and circulators at best, of Jihadi material, which is something of an anachronism to the revolution in 'participatory' audience roles heralded by Web 2.0.
3   Contrary to the established view that Jihadist websites/forums seek to radicalise, results show that most virtual forums exert no considerable or sustained effort in persuasion or legitimation of the ideology or culture of Jihadism.
4   Following on from point 3, there is little ostensive or meaningful debate, discussion, or dialogue amongst members of most Jihadi forums observed.

For example, a statement by al-Zawahiri or a new militant video would be lauded with a string of support, praise and prayers by members, without any critical engagement with the material in question. Consequently, words and deeds of Jihadists are accepted wholesale and go unchallenged.

Instead, the transition of younger, neutral publics from apathy to support has increasingly taken place in more open and genuinely democratising Web 2.0 forums such as blogs, open forums and file-sharing platforms, in which theological legitimation has been superseded by the appeal of emotive audio-visual material. Here Jihadist acts 'speak' for themselves through the 'propaganda of the deed'.

However, as these forums are often outside the purview of Jihadist leadership, they have had the inadvertent effect of undermining an ageing and weakened Jihadist officialdom (see below). This Jihadist core consequently offers little guidance or recognition to potential sympathetic audiences, who instead are often forced to turn to mainstream media such as BBC or al-Jazeera to find out what core al-Qaeda have been doing.

Global Jihadism itself has undergone something of a legitimacy crisis, particularly throughout the duration of our empirical project. Indeed, a number of factors are illustrative of this process:

1   Al-Qaeda has been experiencing a continual waning of legitimacy and a weakening of its support base, particularly as a result of revisionist critiques from ex-Jihadists (Dr Fadl, Noman Benotman, LIFG and so on).
2   The concerted attacks on Jihadist media organs and web forums e.g. downing of the forums and expulsion from YouTube and Facebook) from September 2008 onwards served to remove the principal platforms for the promulgation of Jihadism on the Web.
3   The growth of moderate forums that allow space for extremists to express their opinions and post their material (such as Aljazeeratalk forum) has proven effective in contesting and countering al-Qaeda's metanarrative and religious exegesis.
4   Al-Qaeda seems more likely to tailor its statements and plans, and perhaps future acts, in accordance with the demands of the Muslim public in order not to lose its waning support base. It appears al-Qaeda are bowing to Muslim public opinion, at least rhetorically.
5   Consequently they have engaged in public diplomacy exercises (such as al-Zawahiri's *Ask Aymen* exercise) with a view to engaging with a critical public and becoming more approachable.
6   Increasing use of testimonies of Western officials, analysts, and soldiers that are unfavourable to Western policies to enhance claims al-Qaeda makes.
7   Contraflow of Jihadist material/info; while Jihadist groups may be largely critical of mainstream media, the relationship is more complex; mainstream media are a source of material, and a platform, for Jihadist media products.

Comparative and historical analysis

Analysis of the additional 2002–2005 Jihadist corpus enabled insights of groups and websites banned in Britain today. This reinforced our already existing evidence of the ephemerality of Jihadist forums and the constant 'shuffling' of top sites.

The visual and musical aspect of Jihadist sites and material played a smaller role in the early days of Jihadist media. Multimodal features have become increasingly significant since this period, with the development and command of software and rise of powerful and more professional media wings. A key transformation identified in this respect is a shift from the production and publication of militant and graphic videos to an increasingly documentary-style and even 'glossy' professionalisation of Jihadist output, part of al-Qaeda's increasing focus on seeking legitimacy.

More credible and scholarly (even though radical) figures wrote regularly on Jihadist forums in the 2002–2005 period as well as being some of their prominent members. Members of early sites had titles of Dr, Sheikh and Imam. Today the writings of these figures are present on Jihadist forums only through members who post them (rather than their directly writing on the forum). This clear absence of credible figures among the membership of today's Jihadist sites is oft-reflected in current forums.

Strand B: mainstream media discourse analysis

We identified six key interpenetrating dimensions of the emergence and establishment of the term 'radicalisation' into the British politico-media lexicon across mainstream media discourses. Together, they make radicalisation present without offering certainty about what the phenomenon refers to. Here is a summary of these dimensions:

1   There is a routine **clustering** of terms, phrases and associated discourses (e.g. on paedophilia) by journalists, policymakers and security services, so that the term radicalisation has become part of the rhetorical structure of the waging of the 'War on Terror' with little reflexive interrogation evident of its distinctiveness, genealogy or function, in describing a 'root cause' of terrorist activities which thus requires a policy and/or tactical response (i.e. 'deradicalisation'). Such clustering affords a 'false certainty' to media reporting and commentary. The coherence of these clusters is questioned within the reporting of radicalisation-related stories by those identifying with the 'accused'. For example, following instances in which media identify a 'turn to religion' and outward appearances such as the growing of a beard as signifying radicalisation, these signifiers and claims are contested by members of Muslim communities within news reports.

2   **Uncertainty** is a key dynamic in both journalistic reporting and in the mediation of security service and government discourses on radicalisation. Eclectic elements (clustering, above) were routinely pieced together to form

narratives presented as constituting 'definitive' cases of radicalisation. In this process, less attention is afforded to the logical and the contextual coherence of the clusters. This leads to 'slippage' whereby apparently unrelated concepts – grooming, brainwashing, religious conversion – are conflated into a phenomenon that is presumed as coherent, in that audiences-cum-publics will understand as 'radicalisation'.

3   The language and clustering of 'radicalisation' contributes to a public discourse of **vulnerability** for British society. The mediatised representations and the contextualisations of radicalisation are hooked into a more pervasive discourse or continuum of the everyday and the exceptional, the normal and the extreme. This is apparent at the level of the mediatised construction of and focus upon the normalcy of those who are represented as having been 'radicalised'. Emphasis on vulnerability as a guiding concept could lend credibility to use of the antonym 'resilience' in policy debates which requires scrutiny.

4   **Mediality** is an increasingly dominant frame through which radicalisation (and terrorist threats more broadly conceived) are represented. The 'normal' or the 'everyday' is operationalised and blurred with the extraordinary, by journalists, through a connection made with publics' everyday media practices. Thus, from representations of the Internet as a medium of radicalisation, through to the self-shot home movie of the leader of the 7/7 Bombers, Mohammed Sidique Khan, bidding farewell to his baby, it is the mediality – the continuity and familiarity of these representations and acts with everyday media practices that has created a **new medial style** to the reporting of radicalisation and terrorism in a new media ecology.

5   **Speculative premediation** was found as an increasingly routine prism through which recent and ongoing terrorist and radicalisation news stories are constructed. This is the journalistic or 'expert' speculation on the scale, magnitude and the consequences of terrorist threats. Although speculation is a standard of journalistic discourses, we found that speculation around radicalisation had significantly greater momentum owing to the precautionary principle of reacting to potential threats seen as operated by UK security services (the 1 per cent doctrine – if there's a 1 per cent risk, you respond with 100 per cent force). So, when pressed to justify such precautionary or pre-emptive tactics, officials can necessarily only offer vague claims. These vague claims entered into and propagated a cycle of speculative premediation. By premediation we refer to how (television) news presented viewers with news they had *already seen*. In the first decade of the twenty-first century, the BBC offered regular drama-documentaries or simulations of security crises, with a programme each on a smallpox epidemic, transport catastrophe and terrorist attacks on London. Each of these 'premediations' was used to prepare citizens – and any policymakers, journalists and emergency response workers watching – for how a real crisis might unfold. Indeed, the 'London under attack' terrorist simulation featured the very 'experts' who were used for reporting actual terrorist incidents in the years

to come. This nexus of 'fact and fiction' articulated through repeated blurring of actors and formats constituted an official/media discourse which, Strand C data indicates (below), citizens found difficult to evaluate or engage with.

The media discourse uncertainty patterns around the nature of and the threat posed by radicalisation identified in Strand B, had particular resonances amongst our ethnographic audiences sample, as set out below.

6   **The emergence of security journalism**, a field of reporting which routinely focuses on terrorism-related matters such as violent attacks, apparent cases of incitement to violence, criminal trials, and interviews with former 'radicals'. In contrast to the large body of academic literature and popular iconicity of 'the war correspondent', security journalism is an under-explored but increasingly significant field of journalism.

7   **Jihadists are largely absent from mainstream media**. Breaking news events around radicalised violence are marked by an absence of information. Either officials do have information but are slow to release it, or authorities have acted on the precautionary principle and do not have any confirmed information, having acted in response to an imagined or presumed threat to which the consequences of not responding would be more catastrophic than taking wrong action. This creates a space for speculation about threats in general, and attempts to connect general theories to scraps of information about these particular events. We find discourses of risk, fear and resilience shape what is said and how the events are conceived, *not* Jihadist media content. Their legitimations of violence do not fill the breaking news information-void. It is only through the integration of our three strands of research that this disjuncture becomes clearly visible.

Strand C: audiences' ethnography

Radicalisation appears to be a highly contested expression in ordinary settings and does not possess the relative stability that it does in media and official discourses.

Its current contextualisation, terrorism, although seen as dominant, was also contested: in addition to events and people related to Islamic terrorism and extremism, the contexts of radicalisation refer to all forms of religious fundamentalism, left-wing radicalism, minorities' struggles against forms of oppression, radical thinkers, fascist ideologies and actions by governments and states (See Appendix II). Consequently, the interviews show that 'radicalisation' cannot be taken as a property of Islamic groups and ideologies.

For some, especially in France, the contemporary usage of radicalisation in media and official discourses was seen as a misappropriation or distortion of a term which used to engender much more positive connotations (i.e. to be 'progressive' and to be 'radical'). News media were seen as responsible for the conflation of this and related terms, so that 'radicalism' becomes all-encompassing and 'Al Qaeda' was seen to be the locus for 'terrorism'. There was concern expressed over (a) the media conflation of terminology and its generalisation to emergent acts of violence; (b) the legitimisation and/or increased likelihood of disproportionate responses of the security services; and (c) the impact this would have in encouraging others to act in a similar way but also an over-heightened state of response from wider publics. There is a correlation between negatively connoting radicalisation and expressing concerns about it, versus understanding radicalisation in terms of progressive, radical politics and being unconcerned. Twenty interviewees claimed to personally know people who have been through a process of radicalisation. In keeping with the range of contexts to illustrate what radicalisation is, these 20 cases display a range of settings, including religious fundamentalism, and right or left wing politics.

Reflexivity is needed for interpreting how and why interviewees offered positive or negative connotations of the term 'radicalisation', because interviewees are doing more than just talking about terrorism 'out there'. The disjuncture citizens understand to exist between official and media discourses and their own conceptions of radicalisation is typical of 'news talk' in which audiences-cum-citizens are addressed and understand themselves as part of what Scannell (2000) labels 'for-anyone-as-someone' structures of communication. Interviewees routinely spoke about concepts *anyone* would hear, but they also spoke as *someone*: as not-your-typical-viewer, as more cynical or independent-minded than others in the presumed news public they position themselves within. Such negotiations enabled individuals to establish or maintain their political identity and their sense of ontological security or control over their relation to the threats these discourses both represent and, inadvertently, constitute. This helps when interpreting apparently contradictory data, for instance in making sense of how a majority of interviewees could state they felt threatened by calls for violence such as 'Behead those who insult Islam', yet about a third of the interviewees thought that calls for violence may have some legitimacy. Such ambiguous positions make sense if we account for the identity work being undertaken by interviewees.

Such analysis of *how* interviewees talk about radicalisation and security, not just what they say, illuminates how they understand religious and political identity and affiliations: mainstream and marginal publics, dominant and subordinate cultures, vulnerable and resilient 'types' of people. This data, alongside Strand B analysis of the representation by media of its presumed news publics ('What you need to know', 'How this will affect Britons'), enabled us to map and compare how 'the social' is represented and constituted in and through mediatised contemporary security cultures.

A second point of intersection between Strands B and C concerned representations of technology as a source of threat. This was not an original hypothesis but emerged in the project's duration. Routine news representations of terrorism, identity theft and paedophilia 'over the Internet' contributed to some interviewees' understandings of radicalisation: that although they might not be familiar with Jihadist media or discourse, they experienced a diffuse awareness that the Internet could deliver threats and as such was at once both a useful yet threatening medium. A focus group was convened on this issue. As above, interviewees and participants suggested that *others* would be vulnerable to these threats, not themselves.

A third point of intersection between Strands B and C involved a focus group in which *Newsnight*'s report on the Gaza crisis was shown and discussed. Participants said it did not provide a balanced view of either the Israel–Palestine conflict nor of the nature of Islam. They all found the report to be of a poor journalistic quality and even a piece of propaganda due to journalists' uncritical representation of the UK government's position concerning the conflict and its alleged consequences on domestic politics, i.e. radicalisation of Muslim youth in Britain. The report was also shown at a Digital Media and Security Workshop we convened at the University of Warwick in May 2009 to academic and user experts who articulated similar critical positions. A future research priority we conclude must be to enable journalists to speak face-to-face with expert and lay audiences about why they reach such conclusions about the credibility and politicisation of security reporting.

The findings from the Danish, French and Australian interview contexts confirm the importance of national media and political contexts in shaping understandings of the term, rather than a transnational threat being understood in transnational terms. This complements a finding of Strand A that much Jihadist forum discussion focuses on national concerns and conflicts.

Summary

In this introductory chapter we have set out some of the difficulties in precisely defining radicalisation or finding a consensus as to its meaning. Moreover, it is this intangibility that has been ultimately dysfunctional for those who have promoted its usage, i.e. policymakers, security services and what we call 'security journalists', in terms of its reception by citizen publics. Radicalisation and its related lexicon may though have first served a function in terms of its obscuration of the nature, duration, extent or imminence of the threat posed by terrorism, and thus may have provided some initial cover for British security policymaking, if not just rhetoric, following the 7/7 London bombings. However, there is no doubt that there has occurred over the medium-term a thorough delegitimisation and devaluation of the term 'radicalisation' in media-security discourses, as is evident from their once most certain proponents and indicated by the extract of Baroness Manningham-Buller's evidence to the UK's Iraq Inquiry, with which we opened this chapter.

From setting out our version of the problematic of the term and something of its genealogy, we then outlined our new media ecology approach to the discourses of radicalisation as demonstrated in our two-year New Security Challenges empirical project. The following chapters provide a more detailed exposition of elements drawn from each and also across the three research strands (Jihadist Web 2.0 cultures, mainstream news discourses, audiences).

2   Legitimising Jihadist ideology[1]

Introduction

Al-Qaeda and the Global Jihadists have consistently invoked the image of an ideological battle as being central to the current 'Global War on Terror'. This ideological conflict is almost entirely predicated on issues of legitimacy, in which each side must convince supporters, neutral audiences and even enemy publics of the justness of their cause, the morality of their strategy, the legality of their methods, and the ethicality of their vision for the future. Echoing the hackneyed 'winning the hearts and minds'[2] dictum of Western leaders, al-Qaeda ideologues like Ayman al-Zawahiri have argued, 'More than half of this battle is taking place in the battlefield of the media. We are in a media battle in a race for the hearts and minds of our *Ummah* (community).'[3] The Jihadists have been remarkably prescient in recognising the centrality of the media to this battle, and arguably far more so than their opponents (Tatham 2006; Soriano 2008). In a letter to Mullah Omar in 2002, Osama bin Laden himself wrote, 'It is obvious that the media war in this century is one of the strongest methods; in fact, its ratio may reach 90% of the total preparation for the battles.'[4] However, as a corollary to this profound awareness of the power of the media, the Jihadists have also been pre-occupied by concerns over the grave threat posed to their movement's legitimacy, in light of its increasingly marginalised status vis-à-vis the mainstream media – a problem endemic to all terrorist or revolutionary organisations (Hoffmann 2006). This, Hammond (2003) argues, is a consequence of 'the media war on terrorism'. As early as 2001, al-Zawahiri appealed, 'We must get our message across to the masses of the nation and break the media siege imposed on the Jihad movement. This is an independent battle that we must launch side by side with the military battle.'[5]

To this end, the Global Jihadist movement have employed a range of legitimation mechanisms to successfully propound their ideology and narrative, and have engaged in a number of strategies in order to manufacture legitimacy amongst audiences in the Muslim world and beyond. Essentially, all of this frenetic activity has taken place within the confines of the new media ecology, as characterised in the previous chapter.

This chapter seeks: (i) to explore how aspects of the new media ecology have been employed to propound the Jihadist narrative and disseminate ideas and acts that fall under the rubric of 'radicalisation'; (ii) to analyse the strategies and mechanisms through which these messages, acts and discourses, published or broadcast in this new media environment are supported and 'legitimised' (the ways in which Jihadists convince others of their claims, and persuade others to adopt their worldview); and (iii) to assess the efficacy of these legitimation strategies on radicalisation of audiences of Jihadist material, exploring how legitimacy has been conferred upon, or conversely divested from, radicalising discourses.

Success and failures of the metanarrative

In order to understand how the new media ecology has benefited the narrative, it is important to first discern what actually constitutes this narrative, and assess its successes and failures prior to the emergence of the new media landscape.

When referring to this putative Global Jihadist movement, it is easy to inadvertently imbue the movement with an aura of ideological coherence and homogeneity that is not actually borne out by reality. Rather, the Global Jihad attracts a surprisingly diverse group of individuals, consisting of differences in nationality, ethnicity, language, culture, age, social background, educational level, economic status, religious affiliation, religiosity and criminality (Awan 2008; Sageman 2008; Brachman 2009). Indeed, in recent years, the Holy Grail for many in both counterterrorism and academia has been the identification of a socio-psychological profile of radical Islamist terrorists, which unsurprisingly has been met with little success.

Instead, the ideological cohesion within this eclectic cohort, which provides some semblance of uniformity, is derived from the alluring simplicity of the metanarrative itself. Thus the importance of the metanarrative cannot be overstated; it is the ideological glue that holds the movement together. This overarching narrative compels Muslim audiences to view contemporary conflicts through the prism of a wider historical global attack on Islam by a belligerent 'Zionist-Crusader Alliance', and in response to which the Jihadists claim to serve as the sole and crucial vanguard. This narrative, as Scheuer (2004), Lawrence (2005) and others have recognised, has remained remarkably coherent and consistent over time. Osama bin Laden's earliest message to the world in his 1996 *Declaration of War against the Americans Occupying the Land of the Two Holy Places*,[6] often referred to as the 'Ladenese Epistle', argued:

> The people of Islam had suffered from aggression, iniquity and injustice imposed on them by the Zionist-Crusaders alliance and their collaborators; to the extent that the Muslim's blood became the cheapest and their wealth as loot in the hands of the enemies. Their blood was spilled in Palestine and Iraq. The horrifying pictures of the massacre of Qana, in Lebanon are still fresh in our memory. Massacres in Tajikistan, Burma, Kashmir, Assam, Philippine, Fatani, Ogadin, Somalia, Eritrea, Chechnya and in Bosnia-Herzegovina took place, massacres that send shivers in the body and shake the conscience.[7]

The potency of the Jihadist's alluringly simple metanarrative is bolstered by the stark and unflinching certainty of its interpretational framework for events that might otherwise be perceived as inexplicable. Audiences perplexed, for example, by the fact that terrorist attacks on 9/11, carried out predominantly by Saudi nationals at the behest of a sub-state terrorist entity, nevertheless resulted in the invasion and occupation of two sovereign nation states, namely Afghanistan and Iraq, may be inclined to find coherence and meaning in the acute clarity of the Jihadist's framework for interpreting current events. Revelations of forged dossiers and patent fabrications masking ulterior motives for the invasion of Iraq in particular, not to mention perceived Freudian slips by Western leaders (most infamously, George W. Bush's unfortunate use of the term 'crusade'[8]), only serve to strengthen the Jihadists' reading of events. Exploiting these controversies in the lead up to the invasion of Iraq in 2003, bin Laden argued, 'the Bush-Blair axis claims that it wants to annihilate terrorism, but it is no longer a secret – even to the masses – that it really wants to annihilate Islam.'[9]

For the undecided, the manner in which the Global War on Terror has been conducted, in particular the damning indictments of the United States and Coalition partners in the light of torture claims, extraordinary rendition flights and the lurid excesses witnessed at Guantanamo Bay, Abu Ghraib and elsewhere, have further undermined trust and delegitimised the state-sanctioned interpretation of current events.

Other contemporaneous events, which ostensibly have no bearing on the war on terror, but nevertheless contribute to the perception of a faith under siege, reinforce the Jihadists' contention that Islam itself is being targeted. Actions ranging from European sartorial restrictions on Muslim women, to the deliberately provocative publication of Danish cartoons of Muhammad deemed offensive to Muslims; or from the withdrawal of financial and other support from the democratically elected representatives of the Palestinians in Gaza, to the rise in Islamophobia in the US and Western Europe (Gottschalk and Greenberg 2008; Richardson 2004), all work in favour of al-Qaeda's assertion of a concerted assault on the Islamic faith. The Jihadist movement has sought to gain traction from many of these incidents, for example in December 2009, al-Qaeda's media wing *as-Sahab* released a missive entitled 'Letter to My Muslim Sisters' from Umayma al-Zawahiri (Ayman al-Zawahiri's wife) in which she stated, 'The campaign against the veil represents the most intense battle between Islam and unbelief', no doubt seeking to influence the sentiments of many European Muslim women. Similarly, the Danish cartoon controversy has also been appropriated by Jihadists in the new media ecology hoping to capitalise on feelings of anger and resentment felt by Muslims across the world, in particular by the former head of the *Islamic State of Iraq* – Abu Omar al-Baghdadi, who offered a substantial reward for the assassination of cartoonist Lars Vilks. In an online audio-statement, he calls for the 'liquidation of the cartoonist Lars who offended our prophet … We announce a reward of $100,000 to anyone who kills this infidel criminal. This reward will be raised to $150,000 if his throat is slit'.[10]

But perhaps the greatest strength of the Jihadists metanarrative, is the fact that their Manichean worldview of believers and infidels; of a 'land of war' and a 'land of Islam',[11] is reflected, and indeed corroborated by the equally diametrically opposing dichotomy offered by their ideological opponents, from the infamous Bush dictum 'you're either with us or against us',[12] to Huntington's (1996) 'clash of civilisations' thesis. Indeed, in his 2004 *Message to the American People*, bin Laden alluded to this incongruous synergy, 'it seems as if we and the White House are on the same team', and that this 'truly shows that al-Qaida has made gains, but on the other hand it also shows that the Bush administration has likewise profited.'[13]

This reciprocity of legitimation is helpful in understanding why the Jihadists might have welcomed President Bush's election to a second term, or would endorse Republican Senator John McCain in the 2008 US Presidential election.[14] For example, one message, posted on the al-Qaeda-linked Jihadist forum al-Hesbah wrote: 'if the mujahideen want to exhaust the US economically and militarily, then victory for the impetuous Republican candidate would be an advantage because McCain would continue the failing march of his predecessor Bush.'[15] Indeed the complementary nature of this reciprocal legitimation was aptly illustrated when McCain's endorsement by the Jihadists was followed by the inadvertent admission by one of McCain's own campaign advisors, who suggested that a terrorist attack on American soil would in fact be a 'big advantage' to the Republican candidate's election campaign.[16] Consequently, the success enjoyed by the Jihadists in promulgating their ideological narrative has not only rested to a large degree, on the coherence and cogency of that very ideology, but concomitantly, also on the corroborative reciprocal legitimation of its ideological opponents in the West.

Bearing all of this in mind, it is not difficult to see why bin Laden's emphatic challenge to the *Ummah* to recognise the assault upon their faith, lands, and people, and to retaliate in kind, might strike powerful emotional chords with Muslim audiences everywhere. Indeed, the hundreds of individuals who have heeded bin Laden's fervent calls thus far, are surely testament to the alluring potency of this narrative. Moreover, the carnage wrought by al-Qaeda and its ilk, in places as far afield as New York, Bali, London, Madrid, Casablanca and Riyadh demonstrates in devastating fashion the irrefutable power of this message which compels followers to engage in violent reciprocity. This then has been the resounding success of the ideology so far.

However, although the Jihadists' may have enjoyed considerable success over the years in recruiting and mobilising hundreds of *individuals* to take up the banner of Global Jihad, and despite their spectacular terrorist successes, they have proven themselves unable to persuade wider audiences (namely the Muslim *Ummah* at large) to similarly accept and endorse this polarising worldview. Instead, the Muslim masses, on whose behalf al-Qaeda pretentiously claim to serve as this crucial vanguard, have remained largely immune to the cajoling messages of Global Jihad, with large swathes of the Muslim world in fact having repudiated the message outright (Pew Research Centre 2005, 2009). As al-Zawahiri (2001) laments 'we should realize the extent of the gap in understanding between the Jihad movement and the common people.' This then has been the patent failure of the Jihadist ideology to date.

Averting failure through the media Jihad/legitimising the narrative

The Jihadists themselves have long been cognisant of the potential ramifications a lack of popular support would have for their movement's longevity and indeed survival, as al-Zawahiri argues,

> the victory of Islam and the establishment of a Caliphate in the manner of the Prophet ... will not be accomplished by the Mujahid movement while it is cut off from public support. In the absence of this popular support, the Islamic Mujahid movement would be crushed in the shadows, far from the masses who are distracted or fearful. Therefore, our planning must strive to involve the Muslim masses in the battle, and to bring the Mujahid movement to the masses and not conduct the struggle far from them.[17]

The desire to legitimise the ideological narrative, and engage with and mobilise the Muslim masses then, has been precipitated primarily by the fear of the grave existential threat posed by the impending demise of their movement. The Jihadists have attempted to accomplish this by building grassroots legitimacy amongst the general populace, by mobilising public support, as well as continuing to consolidate their existing constituency, and we shall turn now to explore some of these legitimation strategies and mechanisms employed within the new media ecology.

The primacy of theological legitimation

As one might expect, historically religion has played a central role in the legitimation of Jihadist worldviews and discourses. Bin Laden's statements all begin with a highly ritualised invocation of God and the Prophet. Martyrdom testaments, Jihadist media productions, communiqués, and treatises are all conspicuously preceded by some form of religious sanctification. This is not to implicate religion per se, rather, religious labels are often misappropriated for violent ends; a practice that is neither new nor confined to the Islamic tradition. Moreover, religion has often been employed as a powerful mobilising and legitimising tool in ostensibly secular contexts too (Juergensmeyer 2004; Hoffman 2006). For example, even avowedly secular groups employing terrorism (such as the IRA, EOKA, or the Tamil Tigers to name but a few), have often relied upon a clear religious constituency as their support base. It should come as no surprise then that for Jihadists, who claim to be 'striving in the path of God',[18] and for whom Islam provides (at least in their own minds) the *raison d'être* for their acts of violence, the theological basis for legitimation should take precedence over all else.

The new media ecology has served to reinforce the primacy of theological legitimation in Jihadist discourses, particularly in the more regulated spaces occupied by Jihadism; the Arabic language roster of forums generally thought to be dedicated to the promulgation of Jihadism (*muntadayat*), and to a lesser extent 'official' blogs (such as the weblog of al-Qaeda in Iraq/Islamic State in Iraq).[19] These semi-official spaces appear to be steeped in religious symbolism, imagery and content, displaying an inordinate focus on scriptures and texts, and the valorisation of Islamic scholars or historical Muslim personalities. Similarly, many of the prominent Jihadist media organs within the Jihadist new mediascape also display explicit religious connections. In some cases, the religiosity is explicit in the very name itself, as in the case of the *Global Islamic Media Front*, whereas others have more subtle religious connotations, as in the case of *al-Furqan*, which literally means 'the Criterion' – a word used to also describe the Qur'an;[20] or the *al-Fajr Media Centre*, meaning 'dawn' but also being the title of the eighty-ninth chapter of the Quran. The content of their video and other media productions are similarly infused with religious elements, from Quranic verses emblazoned onscreen, to stirring devotional songs, and from the conspicuous use of religious labels to describe their enemies (e.g. as 'heretics', 'apostates', 'crusaders', or 'worshippers of the cross'), to depictions of men capable of brutal violence appearing serene in prayer and worship.

A cursory review of the most prominent Jihadist forums, such as *al-Ikhlaas*, *al-Firdaws*, *al-Buraq*, or *al-Hesba*,[21] also reveals an explicit association (and indeed preoccupation) with religion. The role of religion in Jihadist forums is particularly intriguing as the content, and therefore the putative religiosity contained therein, is generated (at least in theory) by a diffuse body of individual users. To illustrate this point we might examine the usernames selected by forum users which are often based upon companions of the Prophet, such as *Umar al-Farouq*; historical Islamic personalities, such as *Salahuddin al-Ayyubi*; or demonstrably Islamic names, such as *Saifullah* (lit. sword of Allah). Other identifying markers of forum users may also reference religion in some way – for example, user avatars may display the Prophet's black flag, or signatures may include verses from the Quran or sayings attributed to the Prophet. As forums are intrinsically anonymous environments, revealing little about users except that which they voluntarily disclose themselves, the conspicuous religious saturation of identifying markers is highly revealing. Moreover, the forum vernacular itself is imbued with a strongly religious hue; members greet one another, exclaim joy, elation, grief or praise using a standardised and strikingly religio-canonic language. Whilst the religious character of language is prevalent and indeed commonplace throughout the Muslim world, its frequency and usage here can sometimes appear to be forced and even ritualised, suggesting that membership of these forums engenders conformity through strictly regulated modes of interaction. Communication between members also displays religious undertones; members are overwhelmingly polite, respectful and even affectionate with one another, consciously displaying good *adab* (manners) and ostentatious piety. The language is also highly fraternal, with users referring to one another as 'my beloved brother/sister', reinforcing the strong impression of unity and solidarity encouraged by the Islamic faith.

As one would expect, Jihad provides the *raison d'être* for Jihadist forums; without the perceived need for Jihad and the attendant rise of Jihadism, these spaces would be rendered unnecessary. Curiously, however, the structures of many forums are arranged in such a manner that the 'Jihad' ostensibly only constitutes *part* of the forum's remit, with other sections of the forum being devoted to more patently 'religious' concerns. Other sub-forums, for example, may focus on aspects of *fiqh* (jurisprudence), morality, virtue, and religious guidance or the provision of *fatawa* (legal rulings) on a range of issues. This diversification of Jihadist spaces to incorporate various other issues pertaining to religion is partly pragmatic: these forums help members negotiate daily religious issues, ranging from diverse concerns such as the manner in which to conduct divorce proceedings, to the validity of dealing in the stock market. However, the focus on religious inculcation more generally has another more important ideological purpose too. From the perspective of scholars and ideologues, the legitimation of Jihad is an important part, but crucially, only a *part* nonetheless, of the broader ideology of salafi-Jihadism.[22] Moreover, the intellectuals of the Jihadist movement are understandably wary of the creation of a generation of Jihadists who understand little more than violence, but more importantly, cannot contextualise that violence as an unfortunate but 'necessary' aspect of the broader struggle, as opposed to simply revelling in the violence itself. Al-Zawahiri criticising the youthful Jihadist following of al-Zarqawi for their pre-occupation with bloodshed and brutality, wrote in 2005,

> Among the things which the feelings of the Muslim populace who love and support you will never find palatable, also, are the scenes of slaughtering the hostages. You shouldn't be deceived by the praise of some of the zealous young men and their description of you as the Sheikh of the slaughterers.[23]

In fact, many within the Jihadist movement are acutely aware that this diversification may also help to dispel insinuations from disparaging co-religionists that Jihadists are only obsessed with Jihad, at the expense of all else. The prominent role of religion in these sites, however, may not necessarily be anomalous, but rather may illustrate the uniquely Muslim influence of culture and religion even in the virtual universe (Bunt 2003). As Hoffheinz (2007) suggests, Arabic language websites are unique in that ten out of the top 100 have a decidedly religious orientation.

Legitimising Jihadism through religion

Whilst the fact that Jihadists utilise religion extensively within Jihadist spaces is patently obvious, it is the manner in which Jihadists employ religion within the new media ecology to legitimise their discourses, acts and narratives that is of interest to us here and worth exploring in greater detail. Curiously, although the

Jihadists may appear to be morally compelled to adhere to the Sharia and broader religious precepts, in reality this can prove remarkably problematic for them. In addition to general prohibitions against the taking of innocent life and fighting non-combatants or fellow Muslims (Kelsay 2008), the established rules of engagement for war located within the Islamic Canon automatically place most Jihadist acts outside of the ethical ambit of the Islamic *just war*.[24] Confronted with the overwhelming weight of Quranic injunction, Prophetic tradition (*Sunnah*), historical precedent and scholarly consensus (*ijma*), Jihadist legitimation strategies must then principally focus upon circumventing these religious encumbrances.

The manner in which Jihadists within the new media ecology deal with this quandary is largely dependent upon two factors: (i) their background and competency in issues of religion and theology; and (ii) their interest in religion and/ or their levels of personal piety. These variables allow us to suggest three putative attitudinal motifs vis-à-vis religion and theological legitimation.

(a) **Self-aggrandising:** These include forum administrators and the top tier of forum members who often display little distinction from Jihadist ideologues and leadership in terms of the confident and self-aggrandising manner in which they approach issues of theological legitimation. These individuals are often fairly well versed in religion or, crucially, can at least give the distinct impression that they are (parts of the new media ecology are widely hailed as enabling self-empowerment). Nevertheless, the apparent degree of religious learning does not necessarily always correlate with levels of respect and authority within the hierarchy. For example, Abu Muhammad Asem al-Maqdisi, who is regarded by many as 'the most influential living Jihadi theorist ... and the key contemporary ideologue in the Jihadi intellectual universe',[25] has on a number of occasions been disdainfully criticised by many young Jihadist forum members more supportive of al-Zarqawi's bloody methods.

The conspicuous similarity between the views of Jihadist leadership and forum administrators/senior members may not be accidental, and in fact may be a consequence of the mechanics of Jihadist media processes. For example, the transmission of media from within the 'field' to the wider new media ecology involves processes of editing, incorporation of visual effects, subtitles and logos, and other stages of post-production, before the final end product is uploaded to the virtual environment. The hierarchical and strictly regulated processes of media dissemination on Jihadist forums (Kimmage 2008; Awan and al-Lami 2009) lead us to speculate that a number of the individuals involved in these processes downstream, may be involved in other aspects of the media strategy too.

(b) **Deferential:** The vast majority of forum users do not appear to have sufficient competency in religious subjects, and by extension appear to be far less sophisticated ideationally when compared to the previous group. Nevertheless, they still consider themselves to be staunch adherents of the

Salafi-Jihadist ideology, and fully recognising their 'theological inadequacy' in a fairly self-effacing way, they either display strongly deferential attitudes to more senior members, or pedantically cite Jihadist ideologues on issues of legitimation. In cases where they propound viewpoints on issues of religion or legitimation, they are often careful to attribute these views to 'higher authorities'.

(c) **Ambivalent:** The final motif includes individuals who are not particularly knowledgeable in matters of religion, but crucially for whom religion is not a particularly strong motivator either. It may seem strange to casual observers that Jihadists could be anything other than pious, devoutly religious individuals whose every action hinges on religious considerations. However, one of the enduring contradictions of Jihadism has been the theological illiteracy of many of its adherents (Awan 2007a; Roy 2004). These individuals are far more likely to be attracted to other facets of the 'Jihad' and/or political considerations. This is not to suggest that they do not also employ the 'religio-canonic' lingua franca of Jihadist spaces. This category is far less well represented in Jihadist forums than the previous two, but that does not necessarily imply that they do not make up a significant segment of the Jihadist constituency more generally. Rather, they favour occupying alternative spaces within the new media ecology that do not necessarily expose their perceived weaknesses of faith and religious acumen, or which cater to their specific skill-sets. Consequently these individuals will be considerably more comfortable occupying more generic third tier Islamic or youth forums, or social networking sites and file-sharing platforms (see Chapter 3). If they do inhabit Jihadist forums, they are likely to do so as spectators rather than contributing in any substantial manner to the forum's content.

With this audience stratification in mind, we can return to the Jihadists' dilemma posed by the dissonance between Jihadist actions and Islamic ethical and legal considerations, and examine some of the legitimation strategies that have attempted to circumvent these religious encumbrances. Those individuals that ostensibly command sufficient knowledge of Islamic sources (or once again can claim to do so), most commonly engage in processes of eclectic and ad hoc self-legitimation, employing a highly selective reading of the Quran and prophetic traditions. For example, the Global Jihadists' employment of the Quran to bolster their claims is extremely narrow in its focus and revolves around a subset of less than 75 verses from the Quran's total 6,236 verses. In fact, many of these verses are used partially, and without reference to preceding or following verses which may alter the meaning, or attenuate the injunction to engage in violence considerably.[26] Moreover, these selective religious excerpts are deployed both ahistorically and *sans* context, or without reference to traditional exegetical concepts, such as *naskh* (abrogation), *asbāb al-nuzūl* (the contexts of revelation), or chronological cognisance (particularly vis-à-vis the Meccan and Madinan verses). Unfettered by respect for traditional authority and established learning, or methodological considerations, neo-Jihadists are then free to dispute main-stream interpretations, or indeed formulate novel interpretations that violate clear tenets of Islam, for example, in the unlawful targeting of civilians.[27]

For both these individuals and those with lower levels of religious profi-ciency, this highly skewed reading of the Islamic Canon is reinforced, and indeed exacerbated, by the recourse to quasi-religious 'authorities' who serve to corroborate these aberrant worldviews. Remarkably, these 'religious' authorities are themselves rarely trained in the classical religious sciences and therefore unqualified to pronounce religious edicts or engage in serious exegesis of the Quran and other religious texts. A small number of these conferrers of theologi-cal legitimacy are themselves occupants of the new media ecology, with some indeed acting solely within these spaces. A number of these individuals have even managed to garner considerable prestige in recognition of their presumed religious acumen, being granted honorific titles such as *sheikh*, and include well-known Jihadist forum personalities like Sheikh Abu Abd ar-Rahman al-Yafi and Sheikh Abu Ahmed Abd ar-Rahman al-Masri. The appropriation of religious authority by those perhaps undeserving of it, is made considerably easier by the inherently anonymising nature of the Internet, in which individuals can readily create or assume convincing identities, as many in the security services have dis-covered to their benefit.[28] The widespread availability of searchable databases of the Quran, Hadith collections, *tafsir* (commentary), and the wider democratisa-tion of Islamic knowledge facilitated by the Internet more generally (Bunt 2003), allow novices, the laity and the uninitiated to engage in religious debates with a level of sophistication and competency that belies their more modest back-grounds. A question or comment posed on a forum allows virtually anyone to formulate a considered and erudite response that benefits from extensive open source research online, giving rise to the phenomena of the instant Web expert.

Nevertheless, despite the presumed egalitarian and democratising nature of new media (Castells 2009; Bunt 2003), conducive to the 'levelling' of hierar-chies of knowledge and power, the principle source of theological legitimation and authority remain with the 'traditional' Jihadist ideologues and leadership.[29] However, somewhat surprisingly, these individuals often mirror the startling lack of religious credentials found amongst Jihadist demagogues within the new media ecology more generally. In fact, the absence of religious legitimacy has long been recognised amongst Jihadist leadership, and in whom it continues to be glaringly conspicuous by its absence. Indeed, the vast majority of Jihadist ideologues have undergone modern secular educations, for example, bin Laden studied civil engineering; both al-Zawahiri and Sayyid Imam al-Sharif (one of the founding members of al-Qaeda) studied medicine; Abu Mus'ab al-Suri (the most important strategist of modern Jihadism) and Khalid Sheikh Mohammed (the principal architect of the 9/11 attacks) both studied mechanical engineering; Mohammed Atef (the former military chief of al-Qaeda) was an agricultural engineer and later a policeman; Abd al-Salam Faraj (who wrote the highly influ-ential Jihadist primer, *The Neglected Duty*) was an electrician; Abu Musab al-Zarqawi (the former head of al-Qaeda in Iraq) did not even manage to complete his high school education. Indeed, even Sayyid Qutb, often regarded as the ideological godfather of Jihadism, was a journalist and literary critic.

This fact is not lost on the Jihadists themselves, and thus efforts to adorn themselves in the regalia of religion, most recognisably in their impeccable white robes, pious beards and saintly turbans seen in Jihadist media productions, alongside the employment of a superfluously religio-canonic rhetoric, can serve to cloak what are often highly political or worldly aims, as part of the compensatory mechanism for this theological illiteracy. Moreover, the lack of religious credentials do not necessarily divest Jihadist leadership of this religious mantle, as these quasi-scholars may be considered eminently more trustworthy, more genuine, and more rightly guided than bona fide 'mainstream' scholars, who are perceived instead to have been tainted by complicity with and subservience to secular or despotic regimes. Indeed, the pariah status of individuals like bin Laden grants them autonomy from the political machinations, internecine conflicts and 'worldly' affairs within which mainstream scholars are seen to be embroiled, yielding a potent legitimacy not based on scholarly erudition (Awan 2007a). Consequently, and despite the token reverence afforded to religious validation in the Jihadist new mediascape, the theological illiteracy of Jihadist leaders can be readily compensated for by a presumed level of probity, personal piety and unflinching commitment to the cause.

In some respects, the broader strategies of theological legitimation have changed little in the new media ecology. Legitimation remains inordinately focused on elevating the Lesser Jihad[30] to an individual duty,[31] and indeed an obligatory sixth pillar of Islam (Bonner 2006). These attempts at extolling the virtues of Jihad and convincing fellow Muslims of its centrality to their lives are not new, but rather follow the tone and precedent set by earlier militant works written in the 1970s and 1980s. The most important amongst these included the widely acclaimed *Defense of the Muslim Lands: The First Obligation after Faith* (1979) and *Join the Caravan* (1987) penned by the Palestinian scholar and chief proponent of the Afghan Jihad against the USSR, Sheikh Abdullah Azzam; and the seminal Jihadist diatribe against the established Sunni position on Jihad, *The Neglected Duty* (1981), written by Abd as-Salam Faraj, an electrician and leader of the Egyptian Islamic Jihad group responsible for the assassination of President Anwar Sadat in 1981.[32]

If the Jihadists can successfully persuade audiences in the new media ecology that they are somehow lax in their religious observances as Muslims, or worse, are committing grave sins, they may be capable of engendering a mindset amenable to the broader Jihadist worldview. Mohammed Siddique Khan, the ringleader of the 7/7 London bombers, provides a typically bullying harangue in his posthumously released 'martyrdom testament' video from 2005, produced by al-Qaeda's premier media production wing *as-Sahab*, stating, 'Jihad is an obligation on every single one of us, men and women, and by staying at home you are turning your backs on Jihad which is a major sin.'[33] However, despite the banal exhortation to Jihad, there is no real attempt to convince others that Jihad is indeed an obligation; instead this is presumed to be self-evident. Indeed the seemingly axiomatic obligatory nature of Jihad has been the single most recurring theme amongst Jihadists in the new media ecology. In fact, bin Laden predicated his infamous 1998 'fatwa' on the notion that defensive Jihad as an individual duty was incontestable, invoking authentic historical religious author-ities to pre-emptively silence any dissenting voices,

> Religious scholars throughout Islamic history have agreed that Jihad is an individual duty when an enemy attacks Muslim countries. This was related by the Imam ibn Qudama in *The Resource*, by Imam al-Kisa'i in *The Marvels*, by al-Qurtubi in his exegesis, and by the Sheikh of Islam [ibn Taymiyyah] when he states in his chronicles that 'As for fighting to repel an enemy, which is the strongest way to defend freedom and religion, it is agreed that this is a duty. After faith, there is no greater duty than fighting an enemy who is corrupting religion and the world.'[34]

However, for the Jihadists, it is not simply a case of legitimising the concept of militaristic Jihad, or the obligatory nature of defensive Jihad, which is ostensibly a straightforward task and fairly uncontentious; but also legitimising that which actually constitutes the *ambit* of Jihad. Whilst the former has remained fairly static over time, it is the latter that has been constantly reinterpreted and rein-vented by successive generations of Jihadists, in order to legitimate varying degrees of political violence. For Abdullah Azzam, the seminal philosopher-theologian of the Afghan Jihad against the Soviet Union, Jihad was only permis-sible in *defence* of land which had at some point in its history fallen under Muslim sovereignty. Moreover, the Jihad itself would be ordinarily conducted as conventional or guerrilla-type warfare in recognised theatres of conflict, against military or state targets. Despite Azzam's own considerable scholarly creden-tials, he nevertheless sought out (and received) religious sanction for his fatwa legitimising Jihad against the Russians from prominent Saudi *ulama* (religious scholars) before its publication.

In stark contrast, the Jihad espoused by bin Laden, which in many cases has been reduced to indiscriminate terrorism against civilian targets, bears very little resemblance to the violence sanctioned by Sheikh Azzam. For example, bin Laden's notorious 1998 'fatwa' egregiously reads, 'We pronounce to all Muslims the following judgment: To kill the American and their allies – civilians and military – is an individual duty incumbent upon every Muslim in all countries.'[35]

Moreover, whilst bin Laden similarly sought validation in the mid 1990s from the grand *mufti* of Saudi Arabia, Sheikh Abdul-Aziz bin Baz, his appeal was instead met with derision, with bin Laden being denounced in highly derogatory terms as a *Kharijite*.[36]

It is important to understand how far the ideology of Global Jihadism has diverged from Azzam's pronouncements on Jihad, particularly as Azzam's seminal importance to the Jihadist movement cannot be overstated. As an early teacher and mentor to Osama bin Laden, he first convinced the young Saudi millionaire along with hundreds of other Arab volunteers to lend their services to the Afghan Jihad. Moreover, Azzam established the *Maktab al-Khidmat*, a guest house for the foreign mujahideen, and according to some authorities even coined the theoretical conception of *al-Qaeda al-Sulba*, or the 'firm base' for the mujahideen vanguard, from which the global Jihad could then be waged (Bergen 2006; Lawrence 2006). Indeed, Azzam's crucial status amongst the Jihadists is perhaps best illustrated by bin Laden's hagiographic eulogy, 'Sheikh Abdullah Azzam was not an individual, but an entire nation unto himself. Muslim women have proven themselves incapable of giving birth to a man like him after he was killed.'[37]

Nevertheless, despite these reverent tributes, and despite having laid the ideological foundations for Global Jihadism, the conception of Jihad espoused by Abdullah Azzam often appears diametrically opposed to the actions masquerading as Jihad under the guise of Global Jihadism today.

Framing strategies for dealing with the dissonance in the new media ecology

Recognising this dissonance is central to understanding the manner in which the 'neo Jihad' has been legitimised in the new media ecology. Whilst bin Laden and other assorted neo-Jihadists may unctuously assert that in the event of attack or occupation, defensive Jihad is a religious obligation on every Muslim, this is a premise that is unlikely to be 'religiously' contested, and therefore requires little theological validation. Rather it is the discordance between the classical views and the neo-global views of the nature and form that the Jihad assumes that is most likely to be impugned and thus poses the greatest legitimation challenge for Jihadism today. Morally repugnant actions such as the wanton killing of fellow Muslims,[38] the targeting of non-combatants more generally, the instigation of bloody sectarian strife (as in the case of Iraq), the use of suicide bombings, reprehensible strategies of recruitment,[39] and internecine feuds amongst the Jihadists themselves, cannot easily be subsumed under the sanctifying rubric of a legitimate 'holy struggle'. Indeed, these actions are the most likely to be contested by opponents and thus Jihadists must mitigate the dissonance engendered by these contradictions if they are to legitimise their movement for their existing constituency, as well as successfully radicalise others within the new mediascape.

These endeavours are essentially enabled by strategies of framing/frame-setting; the practice of disseminating and presenting information in certain ways, through preferential selection, emphasis and exclusion, that furnish an internally coherent interpretation and evaluation of events, texts, acts or discourses, and therefore aid in the manipulation of audience opinion. According to Entman (1993: 52), to frame is to select some aspects of a perceived reality and make them more salient in such a way as to promote a particular moral evaluation. These practices have long been recognised as part of the news media paradigm, being particularly associated with the shaping of public opinion (Entman 2004;

Chyi and McCombs 2004). Through framing, Jihadists provide audiences with a schema for interpreting events, through selection and salience, and these practices can have an inordinate influence on the way in which audiences come to understand those events.[40]

The least sophisticated strategy is to simply divert attention from major failings by reference to successes. The practice, often known as 'priming' is well understood within political circles, and refers to attempts by politicians to be associated with issues on which they have the strongest reputation (Iyengar and Kinder 1987). Politicians and their 'media proxies', can thus 'prime' opinions and evaluations of political leaders and policy through the preferential selection of news stories, to the detriment of others.

Through this process of priming then, Jihadists can gloss over contradictions and inconsistencies by focusing efforts instead on highlighting only those acts and discourses that are deemed to be free of controversy, and consequently display without equivocation, the integrity, strength and success of the Jihadists. For example, a video of *Juba the sniper*[41] posted online by the *Islamic State of Iraq* in 2005, which cleverly mimics the reticle of a sniper's telescopic sight, shows the highly adept killing of a heavily armed US marine whilst he stands beside an Iraqi traffic policeman, who is left intentionally unharmed. The message imparted to audiences is clear: the Jihadists are professional soldiers who only engage legitimate enemy combatants in legitimate theatres of conflict, and in a highly discriminatory and even humane manner. Juba in fact is renowned for his highly discerning 'one-shot' kills in which the victim dies relatively quickly – a particularly pertinent point when juxtaposed against the excruciatingly slow and painful deaths of the unfortunate victims of 'video beheadings', as popularised by the likes of al-Zarqawi. Even the Jihadists' harshest critics would grudgingly concede that this is not an unfair depiction of events in this particular instance. Generally, most Jihadists acts and operations carried out against occupying military forces, and employing conventional modes of warfare can potentially be framed and portrayed in this manner. These actions represent the pinnacle of Jihadist operations (particularly if the combatants are killed during the course of battle and can be hailed as 'martyrs'), and in which the valour, upright conduct and self-sacrifice of the Jihadists becomes patently manifest and incontrovertible, even by their enemies' standards. Unsurprisingly, the propagandistic value inherent in productions of this nature is immense, and whilst this may constitute the least sophisticated strategy, it is nevertheless the most difficult to counter as the actions are largely beyond censure.

However, not all Jihadist acts appear to be so idealistic or free from reproach, and thus propagandists must find alternative modes of legitimation for actions that may invite criticism or contestation, and in particular, those that might fall under the rubric of terrorism. In such cases, Jihadists may for example, in order to obscure facts and thus manipulate public opinion, conveniently omit events and facts that might depict their actions in a pejorative light, focusing instead on what they perceive to be the more laudatory, or commendable aspects. We might illustrate this practice by examining a recent *as-Sahab* video production documenting a suicide bombing by the *Islamic State of Iraq*. The video, like many others of the genre, begins with a biographical focus on the persona of the 'living martyr' (*al-shaheed al-hayy*), highlighting his piety, steadfastness, calm demeanour and composure prior to the operation. The camera follows his final preparations, recording a brief but stirring valedictory message before he bids farewell to his colleagues. The camera then switches to an eerily quiet scene only to be abruptly punctuated by the tremendous explosion itself, which is then replayed from multiple viewing angles and accompanied by stirring devotional songs. The video ends without revealing the true consequences of the bombing, save for an exultant message informing the audience that their 'brother achieved martyrdom' in a 'heroic operation against the apostate regime'. The video and attendant commentary, however, do not reveal the rather inconvenient fact that the bombing claimed the lives of scores of civilian bystanders alongside the intended victims, new Iraqi police recruits. Nor does the video show the after-math of the attack or the grotesque carnage wrought in which the faintly discern-ible body parts of innocent bystanders litter the streets amongst the burning wreckage of the destroyed vehicle. Thus the *as-Sahab* video employs a highly distorting prism to depict the event in a manner that omits important factual ele-ments that would no doubt present profound challenges to the legitimation of such actions.

The Jihadists' attempts to propound their narrative, ideology, acts and dis-courses through framing, priming and various other means, have also been aided by the cloistered, yet highly immersive environment of the Jihadist new media-scape itself. The hierarchical and strictly regulated spaces of 'official' Jihadist forums and blogs (Awan and al-Lami 2009), which effectively 'cocoon' audi-ences (particularly new or potential recruits) from alternate realities and interpre-tational frameworks, give rise to an insular virtual community that venerates the ideology of Jihadism at the expense of all else. Moreover, these environments stifle almost any form of debate, discussion, or dialogue instead acting as 'echo chambers' or rhetorical amplifiers,[42] which predispose audiences towards unre-servedly accepting the Jihadists' rendition of events, and thereby inculcating blind obedience to the Jihadist cause.[43]

Countering criticism of Jihadist acts and discourses in the new media ecology

Whilst there is little doubt that these efforts in preferentially framing Jihadist discourses have met with tremendous success, ironically it is the new media ecology itself that has the potential to cause the unravelling of these manufac-tured and contrived narratives and discourses. The general proliferation of sources of news, information and commentary in the new media ecology, coupled with increasingly media-savvy audiences, who are far less likely to accept the veracity of any one narrative and more likely to evince dissatisfaction with conventional modes of mediation, has undoubtedly challenged what Sonwalkar (2004) refers to as 'media imperialism' (Awan 2007b). Indeed the ubiquity of these dynamics in the new media ecology has inevitably meant that Jihadist media organs, who despite their attempts at retaining control of the narrative through traditional paradigms of media production and dissemination, have not proven immune to these developments either.

Consequently, the very openness of the new media ecology has exposed the vulnerabilities of Jihadist discourses in a number of ways. The increasing accessibility to a veritable overload of information from a multitude of sources, particularly online, means that the Jihadists cannot easily falsify or omit those facts and details which might be considered to pose threats to the legitimacy of their discourses. Indeed, despite the Jihadists' best attempts at sequestering their audiences, unsavoury elements that are deemed problematic may still reach audiences, thus making it far more difficult to frame narratives through omission and preferential selection. Moreover, criticisms and condemnation of Jihadist actions, ideology and discourses are also far more difficult to conceal in the transparency offered by the new media ecology. As a result, Jihadist leadership and ideologues have instead been compelled to employ means other than framing in order to counter this deluge of damaging material and criticism. The Jihadists' principle recourse has been to cast aspersion on the sources of these critiques and question the veracity of such reports, labelling them as enemy propaganda designed to tarnish the Jihadist movement's image.

Nevertheless, despite this rhetoric, the critiques have proven difficult to summarily dismiss as enemy propaganda, particularly as they stem from sources far closer to home; from opposition co-religionists (particularly Islamists and non-violent Salafists), from broader Muslim publics, from religious scholars and authorities and, most notably, from credible Jihadists voices who have found themselves increasingly alienated by Jihadism's dystopic trajectory. Joining the cacophony of protest directed against al-Qaeda, prominent ex-Jihadists such as Sayyid Imam al-Sharif (a.k.a. Dr Fadl), Noman Benotman and other members of the Libya Islamic Fighting Group (LIFG),[44] have focused on the evident discord and incongruity between the Jihadists' stated lofty goals and manifest actions, accusing the movement of egregious excess and violating Islamic legal and ethical principles. The authenticity of these and other voices from within the Islamic tradition, and by extension the irrefutable validity of their objections, have become increasingly difficult for the Jihadist movement to simply evade or reject outright. In response, the Jihadist leadership have, in some instances, been forced to adopt what is perhaps their most honest and forthright approach thus far, by responding directly and candidly to the points of contention raised. As a prime case in point, in December 2008, acknowledging the intense criticism directed at the movement from within the Muslim world, Ayman al-Zawahiri solicited questions from Jihadist forum participants in an online question and answer session hailed as the first *Open Meeting with Shaykh Ayman al-Zawahiri.* This highly significant and unprecedented move by the leadership towards transparency and dialogue, although widely welcomed by Jihadist supporters, was seen by many critics to be a desperate attempt to win back their dwindling support base. Al-Zawahiri, citing time constraints, elected to answer only a selection of the questions, perhaps eschewing the more difficult queries that questioned the strategic effectiveness of al-Qaeda or indeed its very existence. Nevertheless, the exercise represented something of a paradigm shift for Jihadists, in that it was an early attempt to acknowledge widespread criticism of the movement in a largely uncensored manner, and somehow render themselves accountable to their putative constituency.

Many of the questions focused upon the deliberate targeting of civilians and the preponderance of Muslim casualties amongst al-Qaeda's death toll. One of the more scathing critics asks:

> Excuse me, Mr. Zawahiri, but who is it who is killing with Your Excellency's blessing the innocents in Baghdad, Morocco and Algeria? Do you consider the killing of women and children to be Jihad? I challenge you and your organization to do that in Tel Aviv. Why have you – to this day – not carried out any strike in Israel? Or is it easier to kill Muslims in the markets? Maybe it is necessary [for you] to take some geography lessons, because your maps only show the Muslims' states.

Another questioner reiterates the widespread aversion to al-Qaeda's convoluted conception of that which falls under the ambit of 'legitimate Jihad':

> With your [al-Qaeda's] reputation of killing innocent people, how do you expect Muslims to trust you and consider your activities legitimate jihad, let alone people of other faiths?

Al-Zawahiri, conscious of the tenor of criticism of al-Qaeda and associated movements, chooses not to ignore the unanimous condemnation of their position on Muslim casualties, instead responding directly on this issue:

> I would like to clarify to the brother questioner that we don't kill innocents: in fact, we fight those who kill innocents. Those who kill innocents are the Americans, the Jews, the Russians and the French and their agents. Were we insane killers of innocents as the questioner claims, it would be possible for us to kill thousands of them in the crowded markets, but we are confronting the enemies of the Muslim Ummah and targeting *them*, and it may be the case that during this, an innocent might fall unintentionally or unavoidably, and the Mujahideen have warned repeatedly the Muslims in general that they are in a war with the senior criminals – the Americans and Jews and their allies and agents – and that they must keep away from the places where these enemies gather. The Crusader-Jewish propaganda claims that the Mujahideen kill the innocent, but the Muslim Ummah knows who its enemy is and who defends it.

Elsewhere in the Open Meeting, he states: 'There is no way they [Jihadists] would intentionally kill an innocent Muslim. However, if that does happen, then it is certainly unintentional or merely a lie fabricated by state-crusader media whose lies you have many times experienced.'

In responding to his interlocutors, al-Zawahiri employs sophistry to reject these critiques. In fact, he first denies the claim outright ('we don't kill innocents'), but later qualifies this statement by countenancing the possibility that civilians may have inadvertently been harmed by the Jihadists' actions. He offers a number of explanations for this patent violation of the sanctity of Muslim life, as enshrined within the Sharia. He resorts to the earlier tactic of disparaging reports of civilian deaths as empty enemy propaganda concocted to denigrate the movement, once again displaying contempt for his audiences' intelligence. He also rather curiously locates the blame for these deaths squarely with the casualties themselves on account of their proximity to the enemy during Jihadist operations. Implicit in this statement is the notion that the 'true believers' will refrain from any interaction or engagement with the enemy. Al-Zawahiri reinforces this intimation by redefining the enemy as 'the Americans and Jews and their *allies and agents*'. Consequently, Muslims killed by Jihadist operations can be posthumously recast as traitors, agents, heretics or apostates, depending on their identities. This is particularly the case for Shiites and others who are accused of complicity with the occupying forces, and thus considered to be legitimate targets. This practice is certainly not new; elements within Jihadist circles have long employed the reprehensible practice of *takfir* (literally the pronouncing of disbelief),[45] as a mechanism for delegitimising their opponents and sanctioning the shedding of Muslim blood. Finally after exhausting these other possibilities and much prevarication, al-Zawahiri concedes that there may have been innocent civilians killed, acknowledging the possibility that errors may have been committed by the Jihadists:

> we haven't killed the innocents, not in Baghdad, nor in Morocco, nor in Algeria, nor anywhere else. And if there is any innocent who was killed in the Mujahideen's operations, then it was either an unintentional error, or out of necessity as in cases of *al-tatarrus*.
>
> ...It is not hidden from you that the enemy intentionally takes up positions in the midst of the Muslims, for them to be human shields for him.

However, he astutely tempers this admission by claiming that the Jihadists may also have acted out of necessity by appealing to an obscure medieval Sharia ruling pertaining to the employment of 'human shields' by the enemy, known as *al-tatarrus*. In the past, enemy forces facing Muslim armies had occasionally placed Muslims before their vanguard in the knowledge that Islamic law forbade the killing of fellow Muslims, essentially rendering the Muslim army impotent. In the face of impending military paralysis, scholars applied the ruling of opting for the lesser of the two evils, and legitimised the engagement of forces, irrespective of the presumed sanctity of the lives of fellow Muslims. Al-Zawahiri's employment of this ruling applies the same principle but in a convoluted and excessive manner that provides both theological justification and a precedent for legitimising violence against Muslim populations in this way. Other Jihadist texts, such as Abu Yahya al-Libbi's *al-Tatarrus in the Modern Jihad*, have similarly sought to capitalise on obsolete and archaic legal positions to justify their actions.

Whilst many of these legitimising tactics may be met with derision and ultimately fail to sway wider publics, they have nevertheless proved immensely reassuring to core Jihadist audiences, for whom they continue to validate the actions and discourses of al-Qaeda and Global Jihadism more broadly. Part of the reason why these mechanisms have proven so successful, has much to do with Festinger's (1957) classical theory of cognitive dissonance which suggests that individuals seek out information confirming beliefs or behaviours while actively avoiding contrary information, in order to mitigate uncomfortable psychological tension. Jihadists ensconced within the reaffirming hyperreality (see Chapter 3) of the new Jihadist mediascape are therefore deliberately and consciously immersed in content that is congruent with existing opinions and beliefs, whilst simultaneously eschewing that which is not. Moreover, the acceptance of rhetoric, sophistry, frame-setting and shrewd strategies which may appear naïve to outside observers may nevertheless allow much of the moral dissonance to be largely negated in core audiences.

Deeds over words and infallibility

Much of the preceding discussion is predicated upon the notion that theological legitimation is paramount, and that moral dissonance can be engendered by failing to uphold religious imperatives. However, it would be erroneous to assume that theological legitimation holds equal validity for all drawn to Jihadism. As our audience stratification earlier has shown, many Jihadists immersed within the new media ecology may display an ambivalent attitudinal motif vis-à-vis religion, and therefore may appear unperturbed by the discord between religious principles and Jihadist actions. Indeed, religious appeals to moderate their actions, and particularly their violence, are unlikely to be heeded by the newer generation of Jihadists. We might demonstrate this point by comparing this attitudinal motif to that of al-Zawahiri, who represents the earlier generation of Jihadists. During his *Open Meeting*, al-Zawahiri is asked, 'Does the doctor consider himself a Muslim scholar of Sharia? If so, upon what basis does he issue his fatwas that oppose those of notable Muslim scholars?'

Al-Zawahiri's responds by modestly stating, 'I do not consider myself to be one of the great Muslim scholars but I highly admire and respect them and try as much as possible to disseminate what I know of their words of wisdom'.

Whereas al-Zawahiri's rejoinders to his critics at least pay lip service to the idea of religious legitimacy and respect for authority and learning, many of the newer generation of Jihadists have no such qualms. Indeed the legitimacy of Global Jihadism, particularly in the new media ecology has been predicated in large part upon the ascendancy of deeds over words, and most Jihadists have attempted to usurp traditional authority from clerics and religious leaders through their acts in this way. Mohammed Siddique Khan's 'martyrdom' video released by *as-Sahab* spoke disparagingly of Muslim scholars in Britain and implied that 'real men' like himself, whose deeds and sacrifices were self-evident, were most worthy of the Prophet's legacy:

> Our so-called scholars today are content with their Toyotas and their semi-detached houses … If they fear the British Government more than they fear Allah then they must desist in giving talks, lectures and passing fatwas and they need to stay at home – they're useless – and leave the job to the real men, the true inheritors of the prophet.[46]

The meteoric rise of Abu Musab al-Zarqawi, the late leader of al-Qaeda in Iraq (AQI), epitomised this trend. Despite being theologically illiterate and hailing from a criminal background, al-Zarqawi gained immense popularity and prestige as a result of his notorious video beheadings and the instigation of bloody sectarian strife in Iraq. Indeed, his violent excesses were so flagrant that even the al-Qaeda leadership found them disconcerting, with al-Zawahiri sharply rebuking,

> Among the things which the feelings of the Muslim populace who love and support you will never find palatable, also, are the scenes of slaughtering the hostages. You shouldn't be deceived by the praise of some of the zealous young men and their description of you as the Sheikh of the slaughterers.[47]

Nevertheless, these grisly deeds continued to propel (now) *Sheikh* al-Zarqawi to international prominence, evident in the bestowal of two particularly dubious honours; the title of 'Emir of al-Qaeda in the Land of Two Rivers', and the US bounty of $25 million for his death or capture, matching that on bin Laden himself at the time.

Placed in stark contrast to the perceived apathy, weakness or inaction of Muslim rulers, clergy and even other Islamists, the Jihadists' engagement in a tangible response to the external threat is uniquely placed in the Muslim world. No matter how odious or counterproductive this response may be (and certainly it has often been both), the Jihadists will never be accused by their opponents of procrastination or indolence. As a result, their manifest deeds enable them to undermine the credibility of other dissenting voices who use words alone, and consequently arrogate to themselves the authority of *Islamic officialdom*.

Increasingly this brazen self-aggrandisement has given rise to claims of righteous infallibility, which insist that Jihadist 'field experience' endows them with the quality of being free from error in judgement and action, and outside of the scope of scholarly criticism (Alshech 2008). Consequently, they do not need to exonerate themselves from accusations and critiques,[48] but rather insist that anyone who seeks to criticise their methods or goals must first serve alongside them on the frontlines, before they are accorded that privilege. This has proven to be a particularly expedient rejoinder to the spate of recent criticisms from renowned ex-Jihadists such as Sayyid Imam al-Sharif and Noman Benotman.

Conclusion

Whilst engaging in discussions of Jihadist legitimacy, we must acknowledge the uneasy truth that a great number of their actions are beyond censure in the wider Muslim world, and to some extent, even beyond. Against the backdrop of military invasion and occupation of two Muslim majority countries, attacks (conventional or otherwise) against military targets within these theatres of the 'classical defensive Jihad', such as IED attacks against Coalition convoys or highly discriminate killings of US soldiers by Juba the sniper, will invariably be considered legitimate. Indeed such tactics cannot even be placed under the rubric of terrorism, and the US military itself has been wary of distinguishing between insurgents and terrorists in this respect. Al-Qaeda do not exist in vacuum; they are principally a reactionary movement that has only been able to exert any influence due to the actions and failings of others. One might posit that the movement's legitimacy is in many ways inversely proportional to that of its enemies (in this instance, the legitimacy of the US in the Muslim world).

Ironically, it is the Jihadists' own penchant for bloodshed and violent excess, allied with a frighteningly dystopic and intolerant vision of a post-Jihadist future that has severely undermined this tacit legitimacy and popular support. This has been a particular challenge for the Jihadist movement whose successive attempts to successfully propound their narrative have been hampered enormously by their engagement in acts of violence and terrorism that ostensibly violate religious and cultural mores. Even many of the Jihadists themselves have not necessarily accepted the legitimacy of Jihadist acts and discourses *in toto* as they may be deemed illegitimate by even their own referential frameworks. Many potential radicals, with romanticised and earnest but largely inchoate notions of defending the *Ummah* and championing the cause of the oppressed, can have their (often laudable) empathies diverted (due to a lack of accessibility to the principal cause) or manipulated to deadly effect. They may initially have been drawn to legitimate forms of Jihad and they may not have had any desire to participate in more 'controversial' operations, but by that point they have long crossed the Rubicon. Mohammad Atta reputedly wanted to travel to Chechnya to defend its Muslims against the brutal repression of the Russians, prior to his involvement in the 9/11 terrorist attacks (Awan 2007a).

Nevertheless, the Jihadist leadership have attempted to confer legitimacy upon their acts and discourses in numerous innovative ways, and have often succeeded in doing so. Whilst this dynamic has been particularly apparent in the new media ecology represented to a large degree by the Internet, many of these strategies in fact function irrespective of the offline/online divide – indeed it make little sense to speak of this ephemeral divide. Moreover, the online world itself is problematic if postulated as a monolithic entity. The new media ecology and online world is in fact composed of a multiplicity of spheres, where, as Manovich (2001: 42) contends, 'every citizen can construct her own custom lifestyle and select her ideology from a large number of choices'. Consequently, it makes little sense to consider the role legitimation plays in the Jihadist new media ecology per se, rather, we must examine the credibility of Jihadism within a multiplicity of spaces within the new media ecology.

Discussions of legitimacy must also take into account the changing character and demographic of the Jihadist movement itself. The newer generation of Jihadists, who are increasingly drawn to the movement in a largely autonomous manner, appear ideologically less sophisticated and display a greater ambivalence towards the religious sphere, whilst simultaneously exhibiting a greater inclination to extreme forms of violence than their predecessors.

3   Media Jihad[1]

Introduction

The previous chapter explored the role of the new media ecology in helping to support and legitimise the ailing ideology of Jihadism in the twenty-first century.

The importance ascribed to the media has allowed the articulation and ascendancy of a very particular form of radical Islamist activism – namely the media Jihad. This chapter sets out how the new media ecology has facilitated the rise of the 'virtual Jihad' or the 'media Jihad', which has increasingly gained prominence and credibility as a legitimate alternative to the traditional militaristic or 'real' Jihad. Media Jihad allows for the production, dissemination, (re)mediation and proliferation of material that serves to reinforce Jihadist leaders' interpretation of ongoing events and the situating of those events within larger narratives of a war on Islam, which may resonate with potential supporters' experience in daily life in whichever country they reside. However, the emergence of Web 2.0 participatory media has diminished traditional Jihadist leaders' control over 'the message', as a diffuse collective of autonomous supporters – including women – have brought Jihadist media culture to broader audiences but at the same time significantly altered the ideology. This process has run parallel to the struggle between mainstream, professional news media, and blogs, social network sites and citizen journalism or what Gillmor (2006) called *We the Media*.

This shift in authority and control has coincided with changes to how Jihadist action is legitimated. This chapter documents how credibility in Jihadist media spaces has in some cases shifted from legitimation through scholarly or religious expertise to 'propaganda of the deed'; several figures have gained popularity and support within this culture by leaving the virtual realm to participate in violent activities 'in the field'. Nevertheless, for many supporters this is not an attractive or feasible option, and the cathartic opportunity to engage in modes of 'info-war' or propaganda battle is deemed sufficient (though this carries its own risks still, such as arrest).

What this history of the recent present demonstrates is that the new media ecology brings risks and contingencies to Jihadists too; Web 2.0 and the opportunity to engage and persuade broader audiences carries with it the danger of the Jihadist ideology or narrative being detached from any core, official or central authority. So, not only does this make it difficult to construct models or general-ise about the effects of Jihadist media or the Jihadist media culture on potential supporters, but Jihadist leaders themselves face difficulties understanding how their ideology could be legitimated in these fast-changing media conditions. The new media ecology enables new connectivities that make it difficult to think in terms of local or global, virtual or real. Indeed, we begin by asking whether 'global' Jihad was even possible before the Internet.

The rise of virtual Jihadism

In order to help contextualise the rise of the media Jihad and to explain why much of the legitimising activity detailed in the previous chapter has taken place within the confines of the new media ecology, it is worth providing a brief over-view of the development of Jihadist media at this stage.

To Western audiences inured to depictions of Jihadists as medieval Luddites whose religious zealotry heralds only self-immolation and destruction of the West, there must be something inherently incongruous and deeply unsettling about al-Qaeda extolling the virtues of twenty-first century mass media cam-paigns, or exhibiting anxieties over being misrepresented by the Press (as illus-trated by the quotes from al-Zawahiri and bin Laden in the previous chapter).

However, these apparent anachronisms are perhaps rendered a little less strange if one considers the fact that Jihadism is a thoroughly modern phenome-non,[2] the rise of which has coincided with the revolution in information and communication technologies witnessed during the early 1990s. Indeed one could argue that the advent of a truly *Global* Jihadism is wholly predicated on the development, availability and affordability of these new technologies (Sageman 2004: 158); satellite phones, digital video recording and editing equipment, PCs, and in particular, on the growth of the Internet and the emergence of the World Wide Web. In the early 1990s, these and other technologies enabled the muja-hideen, heady from victory over the Soviet Union in Afghanistan, to coalesce around radical new, but yet inchoate goals, establishing a loose and decentralised transnational network of sorts. Throughout the 1990s, key events, such as the Bosnian War (1992–1995), the first World Trade Center bombing (1993), the First Chechen War (1994–1996), and the publication of bin Laden's infamous twin 'fatwas' (1996 and 1998), helped to not only strengthen the burgeoning Jihadist community, but also provided the impetus for the gradual migration of these networks to the new virtual havens offered by the emerging World Wide Web.

Whilst the 1998 twin terrorist bombings of US embassies in Dar es Salaam and Nairobi did begin to focus far greater attention of security services on the communicative and operational uses of the Internet by al-Qaeda and affiliated groups, it was only following the momentous attacks of 11 September 2001 that the Jihadist media presence really became an object of intense international scru-tiny (Awan and al-Lami 2009). In this new security climate, these virtual spaces offered unparalleled advantages over conventional media operating in the 'real' world; they provided a free and uncensored medium for communication, mobilisation, recruitment, training, media production and dissemination, as well as a host of other related functions (Weimann 2006; Awan 2007b). The loss of a physical sanctuary in Afghanistan following *Operation Enduring Freedom*, simply expedited al-Qaeda's metamorphosis into this diffuse virtual network, aptly named 'al-Qaeda 2.0' by a number of commentators (Bergen and Footer 2008; Lynch 2006). Indeed, as the Taliban collapsed in November of 2001, bin Laden's biographer Hamid Mir recalled witnessing 'every second al-Qaeda member carrying a laptop computer along with a Kalashnikov' as they prepared to scatter into hiding and exile (Coll and Glassner 2005).

Unsurprisingly, the Internet quickly became the principle platform for the dissemination and mediation of the culture and ideology of Jihadism (Awan 2007b). The Global Islamic Media Front (GIMF), a prominent media organ of al-Qaeda, even acknowledged in 2005 that it was now the *only* platform available to them:

> This is the Internet that God has enlisted in the service of jihad and of the mujahideen, which has come to serve your interests – given that half the battle of the mujahideen is being waged on the pages of the Internet – *the sole outlet* for mujahideen media.[3]

A newer generation of Web 2.0 spaces, including social networking sites and file-sharing portals, helped to consolidate the ascendancy of Jihadist media whilst simultaneously raising the spectre of mediated *self*-radicalisation; the idea that previously unaffiliated individuals could be drawn to the kind of violence and terrorism espoused by al-Qaeda, in a largely autonomous manner through the mediation of the Internet (Awan 2007c; Stevens and Neumann 2008; Bergin *et al.* 2009). Today the *Jihadist counterculture* flourishes in the new media ecology,[4] with virtual propagation of Jihadism proceeding apace; a seemingly exponential growth in 'Jihadist content' over the last decade appearing on websites, blogs, forums, social networking sites and file-sharing portals (Weimann 2006; Awan 2007b).

The rise of the media Jihad in the new media ecology then has arisen from a coalescence of factors: the revolution in information and communication technologies from the 1990s onwards; the loss of a physical sanctuary in Afghanistan following *Operation Enduring Freedom* in 2001; and the urgent realisation by Jihadists of the effect a lack of popular support would have for their movement's longevity and indeed survival.

The media Jihad: providing an evidentiary basis for metanarrative

Today, the functions of Jihadist media in the virtual arena are manifold; communication, mobilisation, recruitment, training, media production and dissemination, as well as a host of other related functions (Weimann 2006; Awan 2007a). However, the principle function of Jihadist media, and indeed its *raison d'être*, has always been, depending on one's perspective, news provision or propaganda; to furnish information about Muslim oppression and grievances, and document the activities of the mujahideen in order to mobilise the masses and rally others to the cause. The earliest Jihadist media emerging during the Afghan Jihad against the USSR (1979–1989), which of course provided the conditions for the emergence of both al-Qaeda and the broader Global Jihadist movement, did precisely this. The *al-Jihad* magazine edited by Sheikh Abdallah Azzam for example,[5] focused on the humanitarian plight of Afghan civilians, denouncing the atrocities committed by Soviet forces, and simultaneously extolled the virtues of Jihad in defence of Muslim lands – all of which greatly facilitated the steady influx of donations, equipment and volunteers, particularly from within the Arab world.

In short, from the very outset, the primary role of the media Jihad has been to provide an evidentiary basis for the metanarrative. If we understand this as the principle, even defining function of Jihadist media, then it is not difficult to appreciate its early limitations too. The *al-Jihad* magazine, launched in 1984, was one of the most successful early examples of Jihadists' own media organs. However, it was plagued by serious problems from the outset. *Al-Jihad* first appeared as an amateurish black and white mimeograph, and required substantial financial resources to keep it afloat. Indeed it only evolved into a full colour glossy from 1986 after a substantial increase in public interest injected funds and resources into the publication. Naturally these problems severely affected its circulation, thereby further circumscribing an already limited potential readership. To make matters worse, *al-Jihad's* potential ambit was circumscribed further by countries in which its message was considered to be illegal or incendiary (Lia 2006). Indeed there is anecdotal evidence to suggest that at the height of its popularity, around half of *al-Jihad's* readership was to be found not in the Gulf States, as one might assume, but instead in the United States where its dissemination was protected by constitutional freedoms. So although *al-Jihad* could control its *message* very strictly, and thus tailor the evidentiary basis for its claims, the *medium* itself proved to be the limiting factor in terms of audience size, scope, reach and the lack of audio-visual content.

The only real alternative to the shortcomings evident in the Jihadists' own media organs, was to attempt to manipulate and exploit the mainstream media as unwitting communicative agents for the message. As we have already noted from al-Zawahiri's lament over the 'media siege imposed on the Jihad movement', this was rarely possible either. To illustrate this point, we might consider one of the earliest attacks by al-Qaeda: the twin US embassy bombings in Dar es Salaam and Nairobi in 1998. Whilst these attacks convincingly displayed al-Qaeda's competence, technical prowess and a certain flair for the 'theatre of terrorism' (Stohl 1988), they also displayed how utterly reliant terrorists remained on the symbiotic relationship with mainstream news media identified by Schmid and De Graaf (1982). Indeed, Jihadist media organs had made little effort to consolidate their 'propaganda of the deed', or communicate their actions to rapt international audiences who had witnessed the spectacles of violence onscreen. In hindsight, damning critiques from within the Jihadist movement lambasted the 'horrible informational and political shortfall regarding these events', decrying the fact that audiences resorted to 'western foreign media to quench their thirst for the true news'.[6] Here, whilst the Jihadists had managed to temporarily usurp the *medium*, their *message* was controlled by myriad factors outside their control; editorial controls, commercial and political considerations, news agendas, media frames, governmental pressure, censorship and audience sensibilities amongst other factors. If we understand terrorism to be ineluctably political, and following McLuhan's (1978) famous phrase, 'without communication, terrorism would not exist', then the abstract depictions of spectacular terrorist acts did little to politicise Jihadist violence, or communicate the underlying reasons behind that violence. Unsurprisingly, al-Zawahiri (2001) concluded the pernicious effect of this 'complicity' noting, that amongst the tools that Western powers use to fight against Islam are 'the International news agencies and satellite television'.

Image warfare

The capacity of an image to 'cut through' prior understandings of an event and influence a person's viewpoint or even worldview is relational: images are 'read' in relation to other images seen before in relation to words and captions which might anchor the meaning of the image within that text, and in relation to a person's understandings of the larger historical processes the image may indicate (an event snapshot within a longer story). There is hence nothing intrinsically shocking about an image, no given power, so to understand the role of images projected by Jihadist media we need to account for the context vis-à-vis other media the target audience may be familiar with, the textual composition, and the events the image is taken to denote or authenticate (O'Loughlin 2010).[7]

If the role of the media Jihad has been to provide an evidentiary basis for the metanarrative, then the role of images has proven to be absolutely central to this endeavour. If we return to the *Ladinese Epistle* cited in the previous chapter, we can appreciate the power of the image quite clearly. The potency of bin Laden's discourse in his 1996 statement, replete with visceral imagery of 'Muslim blood being spilled' may be undeniable, however, it is only when it is substantiated by the role of the image that it takes on any tangible meaning in the minds of audiences. Bin Laden, cognisant as ever of the role of images, pointedly alluded to the 'horrifying pictures of the massacre of Qana', which only four months earlier had shocked audiences worldwide. Bin Laden was well aware of the startlingly graphic reports of the carnage wrought in Qana by the Israeli Defense Force, and which had been widely circulated in the news media at the time. The extraordinary coverage was due in part to the persistence of journalists like Robert Fisk,[8] but also because it had in fact been a United Nations (UNIFIL) compound, in which Lebanese civilians had sought refuge, that had been shelled with apparent impunity. Consequently, in the context of the mainstream news media delivery of sanitised, carefully edited and censored coverage of conflict (Theobald 2004), implausibly grotesque images, like that of the Fijian UN peacekeeper silently holding aloft a decapitated baby, appeared onscreen. These images and others, such as footage of residential apartment blocks in Beirut being levelled by F16s, were immediately seared onto audience memories, eliciting strong and angry reactions in parts of the Muslim world, not least of which included the radicalisation of Muhammad Atta. According to Lesch (2003: 523) Atta, the ringleader of the 19 hijackers on 9/11, committed himself to 'martyrdom' after witnessing these images from his dorm room in Germany, choosing to write his 'martyrdom will' the very same day.

For bin Laden these images were a means to corroborate the massacre, and attempt to evoke sufficient moral indignation and umbrage in his potential audience, thereby giving credence to his narrative in a way that he could not possibly have envisaged for the list of other exotic sounding Islamic conflict zones that formed his litany of grievance. Conversely, he did not (and could not) point to 'horrifying picture' of 'Tajikistan, Burma, Kashmir, Assam, Philippine, Fatani, Ogadin' *et al.*, and without an evidentiary basis to substantiate these claims, he is vulnerable to accusations of propaganda and empty rhetoric. This is not to dispute or deny that massacres or serious human rights violations might have occurred in these places. Rather many of the conflicts occurring on the peripheries of the Muslim world,[9] have been conspicuously, and from the perception of Jihadists' (al-Zawahiri 2001), wilfully neglected by the mainstream Western news media. Nevertheless, setting aside their veracity for a moment, the absence of commensurate images and reportage from these contexts attenuates the potency of the narrative in a staggeringly disproportionate manner. Taylor (2007) commenting on the Abu Ghraib prison scandal, identifies the same asymmetrical relationship between the effects of pictures and words. Taylor contrasts the unprecedented furore over the photos of prisoner abuse, and the prior imageless reports of torture and serious human rights violations from *Amnesty International* which went virtually unheeded. Consequently, it is the mediated image that is the most effective modality for directing audience to the event that the photograph of video footage serves as an authenticator for.

The beguiling notion that images embody truth (or put differently, 'the camera does not lie'), also offers audiences an alternative to the apparent obfuscation of reality provided by mainstream media aphorisms: contractors as opposed to mercenaries; collateral damage as opposed to killing civilians; regime change as opposed to invasion and occupation. Of course, this is not to suggest that the camera does not distort the truth in even more mendacious ways. Instead, as Bracewell (2002: 66) commenting on the contemporary status of the image suggests, 'there is now the sense that authenticity itself can be sculpted to suggest veracity as an image, in which truth remains ambiguous'.

The hyperreality of Jihadism

The circulation and flux of images is one indication of the capacity of the new media ecology to buttress ideologies and grand narratives, such as that offered by Jihadism. The unique multimedia environment of the Wold Wide Web in particular lends itself to the construction of a *hyperreality*; the paradoxical notion of a mediated phenomenon that appears more real than the reality itself (Eco 1987; Baudrillard 1983). This *hyperreality* can be envisaged as an enhanced reality that places the participant in a wholly mediated environment constituted by a surfeit of images, texts and videos, all filtered through the lens of Jihadism, and through which the individual unwittingly experiences reality by proxy. This cloistered 'cocooning' effect of Jihadist spaces in the new media ecology referred to in the previous chapter is immensely important in the construction of this hyperreality, particularly as it has enabled the Jihadists to assuage the discordance between the classical views of Jihad (as propounded by Azzam *et al.*) and the Jihad espoused by al-Qaeda and its ilk, particularly with respect to the nature and form that the Jihad can legitimately assume.

In addition, the new media ecology enables the manipulation of all forms of content in a myriad disingenuous ways; a host of widely available editing tools allow producers to crop, resize, copy, paste, assemble, blur, airbrush, superimpose and generally alter textual and audio-visual content. These tailored depictions enable the Jihadists to further validate the metanarrative, manufacturing legitimacy along the way. The veracity of the content is almost inconsequential, as the cumulative effect of this unremitting barrage of images and videos, and the selective framing of events, all presenting either a simulacrum of Muslim suffering or Jihadist success, can interact and mesh with other worlds or realities a person experiences, such as day to day discrimination, oppression, political inefficacy and so on, such that a dogmatic and singular set of causal beliefs or ideology becomes the sole perspective for making sense of the world. Hence, when these non-mediated conditions are in place, it can make sense to speak of media as 'primary definers' of social reality (Schlesinger 1991).

Jihadists, recognising the immense potential of the new media ecology, have responded to these manifest opportunities with alacrity, churning out increasingly sophisticated media productions, and employing professional techniques and methods of audio-visual production and dissemination, as well as shrewdly framing narratives and events in ways sympathetic to their cause. Much of this frenetic activity has taken place in prominent or 'official' Jihadist spaces, represented primarily by an ever-changing roster of Arabic forums (*muntadayat*) which have served as semi-official mouthpieces for al-Qaeda over the years, including a number of forums sponsored by the *al-Fajr Media Centre* (al-Qaeda's key media wing) such as *al-Ikhlaas*, *al-Firdaws*, and *al-Buraq*, as well as other such as *al-Hesba*, *al-Faloja*, and *Shumook al-Islam, and al-Ansar*; and to a lesser extent 'official' blogs (such as the weblog of *al-Qaeda in Iraq/Islamic State in Iraq*).

Despite the fact that these platforms represent early Web 2.0 technologies, which are ostensibly conducive to the 'levelling' of hierarchies of knowledge and power (Castells 2009; Bunt 2003), they have nevertheless been hierarchically organised and strictly regulated with actors (e.g. al-Qaeda in Iraq – ISI), producers (e.g. al-Furqan), distributors (e.g. al-Fajr), and specific forum posters controlling every stage of the process (Kimmage 2008; Awan and al-Lami

2009). By following broadcast-era paradigms of media production, with passive media consumers, and top-down media production and dissemination, Jihadists have in the past managed to retain control of the narrative and maintain ideological coherence to a large degree.

However, the growth of Jihadist media has increasingly been shaped by the revolution in audience roles heralded by later Web 2.0 or post-broadcast technologies, where a wide range of second generation services on the Web have allowed users contribute as easily as they consume.[10] Consequently, Jihadist media efforts have also included autonomous user-generated content, often without official Jihadist sanction. This diffuse dissemination of Jihadist content across Web 2.0 platforms, outside of the ambit of 'official' forums, has not necessarily been welcomed by Jihadist media organs, Indeed, in September of 2006, *al-Boraq Media Institute* published a detailed policy document entitled *Media Exuberance* which sought to curtail the unsanctioned and 'exuberant' proliferation and production of unattributed Jihadist media by freelance amateurs, which it felt was divesting key Jihadist media organs (*as-Sahab, al-Fajr, Global Islamic Media Front* and so on) of control over production, mediation and dissemination of Jihadist content. The principal concerns appeared to have been fears of unpolished and unprofessional content undermining the credibility of Jihadist media and diverting attention from 'official' sources (Kimmage 2008; Awan and al-Lami 2009).

Nevertheless, despite the remonstrations of 'official' Jihadism, freelance media Jihadism has flourished. These media efforts avoiding the niche and strictly regulated platforms of 'official' Jihadism, have instead appeared on a range of new, more mainstream platforms, relying far more on emotive imagery and other affective content in engendering solidarity and allegiance to the counterculture of Jihadism. Rather than present cogent theological or ideological arguments designed to appeal to one's reason, polished montages of Jihadist images and video clips, accompanied by stirring devotional songs appealing to the senses, render issues of theological or ideological legitimation far less important, for some audiences perhaps even obsolete. This virtually mediated imagery and propaganda of the deed is crucially important to young web-savvy audiences, and non-Arabic speaking, diasporic Muslim audiences, both of whom contribute disproportionately to the Jihadist demographic (Awan and al-Lami 2009). Indeed, as Bolt *et al.* (2008) argue, imagery does not respect linguistic barriers and has itself become part of the message.

This has enormously important repercussions for Jihadist ideology in the twenty-first century too. The nexus between the new media ecology and the autonomous media Jihadist has not only facilitated the wider dissemination of Jihadist ideology, but significantly, outside its traditional ambit too. Mainstream file-sharing platforms like YouTube, which host Jihadist videos, such as the statements from al-Qaeda leaders and IED attacks on Coalition forces, have granted the material a considerably higher publicity profile than could have possibly been envisaged by traditional Jihadist media organs (Awan 2007b). The dissemination of the culture, ideology and media of Jihadism across communities on social networking sites like Orkut and Facebook, and virtual worlds like *Second Life*, is significant in that these constitute novel arenas that have thus far proven to be beyond the scope of official Jihadist media organs. Consequently, the Jihadist message, intended for, or only available to, smaller parochial audiences in the past, is increasingly being granted much more diffuse audience penetration (Awan and al-Lami 2009).

Real versus virtual Jihad

One of the underlying factors behind this increase in autonomous user-generated Jihadist media content has been the changing demographic of the Jihadist movement itself. Jihadism today is generally understood to be a phenomenon associated with young males (Awan 2007a; Sageman 2004), and consequently many of the new generation of virtual media Jihadists are, following Prensky (2001), 'digital natives' rather than 'digital immigrants'. Prensky defines the former as native speakers of the digital language of computers, video games and the Internet. Conversely, those who were not born into the digital world but have, at some later point in their lives, adopted many or most aspects of the new technology are, and always will be compared to them, digital immigrants.

Consequently for many media Jihadists, there is little *new* about aspects of the new media ecology. Rather, it is the *only* media environment with which they are familiar. For this newer generation of Jihadists, much of their social and other interaction already takes place within a new media ecology, whether it be social networking, shopping, dating, playing videogames, watching movies, reading news, listening to music or learning. In fact any activity in the 'real' world now has a virtual counterpart that may appear to be more appealing to a certain age cohort that represents this 'digital native' and so it is unsurprising that their political activism should similarly take place within this arena.

Sanctioning the virtual media Jihad

One of the previous perennial debates in Jihadist circles had focused on the status of those who fail to physically engage in the 'Jihad'. Such individuals had, in the past, been reproached for remaining behind and limiting their contribution to words or funds rather than deeds. During Ayman al-Zawahiri's *Open Meeting*, he was asked by a questioner:

> Our beloved Sheikh, what are the duties and obligations of those of us who support jihad but live in the non-believers' lands, such as Europe and North America, especially those who have troops fighting in Muslim lands? Should we individually engage in jihad in whatever form we can, as our Sheikh Abu Musab al-Suri recommends, or try to set out to conflict zones by any means possible? Is our engagement in jihadi media [in these non-believers countries] a sufficient reason for us to stay behind, knowing that most of us pay these countries taxes that are used to arm their troops to kill Muslims?

To which al-Zawahiri responded:

> The best solution is for you to get in touch with the mujahideen in the safest way possible in order to coordinate your efforts with them. If you fail to make such communication, you have two choices: either you engage in jihad individually or in the form of small cells, or you yourself set out to the mujahideen. As for jihadi media, it is *no excuse* to stay in the land of the kuffar, unless it is upon the request/ instructions of the mujahideen.

Curiously, despite al-Zawahiri's own earlier pronouncements on the urgent need for Jihadist media organs to counter 'the media war on terrorism' (Hammond 2003), and mobilise the *Ummah*, he declares in no uncertain terms that media Jihad is not a legitimate endeavour for *individual* aspiring Jihadists to engage in. However, al-Zawahiri's views do reflect an earlier, perhaps more quixotic attitude, particularly as he perhaps best epitomises the early generation of Jihadists forged from the Soviet-Afghan war.

Conversely, various other Jihadists have had no qualms about legitimising this activity, and have even drawn upon historical or religious precedents to do so. Abu al-Harith al-Ansari's categorisation of the types of warfare sanctioned by the Prophet, for example, cites 'media warfare' as a legitimate endeavour,[11] whereas Muhammad bin Ahmad al-Salim's highly popular text, *39 Ways to Serve and Participate in Jihad*, extols 'performing electronic Jihad' as 'a blessed field which contains much benefit'.

He states that,

> Believers are called upon to join the jihad by participating in Internet forums to defend Islam and to explain and recommend the duty of jihad to all Muslims.... Internet offer [sic] opportunity to respond instantly to false allegations and to reach millions of people in seconds; those who have internet skills are urged to use them to support the Jihad.

This effort he suggests 'can be divided into two major parts: discussion boards and hacking methods.'[12]

Perhaps the most infamous recent jihadist ideologue to contribute to the debate is Anwar al-'Awlaki, who gained notoriety after being implicated in the potential radicalisations of the 'Fort Hood shooter', Major Nidal Hassan, the 'Christmas Day bomber', Umar Farouk Abdul-Mutallab, and the 'Times Square bomber', Faisal Shahzad. Al-'Awlaki suggests in his *44 Ways to Support Jihad*, 'Fighting the lies of the Western Media'. 'Following the news of Jihad and spreading it', and 'Spreading the writings of the mujahideen and their scholars'.[13] Yet perhaps al-'Awlaki's most interesting contribution is number 29 on the list: 'WWW Jihad'. According to al-'Awlaki,

> Some ways in which the brothers and sisters could be 'internet mujahideen' is by contributing in one or more of the following ways: Establishing discussion forums that offer a free, uncensored medium for posting

information relating to Jihad; Establishing email lists to share information with interested brothers and sisters; Posting or emailing Jihad literature and news; and Setting up websites to cover specific areas of Jihad, such as: mujahideen news, Muslim POWs, and Jihad literature.[14]

Contemporary Jihadist strategist and key proponent of a decentralised, leaderless Jihad, Abu Mus'ab al-Suri, even acknowledges the underlying reasons why this mode of action may be appealing in his seminal *Call to Global Islamic Resistance*.[15] Al-Suri concedes the existence of large numbers of individuals within the Jihadists' ideological support base who are nevertheless unwilling to countenance or engage in violence on a personal level. Addressing these individuals directly, al-Suri articulates expanded opportunities for participation in Jihad for those individuals who may agree with the grand narrative, discourses and acts of Jihadism, but will not cross the threshold into violence themselves. Instead he proposes a number of alternative modes of non-violent action to support the Jihad, one of which entails the 'media or informational battle'.[16]

In some cases there may be pragmatic reasons for sanctioning a virtual or media Jihad. A posting on a Syrian Jihadi site in 2005, entitled 'Advice to Brothers Seeking Jihad in Iraq', rather pointedly stated that raw recruits offering only 'enthusiasm or impetuousness or love of martyrdom' were no longer wanted. The obvious implication was that untrained and ill-equipped volunteers actually posed a liability to the movement and should either prepare themselves or find some other method of aiding the cause.

As a result of these varying legitimising mechanisms, the 'media Jihad' has gradually gained respectability as a legitimate endeavour in itself. A communiqué authored by the Ministry of Information for the Islamic State of Iraq and posted on several Jihadi forums in September 2007, for example, hails the uptake of the media Jihad as the 'awakening':

Praise be to God for [the mujahideen's] great efforts in triggering the jihadi awakening among the children of the ummah. How great [are the] fingers which sit behind the computer screens, day and night, awaiting a statement or releasing a production for their mujahideen brothers in the forums.[17]

Moreover, the media Jihadists have taken these accolades to validate their long held, overinflated sense of self-importance and worth. Recognising the immense potential of these technologies and forums, and the considerable power it grants them, some media Jihadists have placed themselves on a par with real-life Jihadists, adopting the slogan 'keyboard equals Kalashnikov'.[18] Indeed in some instances, the work of the media Jihadists has even raised above "martyrdom" operations; for example, the prominent media Jihadist Younis Tsouli (aka Irhaabi 007 or Terrorist 007) is frequently lionised by fellow forum members for distributing Jihadist videos and messages, and thus having been highly instrumental in the successful radicalisation and indeed 'martyrdom' of many others. The implicit suggestion of course is that although Tsouli has not 'achieved martyrdom' himself, he has been of far greater benefit to the Jihadist cause in enabling the 'martyrdoms' of many others in his stead.[19] Tsouli, whose autonomous media efforts placed him in the virtual company of Jihadist 'luminaries' like al-Zarqawi and Abu Maysara al-Iraqi (Zarqawi's highly regarded 'press secretary'), perhaps best understands the potency of the media Jihad,

> Film everything; this is good advice for all mujahideen. Brothers, don't disdain photography. You should be aware that every frame you take is as good as a missile fired at the Crusader enemy and his puppets.[20]

If 'radicalisation' is considered to include some reference to violence, can those drawn to virtual Jihad be characterised as radicalised? Do the attitudes of individuals who are unwilling to countenance violence themselves nevertheless pose a security risk, as Western security discourses about radicalisation claim?

Perhaps what attenuates this characterisation to some degree is the employment of similar referential frameworks by those located firmly outside the Jihadist movement. Yusuf al-Qaradawi, perhaps the most important living mainstream Islamic scholar in the Muslim world offers an intriguing broadening of the concept of Jihad, away from violence 'to the realm of ideas, media, and communication', which he calls the 'Jihad of the age, a great Jihad, and a long Jihad'. He suggests the weapons of this Jihad should be TV, the Internet, email and the like rather than guns. Persuading Muslims of the message of Islam and the importance of this Jihad in the path of God, he argues, should be the first priority.[21] Although al-Qaradawi is surely encouraging an entirely different form of political activism, it would perhaps be easy for policymakers or journalists to confuse or blur together various manifestations of virtual Islam per se with Jihadist sites inciting violence. Instead, what al-Qaradawi's example shows, is that all aspects of social life are inevitably becoming mediatised (see introduction) including religion, and the Jihadist media vanguard may just be a smaller element within the broader dynamic of the mediatisation of religion.

The catharsis of the virtual/media Jihad

The sanction offered to the 'media Jihad' has proven to be particularly important as it also helps assuage cognitive dissonance in the media Jihadists themselves. Whereas in the previous chapter, the dissonance identified arose as a result of the discord between Jihadist actions and Islamic ethical and legal considerations, the dissonance here stems from the internal conflict arising from an inconsistency between the Jihadist's own beliefs and actions. Thus, a Jihadist who wishes to contribute to the conflict, but is unable or unwilling to partake in actual warfare (for any number of reasons, ranging from inaccessibility to the theatres of conflict, to indolence or cowardice) is given a vindicatory rationale for this alterative, entirely legitimate mode of action. Media Jihadists, for their part, have responded to these overtures with enthusiasm and unsurprisingly great relief –particularly in the knowledge that they are no longer relegated to their previous roles of voyeuristic passivity.

This cathartic function of the Jihadists' new media spaces, which allows would-be Jihadists to be part of the broader Global Jihad, but crucially without engaging in direct violence, cannot be overstated. Indeed, the virtual or media Jihad has served an increasingly important function in subsuming diverse strains of political activism, unrest and dissent, thereby providing a purgative conduit and framework for its non-violent expression. Audiences can vent their anger and frustration at the various ills plaguing the Muslim world, or perhaps more importantly redirect their energies in an ostensibly useful way, without resorting to violent means.

There is little doubt that the media Jihadists in these new roles have proven immensely useful to the growth of the movement and the dissemination of its ideology. One of the most celebrated virtual Jihadists, Younis Tsouli (as mentioned above, also known as Irhaabi 007), whose contributions to the Global Jihad may have been confined to media production efforts from a bedroom computer in the United Kingdom, nevertheless received considerable acclaim from Jihadists around the world, including from prominent individuals such as Abu Mus'ab al-Zarqawi (the previous head of *al-Qaeda in Iraq*). The important role played by media Jihadists is acknowledged candidly in Tsouli's exchange with a fellow forum member, 'Abuthaabit', who attempted to convince a self-effacing Tsouli of his immense contributions to the Jihad:

This media work, I am telling you, is very important. Very, very, very, very ... Because a lot of the funds brothers are getting is because they are seeing stuff like this coming out. Imagine how many people have gone [to Iraq] after seeing the situation because of the videos. Imagine how many of them could have been *shahid* [martyrs] as well.[22]

The virtual media Jihadists have also increasingly understood that immersion in the virtual conflict does not necessarily render them immune to repercussions in the real world, such as arrest and prosecution under charges of materially abetting terrorism, encouraging or glorifying terrorism, or disseminating terrorist publications (as proscribed at least in the United Kingdom by the UK Terrorism Act 2006, Part 1).[23] The successful arrest and prosecution of a number of individuals in Europe on such charges have shown these to be genuine concerns that must be considered by media Jihadists before engaging in any potentially incriminating activity. The case of Babar Ahmed provides one of the earliest examples of the serious dangers inherent in conducting 'media Jihad'. A British IT support specialist, Babar Ahmed was arrested under the UK Terrorism Act 2000 in 2003 in connection with running the 'mujahideen news' website *azzam.com*. He was severely brutalised in police custody before being released without charge, but then rearrested shortly thereafter following a US extradition request on charges of 'providing material support to terrorists and conspiring to kill persons in a foreign country'. In a damning indictment of British justice, Babar Ahmad has now been held for almost six years without trial or charge by British authorities whilst awaiting his pending extradition.[24]

In addition to the dangers in the 'real' world, Jihadists online have also long been cognisant of the threat posed by the presence of security agencies and civilian 'spies' within the new media spaces of the Jihad. Many Jihadist forums dissuade individuals from communicating sensitive information over the Internet and encourage users to employ methods for masking their identities online. A post on a Jihadist forum in 2005, dissuaded individuals from communicating sensitive information on the Internet, warning that 'this forum, like the others, is under ... surveillance; any information is obviously not secret, so any individuals you meet and correspond with on the forums cannot be trusted at all'.[25]

For some, these elements of danger provide further justification that they are indeed engaging in a legitimate aspect of the conflict, evident from the 'enemy's' usage of the very same spaces and from the personal hazards to which they are themselves exposed.

Gender

For the numerous young men drawn to the virtual or media Jihad, its appeal is not difficult to understand. Individuals unable or unwilling to engage in the physical or militaristic Jihad for any number of reasons can nevertheless continue to support the cause without leaving the comfort of their homes and without exposing themselves to any significant danger. Moreover, with sanction from various Jihadist ideologues, providing crucial legitimation for these activities, there is little or no moral discordance in failing to travel to the frontlines oneself. However, we have not yet taken into consideration the appeal of the virtual media Jihad to women, particularly bearing in mind the various sociocultural restrictions placed upon women that prevent them from joining the actual Jihadist frontlines.

In the early 1980s, Abdullah Azzam attempted to convince the Muslim world of the obligatory nature of a defensive Jihad against the Soviet Union. He argued forcefully in favour of women being allowed to take part in the Jihad. In his *Defense of the Muslim Lands: The First Obligation after Faith* (1979), he writes:

> a boy is permitted to go out to fight without his father's permission, a wife without her husband's, and he who is in debt without his creditor's[26]

Nevertheless, perhaps in the face of criticisms from his generous, and more puritanical, Gulf Arab benefactors, Azzam later tempered his progressive stance in *Join the Caravan* (1987) by stating that 'Arab women cannot take part in fighting, because Afghan women have not yet done so'.[27]

Ayman al-Zawahiri's *Open Meeting*, he is asked by a questioner:

> Who is the highest-ranked woman in al-Qaeda? You don't have to state names, but what are their positions in the organisation?

Al-Zawahiri responds by stating:

There are no women in the al-Qaidat al-Jihad Organisation, but the wives of the mujahideen play a heroic role in managing their homes and sons despite the hardships of immigration, moving from place to place, fighting and expecting the strikes of the crusaders.

Others have similarly reinforced the notion that women traditionally do not partake in Jihad. Al-Zarqawi, for example, attempts to embarrass his audience into action by declaring:

if you [men] are not going to be chivalrous knights in this war, make way for women to wage it ... Indeed, by God, men have lost their manhood.[28]

In light of these social and cultural mores that restrict access to theatres of conflict, women with inclinations towards Jihad have naturally gravitated towards online forums, where they can simply mask their gender or fail to disclose it completely. Increasingly, however, it appears that women are displaying increasing confidence in revealing their true identities, and expressing their femininity as can be evinced through the growing proportion of female usernames and avatars on Jihadist forums. Moreover, their disclosure in fact is often met with great respect and courtesy by other forum members and they can enjoy what they consider to be permissible forms of interactions with fellow Jihadist males. Consequently, some women have welcomed access to media Jihad opportunities and proven themselves to be equally capable to their male counterparts in many arenas. For example, an article titled: 'Jahid: Your Enemies Online' in the April 2008 issue of the publication *Jami* of the Islamic Front of Iraqi Resistance had prominent contributions from Hiba Zakariya, described as 'a female activist in electronic Jihad'.

The growth in female media Jihadism was suggested in 2007 by the Dutch Intelligence and Security services (AIVD) who reported there had been a clear rise in the number of women that participated in spreading radical material over the Internet (AIVD 2008, pp. 46–7).[29] This is corroborated by Awan (2007b) who has shown that at least 20 per cent of registered users on the now defunct Mujahedon. net forum chose female-gender-specific usernames. Indeed, there have even been attempts by the Jihadist leadership itself to incorporate women's voices. In December 2009 for example, al-Qaeda's prominent media wing *as-Sahab* released a communiqué entitled 'Letter to My Muslim Sisters' by Ayman al-Zawahiri's wife, Umayma al-Zawahiri. The gendered aspect of Jihadist culture is absent from much media discourse around 'radicalisation'; gender would add one more axis of uncertainty, undermining stereotyped profiling of 'vulnerable' young men, contributing to the generalised condition of hypersecurity present in Western media-security discourse in the 2000s.

Transitions to the real Jihad

Despite the considerable means employed to legitimise the media Jihad, it would be imprudent to assume that the media Jihad will completely supplant the physical Jihad, which has continued to prove irresistible to some. In fact, Jihad-ist ideologues like Abu Musab al-Suri had almost always expected an inevitable transition from operating in a virtual capacity to a real capacity from those ensconced within the hyperreality of Jihadism. Al-Suri presciently described al-Qaeda's role as that of an ideological vanguard: 'al-Qaeda is not an organization ... nor do we want it to be ... It is a call, a reference, a methodology'.[30] Con-sequently he could propound a theoretical framework for autonomous cells and 'leaderless resistance' which envisioned that the,

> next stage of jihad will be characterized by terrorism created by individuals or small autonomous groups, which will wear down the enemy and prepare the ground for the far more ambitious aim ... an outright struggle for territory.[31]

Others have also been quick to adopt this framework. The al-Qaeda magazine *Muaskar al-Battar*, or Camp of the Sword, wrote in its 2004 debut,

> Oh Mujahid brother, in order to join the great training camps you don't have to travel to other lands ... Alone, in your home or with a group of your brothers, you too can begin to execute the training program.[32]

The first issue of *al-Battar* went on to outline its purpose:

> because many of Islam's young people do not know how to bear arms, not to mention use them ... your brothers in Mujahideen in the Arabian penin-sula have decided to publish this booklet ... and [the young Mujahideen] will act according to the military knowledge in it.[33]

A number of resources have also long been available for enabling this transition and include the now infamous and continuously expanding 700 megabytes-size file known as the *Encyclopaedia for the Preparation for Jihad (mawsu'at al-i'dad)*, which was first compiled during the 1979–1989 Afghan war. Indeed some virtual Jihadists appear to have focused almost entirely on virtual training. Despite the sanction afforded to media Jihad endeavours, the considerable weight of expectation from ideologues and fellow members to act upon their putative Jihadist aspirations, appears to have compelled a number of individuals to become dissatisfied with their current roles.

Despite garnering considerable acclaim in the virtual world, and being greeted on the forums as 'The hero – God salutes you', Tsouli nevertheless continued to harbour yearnings for 'martyrdom' on the 'real' battlefield. Although Tsouli was one of the most significant virtual Jihadists to emerge thus far, he nevertheless often lamented to his fellow forum users, 'Hero? I am only half a man now ... my heart is in Iraq.'[34] Tsouli's desire for 'real' Jihad appears to have led to his eventual demise; he was sentenced to 16 years' imprisonment in 2007 for his involvement in a decentralised web of terrorist plots.[35]

Numerous other examples exist of successful transitions from the virtual world to the real world. The most celebrated recent case is that of Abu Dujana al-Khurasani (the *nom de guerre* of Humam Khalil Abu Mulal al-Balawi), a well-known administrator of the al-Hesbah Jihadist forum. Abu Dujana was at some point recruited by the Jordanian General Intelligence Directorate (GID), but instead, serving as a double-agent, he conducted a suicide attack against US Camp Chapman near Khost in Afghanistan in December 2009, killing seven CIA operatives and a member of the GID. In interviews given by his wife after the event, al-Balawi is portrayed as someone 'obsessed with Jihad', who spent an inordinate amount of time on Jihadist forums:

> He followed all of them, but from a distance.... He was constantly reading and writing. He was crazy about online forums. He would go onto them and write severe, extremely hardline comments. He would cite verses from the Quran that talked about the need for jihad, and then write very tough comments based on those verses or on the sayings of the Prophet.[36]

But despite his clear attraction to the Jihadist cause, and his considerable writings on the Jihadist forums, he was nevertheless left feeling increasingly guilty over his self-induced torpor:

> My husband was also like them. He would talk and write about jihadi subjects a lot. But when we talked with his family among ourselves, we would always talk about his conversations. We would say 'he always talks but never does anything.' Despite all [his] talks and writings he was always criticized for doing nothing.[37]

It appears that al-Balawi was at some point early in his online career, content with supporting the Jihadist cause virtually, as this post of encouragement to his fellow forum users following the concerted assault on Jihadist forums shows,

> I say to my brothers in the jihadi media trench to rise up and support your mujahideen brothers with your pens, wealth, and time. Dust off the dirt of laziness, as the situation is not a happy one, and [the] Jewish Haganah dogs have attacked us, closed the forums, and have manipulated the download links of jihadi media productions – so is it that they are more patient and determined than you are? If you are familiar with your reputation amongst the mujahideen, then you would not sleep or enjoy living before you can reassure them with the return of the al-Hesbah, al-Ekhlaas, and al-Boraq forums, so will you do this now that you are aware?[38]

However, his own internal conflict over his inaction remained. This eventually precipitated the transformation to a real-world Jihadist:

The point my husband mostly complained about was this: why do we not go toward jihad? He was focused on this point. 'We always write, we always read but we do nothing,' he wrote.[39]

His experiences resonate strongly with many Jihadists confined to the virtual or media arena, and perhaps al-Balawi's eventual transformation may provide some form of vicarious validation for the media Jihadists' own current passivity. Certainly, al-Balawi's actions have been widely hailed within the virtual Jihadist community, with Abu Dujana quickly immortalised in videos, photo montages and even poetry, including an almost farcical ode to al-Balawi entitled 'Our James Bond'.[40]

Others appear content to remain within the virtual media sphere, enjoying the catharsis afforded by virtual action, unless of course they are compelled to leave, which may lead to actual physical violence and terrorism. The unprecedented attack on Jihadist media spaces from September 2008 onward, which included the disruption of major Jihadist web forums, severely curbed the opportunities for 'media Jihad'.[41] One forum member lamented,

> with the closure of all our sites, you [the Crusaders and their agents] have left us with no choice but to physically join the caravan of Jihad. With no Jihadi sites through which we can support our brother Mujahideen, there is no point for us to stay behind. We shall join them. Your act has shamed us and caused us to think 'what is left for us?'[42]

Ironically, individuals who may not have countenanced actual violence in the past may in the absence of these virtual arenas feel compelled to relinquish their virtual personas in favour of real-life Jihadist operations (Awan and al-Lami 2009). Indeed, we might postulate that the disruption of the al-Hesbah forum in late 2008 may have even played some small role in providing the *casus belli* for Abu Dujana's transition to the 'real Jihad'.

Conclusion

The virtual or media Jihad has not only gained prominence and credibility as a wholly legitimate alternative to traditional conceptions of Jihad, but has also progressively outpaced the militaristic or physical Jihad in the modern era. While the 'real' Jihad continues to hold a certain level of aspirational appeal, the catharsis offered by the media or virtual Jihad has proven sufficiently efficacious to supplant traditional notions of Jihad for a new generation of Jihadists, unwilling or unable to engage in actual violence themselves. Consequently, while the occasional transitions from virtual to real actions will remain a distinct and disconcerting possibility, they are unlikely to be adopted as praiseworthy precedents by significant numbers of virtual Jihadists, despite whatever rhetorical validation they might be accorded publicly. Moreover, the uncertain dynamics of these processes, typically articulated as 'radicalisation online' or 'virtual radicalisation' remain uncertain and contested, particularly as the linkage between words and acts online and deeds offline is exceedingly problematic (Awan 2007c; Stevens and Neumann 2008; Bergin *et al.* 2009).

The nexus between Web 2.0 in particular, and the media or virtual Jihadist, has had enormously important repercussions for Jihadism in the twenty-first century, rejuvenating its ailing ideology, and facilitating the dissemination of its counterculture to new and diffuse audiences, many of whom are beyond the traditional ambit of official Jihadist media organs. Crucially, however, the ideology of Jihadism has to some extent been distorted and recast along the way, for a new generation. Although Jihadism has survived, albeit in somewhat attenuated form, and indeed spread unimpeded across other the new media platforms, the ideology itself has lost some of its coherence and cogency along the way, tremendously warping the signal to noise ratio. Marshall McLuhan's well-known and prescient maxim 'the medium is the message',[43] can perhaps help us to better appreciate how the promotion of a virtual or media Jihad within the new media ecology has fundamentally recast the ideology of Jihadism in the twenty-first century, in order to retain its relevance to a new generation of 'digital natives'.

4 Media events
Televisual connections 2004–2006

Critical events trigger the most intense consideration of security, identity, and legitimacy. Pearl Harbor, the Cuban Missile Crisis, and more recently the 9/11 attacks were each catalysts for reflection and reaction concerning national and personal security, who 'we' are and what 'our' values are, and what security policies would be a legitimate and efficacious response to the situation as understood. Following the launch of the 2003 Iraq War, the UK then appeared to be beset with critical security events, each brought to citizens by media but which also directly affected many people's lives. Here, our focus falls upon the 7/7 London bombings of July 2005, the Forest Gate police raids on homes in June 2006, and the transatlantic air plot that paralysed Heathrow airport in August 2006. All involved apparently 'radicalised' individuals who committed or were believed to be about to commit violence. These events were part of a series of international attacks or counterterrorism responses presumed to constitute and lend narrative coherence to the 'Global War on Terror' and discourses of global fear, risk and resilience. Such incidents are crucial test cases for the assertion that radicalisation lies at a nexus of global Jihadist discourses and local security concerns, since we might expect to see the motives and background of Jihadist perpetrators made visible by mainstream media for audiences to understand who is carrying out the attacks being reported. If there is a nexus through which Jihadist discourses cascade from the Jihadist online world and translate through reporters and analysts into mainstream public understandings, it is through breaking terrorism events that such connections might occur.

This chapter explains why mainstream television coverage of breaking news events connected to terrorism and radicalisation took on a certain consistent form and content. Edward Said noted the pun in the title of his book *Covering Islam* (1981). His analysis of Western media coverage of Islam and Muslims suggested such reporting obscured or covered as much as it made clear. We suggest media coverage is more than a matter of obscuring/revealing: media construct particular forms and audience relations to such forms, in order to create imperatives to keep watching. We must investigate such forms to begin to identify how audience understanding, concern and perhaps anxiety or insecurity might be generated. We find that, first, the form these events took in media were shaped by the representation of a certain temporality. These media events offered an 'event time' (Gitlin 1980) characterised as an *extended present* (Nowotny 1994). The past and the future were represented as extensions of the ongoing crisis, the breaking news moment. The future was presented as an empty space or plane upon which the implications of the event would unfold, and the past was interpreted for 'signs' of danger leading to the present crisis. As news, the extended present created an imperative to keep watching and following the story. As news about terrorism, this format offered a representation of a future foreshadowed by the threat of similar or greater attacks to come. However, in addition to the extended present, television news presented the viewer with news they had *already seen*. In the first decade of the twenty-first century, the BBC offered regular drama-documentaries or simulations of security crises, with a programme each on a smallpox epidemic, transport catastrophe and terrorist attacks on London. Each of these 'premediations' was used to prepare citizens – and any policymakers, journalists and emergency response workers watching – for how a real crisis might unfold. Indeed, the 'London under attack' terrorist simulation featured the very 'experts' who were used for reporting actual terrorist incidents in the years to come, resulting in a merging of real and fictional representations.

If the form of television coverage suggested a particular orientation to the past, present and future, the content of the coverage was shaped by discourses of security prevalent among security analysts, practitioners and academic analyses since the 1990s. A discourse is a set of practices through which certain statements count as meaningful. Hence a discourse 'constrains and enables what can be said' (Barad 2007: 147). We examine how analyses of security and terrorism created discourses in which certain descriptions of terrorists, governments, citizens and fear are presented as meaningful and valid. The 'global risk' analysis of Ulrich Beck presents a world of contagious threats generated by human activity but now beyond human control, requiring a fundamental shift in the arrangement of world politics. A parallel 'global fear' analysis produced by scholars as well as journalists and some policymakers suggests we have entered a 'post-9/11' era, a distinct, dangerous new period, in which anxiety about threats is universal. Finally, television news coverage of breaking terrorist events is marked by a 'resilience' discourse, in which is it is assumed that public authorities need to instil resilience in citizens so that they are less vulnerable to mass panic or residual anxiety in the face of global risks and fears. Journalists and officials appearing in media coverage in the 2004–2006 period largely operated within these discursive parameters of risk, fear and resilience. Such discourses reinforced the temporal formats of the extended present and premediation, resulting in the projection of an understanding of the present and future as a 'war without end', thereby reinforcing – inadvertently – the 'war on terror' framework of the US and UK governments of the time.

Jihadists are largely absent from mainstream media, however. Breaking news events around radicalised violence are marked by an absence of information. Either officials do have information but are slow to release it, or authorities have acted on the precautionary principle and do not have any confirmed information, having acted in response to an imagined or presumed threat to which the consequences of not responding would be more catastrophic than taking wrong action. This creates a space for speculation about threats in general, and attempts to connect general theories to scraps of information about these particular events. We find the discourses of risk, fear and resilience shape what is said and how the events are conceived. Hence, the chapter identifies the nexus of discourses that enable radicalisation to be framed as a significant problem.

After establishing the centrality of mainstream television to audience-cum-citizens' engagement with breaking security events, this chapter offers analysis of the 7 July 2005 London bombings, June 2006 Forest Gate police raids, and August 2006 Heathrow transatlantic bomb plot arrests.

Watching media events

When breaking news events such as terrorist attacks occur, audiences' patterns of news consumption also break with routine.[1] On an ordinary day, people continue to have news routines interwoven into their social lives. What news they consume depends on what they are doing, whether it is getting ready for school, going to work, eating dinner and so on. These consumption routines have been transformed to an extent by the advent of the Internet and the mobility afforded to digital media consumers. However, the hierarchy of use gets turned upside down when a major terror event happens, with TV suddenly the choice source, and then broadsheets for authoritative analysis the next day. Hence in this chapter we focus on mainstream television news as the primary medium connecting citizens to radicalisation-related events.

In this period marked by critical security events, we must also situate the subsequent analysis in terms of the experience individuals accumulated in making sense of such events. For instance, by the time we get to the transatlantic air plot arrests in August 2006, audiences have become familiar with actual acts of violence such as the 7/7 bombings and failed 21/7 bombings, as well as false alarms such as police raids on homes in Forest Gate, East London, in June 2006. Although the transatlantic air plot arrests led to convictions, the authorities' actions on the day were met with some cynicism. For instance, in the following exchange from an interview the next month, a group of friends have been discussing the Israel–Hezbollah conflict of August 2006 and its relation to the events at Heathrow. Alper is a Turkish sports journalist, age 25, living in London. He is a non-practicing Muslim. Raphael is an administrative assistant, age 24, born in Israel, he also speaks Turkish and lives in London. He is Jewish. Also present is Darren, a 22-year-old London travel agent, also Muslim, non-practicing, from Turkey:

ALPER: Yeah and, for example, during that conflict there was a bomb scare at Heathrow airport. And when that happened, I remember I even said to Darren, it came to the end of the day and I hadn't heard a single thing of what was happening in Israel, and I thought the biggest bombings could have occurred there today but we haven't heard because it has been *pushed down the agenda by some fake bomb report*. There may have been major atrocities going on and it could have been *a planned act* to have this happening here *to completely divert all the media attention* which is exactly what it did. They just showed some planes standing on the runway for hours on end saying 'bomb alert' in complete Fox News style.[2]

Alper interprets the very happening of the Heathrow bomb plot as a ploy to divert attention of audiences away from the Israel–Hezbollah conflict. The British government, though not named, is presumably the actor behind this diversion, and 'They' refers to the mainstream media. Alper and Raphael link the Heathrow bomb plot coverage to a series of geopolitical events in the UK:

RAPHAEL: Same argument could be said when 7/7 happened, the London bombings happened, and a couple of days later [the] London Olympics, and then a day later the G8. Everything was perfectly set.

ALPER: Yeah exactly, I totally believe in that.[3]

The issue is not whether the connection Alper and Raphael make between these events is valid. Rather, in the 2001–2006 period, audiences, media and policymakers habitually made such connections. Such a series of apparently connected events became 'schemata' through which any new event, or imagined future events, could be interpreted (Hoskins and O'Loughlin 2007). The period was marked by media events such as the 7/7 London bombings, the Asian tsunami, Hurricane Katrina and the Heathrow bomb plot. One thing these events had in common was blanket, 24-hour media attention. As such, the expectation of such events and the predictability of massive media attention created the possibility for the construction of an event so that, in Raphael's terms, it is 'perfectly set' to receive blanket media coverage. The very predictability of media attention constituted a crisis for journalists because they could easily be manipulated by policymakers who knew how to create a story fulfilling the news values that would compel journalists to cover it. Journalists had become weapons of both terrorists and governments.

Hence the suspicion, even conspiratorial air, evident in this interview. It was this context of media events, spontaneous or constructed, within which the 7 July 2005 bombings, Forest Gate raids and Heathrow bomb plot analysed below were made sense of.

In our introduction we discussed several key discourses through which terrorism and radicalisation were discussed in this period, in which the concepts 'risk', 'fear' and 'resilience' were central. The chapter now identifies how these shaped the consideration of a series of breaking news events related to radicalisation in the UK.

The 7/7 London bombings: premediation, the event, the retrospection

A year before the attacks of 7 July 2005, the BBC broadcast a drama documentary or simulation, 'London under attack', which anticipated the eventual actual attacks with some accuracy. The programme was part of a string of simulations, broadcast by the BBC, of catastrophes befalling the infrastructure of Britain. On 13 May 2003, 'The day Britain stopped' was aired,[4] a 'what if?' dramatisation depicting how transport gridlock caused by a train strike could cause unexpected effects on car and air travel, leading to a major air crash. A little over a year earlier, on 5 February 2002, the BBC had broadcast 'Smallpox 2002',[5] a docudrama about the release of the smallpox virus by terrorists in New York and the contagious spread of catastrophe around the world that followed, including its effects upon London. These dramatic simulations ask audiences to consider whether they or their governments are prepared for such crises rather than how likely such crises are. The political nature of risk evaluation is subsumed by the logic of hypersecurity, the 'war against contingency' (Dillon 2007: 14). The presumed certainty is that since catastrophes can happen, they will. What is uncertain is how citizens and governments will respond. Such programmes are presented as helpful premediations enabling awareness to be raised and contingency planning to be thought through.

The programme begins in the studio with the headlines at 8 a.m. from newsreader Kirsty Lang, interspersed with comments from longtime BBC News presenter Gavin Esler that what the viewer is watching is 'well researched but fictional'. Over the morning we learn of three terrorist attacks on the London underground train network, before a chemical tanker carrying chlorine is blown up releasing a poison gas cloud into the streets later in the day and, finally, news that a second tanker is missing and possibly hijacked by what by then seems a coordinated terrorist group. By the end of the programme, over 3,000 people are dead. The studio is filled with assorted experts, including David Gilbertson (former Commander, Metropolitan Police), Crispin Black (former intelligence officer), Ian Hoult (Emergency Planning Officer), Michael Portillo (former Secretary of State for Defence), Peter Power (former Metropolitan Police and government advisor) and Lance Price (former Deputy Director of Communications, 10 Downing Street). Each offers their diagnosis on what the respective branches of government should be doing as the crisis develops. Price and Portillo suggest opportune moments for the Prime Minister to use media to offer the public reassurance, both for the symbolic value of illustrating the presence of a leadership figure and because it is presumed citizens would seek to be addressed in emotional terms, rather than simply being provided with information. Gilbertson considers the point when mobile phone networks should be commandeered for emergency services only. Hoult wonders how the state should deal with the 'tens of thousands of people on the streets' who cannot use public transport and may need to be evacuated. The focus, overall, is resilience, and Furedi's analysis (see Chapter 1, this volume) that government understands resilience as something *it* must do, and that citizens are relatively helpless, appears accurate. Indeed, when the actual 7/7 attacks occur a year later, the 'tens of thousands of people on the streets' simply walked home. When the second chemical tanker goes missing, Price raises the question of emergency powers:

> If there are now bombs going off above ground, in this case a lorry being attacked, it could happen anywhere, so the potential for mass panic across

not just the capital but the whole country is very much with us. I think therefore we need to look at more serious measures. We do have reserve powers
in effect to take over the BBC if we were to wish to, and to get them to
broadcast whatever we wanted them to broadcast. Those powers are there in
the Broadcasting Act.

Price does later equivocate, 'the public have got a greater capacity to deal with
uncomfortable truths and uncomfortable possibilities and scenarios than perhaps
we give them credit for'. Nevertheless, the thesis of the programme is that Britain's emergency services and planning for multiple attacks is lacking; as such,
the problem of resilience lies with better state organisation rather than improved
social relations. This is demonstrated through interviews with anonymous
London underground workers asserting they have had no training in emergency
response, and the presentation of apparently damning, authoritatively sourced
statistics scattered throughout the programme, including, for instance:

Metropolitan Police radios do not work in one third of the underground
network.

Source: London Resilience

The Civil Contingency Reaction Force communications system is not compatible with those of the emergency services.

Source: House of Commons debate, October 2002

It has been estimated that it would take 12 hours to mobilise 100 people.

Source: Evidence to Defence Select Committee 2003

More than half of businesses in the UK have no emergency plans in place.

Source: Business Continuity Institute and Chartered Management Institute

The programme is notable for offering little analysis of who the perpetrators of
the attacks might be. There is no explicit mentioning of radicalisation or 'Jihad'.
Instead, it *implies* the attackers must be Muslim as the studio experts warn about
the possibility of reprisal attacks on Muslim communities and the need to consult
Muslim community leaders. Almost exactly anticipating how Home Secretary
John Reid would respond to the actual 7/7 attacks, Price suggests, as the
simulated attacks occur, 'I think we have to look at getting people up on
the media who are able to offer some degree of reassurance and try to explain
that this isn't a sort of Muslim attack against the West, that people need to be
responsible and measured in the way in which they react to it.'

The simulation ends by amplifying fear through the depiction of an extended
present in which larger attacks are likely. The fictional killing of 3,000 people or
the possibility of this actually happening means, for Gilbertson, that 'the world
changed'. 'When we've got something like this, there's no normality other than
the new normality,' Power adds, and 'It's going to have a resonance that will go

on for decades'. Gavin Esler concludes that 'what we saw on film today might be at the lower end of the spectrum of what terrorists might on a good day achieve'.

By the time of the evening of the 7 July 2005, BBC News at 6 p.m. began:

> Londoners have been worried about an attack they hoped would never happen, but today it did. It was still rush hour when the attacks began. Police say there were four bomb explosions, three on the underground and one on a bus.

As with the 2004 'London under attack' simulation, an early morning attack hit three tube trains and one vehicle above ground, in this case a bus. Acknowledging the premediation of the event, a BBC News 24 presenter added, 'This was something the capital had rehearsed for but had hoped would never have to be implemented.' The coverage then centred upon the theme of resilience. By focusing on the response of emergency services and citizens, London was presented as resilient. However, if such coverage contained terror, the subsequent analysis of the operations of al-Qaeda would go on to amplify the threat again.

The question of resilience was raised in terms of the efforts of emergency services: their practical effectiveness, and the emotional effect on its workers. 'It must be very traumatic for them', a BBC reporter asked Brian Paddick, Deputy Assistant Commissioner of the Metropolitan Police. 'How do they cope with it all?' Paddick replied:

> It's been very traumatic for our officers and for those people from the other emergency services. They are determined to do a professional job. Clearly we are going to give them plenty of support to make sure they can cope with the terrifying scenes that they've seen. But I have to say, the emergency services and the people of London have responded magnificently to this terrible, terrible atrocity.

The BBC Home Correspondent Mark Easton reported that the emergency services workers had 'managed to suck the terror out of terrorism this morning', and 'if indeed this was the work of al-Qaeda and they were trying to terrorise London and Londoners, my impression here ... is that they've failed'. Would this mean a 'new normality', as Peter Powers had suggested in 'London under attack'? This suggestion was discounted in a discussion later on Channel 4 News between presenter Jon Snow and Professor Michael Clarke, a security expert. Snow noted that Prime Minister Tony Blair, by this point in the day, had asserted that the attacks would not affect the daily lives of British citizens, but was part of a government looking to introduce identity cards and extended police powers. Clarke argued that identity cards would not have stopped that day's attacks. Channel 4 News also broadcast an interview with Rudolph Giuliani, Mayor of New York City during the 9/11 attacks. Giuliani also refrained from sensationalising the events:

PRESENTER: Is our way of life inevitably going to be affected?

GIULIANI: Uh, yes, it will be affected but not in a draconian way or a dramatic way. Honestly, there isn't too much more that you can do. Yes, there are a few things more you can do, but the reality is that in a city as large as London or New York or Washington or Paris you can't have perfect security. I mean it's just never going to exist. In fact in life we don't live without risk, so you can't create perfect security in the city.

Nevertheless, imperfect security could be interpreted as a permanent risk of terrorism. And rather than containing the drama of the attacks, Giuliani proceeded with an analogy that inflated the historical significance of the day:

> But people of London are very calm. They seem very measured and very determined. They remind me very much of their parents, uh, grandparents and great-great grandparents whom they must've inherited this from, this sense of strength because they had to live through the Battle of Britain, which is far worse than anything we've had to face.

Imperfect security marked by periodic events reminiscent of 'the Blitz' suggests a 'new normal'. Sky News presented a visual sequence of attacks in Bali in 2002, Istanbul in 2003, Madrid in 2004, and finally London in 2005 (Hoskins and O'Loughlin 2007, Chapter 5). Sky News also presented 'Terrorism Expert' Nick Kochan, who suggested authorities should be 'looking for a group of sleepers. People who have been here [in the UK] for many years, who have given no evidence of criminality or suspicion, who would have been accumulating money and accumulating material of some kind. But, um, *behaving in a normal way* and *merging* with the rest of the Muslim community' (italics added). A clip is shown from 2004 of Ken Livingstone, Mayor of London, saying 'It would be inconceivable really that one day some [terrorists] will *not* get through'. Earlier, BBC News asked Professor Jose Ignasio Torablanca about the security implications of the Madrid attacks and parallels with London. Torablanca replied:

> Yes ... this shows that nobody is safe, that public transportation [is] very easy to hit. You have a feeling that after this second attack on London that it could happen to you again, that there's nothing you can do to stop it if the terrorists set the target on you. So there is a sense of helplessness, of being, you know, unable to do anything.

Such comments reinforce the global risk and fear discourses, presented terrorism as unstoppable and both governments and citizens as passive victims with no choice but to wait to be attacked.

Here, at last, the nexus with Jihadist discourses of violence becomes apparent. The perpetrators were by now described as potential sleeper cells, merging into British Muslim communities, their actions fitting the template of previous al-Qaeda attacks. In the Channel 4 News studio filmmaker Paul Eedle, who had been tracking communications on Jihadist websites at the time, noted that no credible al-Qaeda actor had claimed responsibility for the attacks but this was common; no responsibility had been claimed for the 2004 Madrid bombings. Professor Michael Clarke argued that the attacks had a political point: 'to indicate that even in the middle of a G8 summit they can get bombs going off in the middle of London. That's the point'. The Sky News Political Editor, Adam Boulton, argued that 'the attacks have in a way succeeded' because world leaders at the G8 summit were forced to respond. In a significant slip from the official register of solidarity between civilised nations presented at the G8, Boulton said the attackers had:

> got this very fierce response, uh, *united* response from all the world leaders, which has of course elevated the publicity for the story and the public attention to a new level around the world.

World leaders had amplified the impact of the 7/7 London bombings, with Sky, the BBC and others also providing the very publicity he mentions. Media and political actors acknowledged and thereby offered credibility and potentially authority to the then-unknown perpetrators of the act and to al-Qaeda, whether as a direct co-ordinator or indirect inspiration for the attacks. The terror of the attacks had been partially contained by praise for the resilience of Londoners and emergency service workers. However, despite remaining invisible and rarely mentioned in those terms, on the 7 July 2005 Jihadist violence was a central matter of concern, and the potential for future attacks was presented as inevitable, unstoppable and diffuse.

Three days later, on 10 July 2005, BBC One broadcast a new documentary presented by Peter Taylor called – confusingly – 'London under attack'. Taylor had been investigating al-Qaeda in the year previously, and presented the interviews and research he had compiled. As with the original 'London under attack' and the coverage on the day of 7/7, the thesis of the report was that future attacks were inevitable. This was because intelligence services were 'blind', unable to trace the sleeper cells indicated by Kochan. Taylor interviewed the former head of the CIA's Bin Laden Unit, Michael Scheuer, who claimed 'al-Qaeda's first role is inciter and instigator rather than command control'. 'That may explain why the cell got under the wire', said Taylor. 'There was not a scrap of intelligence. No tell tale "chatter" over the airwaves'.

That attention to sleeper cells entailed some analysis of the radicalisation process. Taylor noticed the lack of pattern to *who* had been radicalised at that time. Sajid Badat and Richard Reid had planned to attack aeroplanes, but Badat was 'a middle class grammar school boy' whereas Reid, the 'shoe-bomber', had a less affluent background. Turning to *how* radicalisation happened, Taylor fully implicates the Internet:

TAYLOR: Some jihadi supporters have twisted the news coverage of Thursday's attacks to their own propaganda advantage. And the Internet carries their message that it's revenge for Iraq.

And it's the Internet, the World Wide Web, that drives the radicalising power of Iraq. Few attacks take place without a camcorder, computer and Internet access – to send the images spinning around the world. In Britain there's an audience too.

EVAN KOHLMANN (US Government Advisor): While a picture may be worth a thousand words, a video, uploaded to an Internet site, is worth 10,000.

TAYLOR: Evan Kohlman studies the Internet traffic from Iraq for clients that include the US government.

KOHLMANN: Show a video of someone blowing themselves up, killing Americans, spreading American blood. *That has an incalculable effect* in terms of recruiting future terrorists.

Taylor does not scrutinise these claims. For instance, a sceptical viewer might ask: *who* are the Jihadi supporters? Is it the Internet 'driving' the 'radicalising power' or people using the Internet? Attacks are recorded and sent 'spinning around the world', but most aspects of social life are now recorded – think of family events, or even routine uploadings – so why remark that the attacks are? It would be more surprising that they are not, and it seems like Taylor is part of a generation of journalists, policymakers and 'experts' who find remarkable a media ecology which to younger generations is taken for granted. Is a video 'worth 10,000' words? Is there any evidence that moving images have a quantifiably measurable impact on, say, potential supporters or terrorised publics? And then, after have a 10,000-word impact, the viewer is told such videos have 'an incalculable effect'. In sum, such a report is not informative to citizens. It perpetuates several myths about dangerous technologies and media effects that might feed into audience anxieties or simply increase mistrust in BBC reporting. Indeed, these ambivalent responses are what we find in analysis of audience engagement with such news in Chapter 6.

Taylor points to the Internet as a source of information on how to commit violence as well as a source of material that inspires violence. This is represented as an easy, routine opportunity; if Beck points to global risks such as terrorism as the 'dark side' of globalisation, then the Internet is a central mechanism:

TAYLOR: ...there would have been no need for Thursday's bombers to travel to learn how to make explosives. Would-be jihadis *just have to log on*. Training videos are there *at the click of a mouse*, with detailed instructions of how to make and detonate bombs, carry out kidnappings and make homemade weapons. These images were found on the hard drive of a suspect allegedly to be connected to the Madrid conspirators. The train bombs were detonated by alarms on mobile phones.

KOHLMANN: Even at home you have a how-to guide to terrorism available *at the touch of a button*, how to build a suicide bomb vest, how to build a suicide car bomb, the motivation and the tools to commit terror.

SCHEUER (Former Head, CIA Bin Laden Unit): They mounted a great number of these things, one of them called the Encyclopaedia of Jihad, it's apparently about 12,000 pages long, based primarily on US and British Special Forces and Marine Corps manuals. You can now, *in the comfort of your home* download those parts of the manual you want to study, whether it's bomb making or small unit combat tactics [...]

TAYLOR: It's like a jihadi do-it-yourself correspondence course.

The Internet becomes a source of insecurity but also a space of danger, in which terrorists lurk:

KOHLMANN: In fact, it is the terrorists who have the technological advantage when it comes to the Internet – it is the terrorists who were able to *mysteriously move through the Internet* without being detected, without being seen by law enforcement, and able to distribute these materials in many cases without any consequences happening to them.

The BBC's primary analytical response to the attacks of 7 July 2005 amplified the danger posed by creating a tenuous connection between technology and terrorism. Taylor closed the programme by noting that the recovered computers of the Madrid bombers contained plans for 'future, high profile targets – like Real Madrid's stadium'. However, the bombers blew themselves up rather than face arrest by Spanish police. Did the London bombers – their identity still unknown at that time – plan future attacks or would the police find them first? For Taylor, 'No one knows what will happen between now and then'.

The Forest Gate raid: 'if you grow a beard, you're a terrorist'

On Friday 2 June 2006 Metropolitan Police raided two houses on a street in the Forest Gate area of East London, arresting the brothers Mohammed Abdul Kahar, 23, and Abdul Koyair, 20. Police were acting on intelligence that a chemical weapon was being hidden in one of the houses (BBC News 2006a). The men were released without charge on 9 June 2006, and the police apologised (BBC News 2006d). The police said they had 'no choice' but to act once 'specific intelligence' had been received (BBC News 2006b), and Prime Minister Blair reaffirmed the precautionary logic: 'You can only imagine if they fail to take action and something terrible happened what outcry would be then, so they are in an impossible situation' (BBC News 2006c). It was significant that one of the brothers, Kahar, was shot in the shoulder in what an independent police report later declared was an accidental shooting. On 22 July 2005, following the 7/7 London bombings and failed 21/7 bombings, a Brazilian plumber, Jean Charles de Menezes, had been shot by police on the London underground while boarding a train after he was wrongly identified as a suspect from the previous day's failed attacks. Armed police had until then not been a feature of UK society, and the use of firearms by police had become a matter of public controversy. The misidentification of de Menezes raised the possibility that one might be shot for 'looking Muslim' as well as knowledge that police make mistakes with fatal consequences for innocent people. This was the context for the Forest Gate raids. We analyse coverage of the day from 10 a.m. until 10 p.m. on BBC1, ITV, Sky News and Channel 4 News.

Officials had not released information about the intelligence being acted upon on the day, so the possible presence of a chemical weapon is absent from the news coverage. At 10.45 a.m., the BBC correspondent decodes the information made available for the viewer by focusing on what kind of incident officials say this *is* and is *not*. Note that the viewer is not told where this information is from, only a mysterious 'security world':

> Going back to the seriousness of this raid, when a question is asked and it's early days yet, a man's in custody who hasn't been charged, but when asked 'well, what's this all about', the answer from people in the security world is that this *is* an anti-terrorist raid. It relates to international terrorism, that's the code for *not* Irish terrorism, and if there were targets involved then those targets *were* here in the UK. In other words, they are *not* talking about people who might have gone off and fought overseas. So clearly, no suggestions of who may or may not be guilty of anything. But what the police are dealing with are suspicions of international terrorism with targets in the UK and that's the indication of why it's being taken so seriously.

In this information vacuum, attention is focused on the brothers and how they might have been radicalised. The primary theme is that the two brothers had gone through a sudden transformation following the 11 September 2001 attacks. Neighbours and local people commenting on the street remarked that the brothers had grown beards, started wearing Muslim clothing, and regularly attended mosques. This speculation is not about whether those commenting thought the brothers could be involved in terrorism or if they had shown any behaviour that might indicate activity related to terrorism, but instead focused on them becoming religious. It is as if a turn to religion is a proxy for turning to terrorism. On Channel 4, a young female witness who had previously appeared on BBC and ITV said, 'One of them used to go to my school and before 9/11 he was pretty normal looking, you know, Western clothing. And suddenly after 9/11 I saw the boys with beards and hats [skullcaps] and stuff and I thought that was weird'. This connection is refuted on BBC News at 9.03 p.m., where one of a group of Muslims being interviewed said, 'Basically freedom of speech doesn't apply to Muslims. If you grow a beard, you're a terrorist'. ITV News addresses that apparent connection between religiosity and terrorism, its Security Correspondent James Mates summarising the views of the brothers' 'families and friends': 'one thing they all agree on is that none of the three mosques they attended were radical mosques and there was nothing in these men's lives that suggested in any way that they were connected with terrorism'.

How did media represent the reactions of the local community on this day in mid-2006, a year on from the 7/7 bombings and the Jean Charles de

Menezes shooting, a climate in which British Muslims and other ethnic and religious minorities felt securitised and racialised while a majority of British citizens supported increased police powers, a more aggressive foreign policy, and felt the 'war on terror' would last over 20 years and 44 per cent 'beyond their lifetimes' (Gillespie and O'Loughlin, forthcoming)? The way in which television operates privileges the visual, and across the channels analysed, on the surface there appears a relatively tranquil scene. Against a split screen backdrop depicting policeman in one screen and emergency services, vans and forensic tents extending down the street to the houses, the BBC News correspondent says:

> it's a beautiful sunny day in East London and the atmosphere is very, very relaxed. You might think there would be tensions in an area like this when a raid like this happens, but that certainly has not been what we're seeing this morning ... there's a level of curiosity, people are fascinated about the fact that this has happened in their community ... People who lived on the street whom we've been speaking to say that these were fairly normal people who lived in this house ... this is not a tense feeling and certainly not one of imminent danger from anything that might be down the road there.

The people being interviewed appeared to represent what ITV described as, 'a very lively mixed area ... Pakistanis and Bengalis are communities living side by side'. Young people stand around, several laughing, some talking on mobile phones. Some are shown playing tennis next to the cordoned off area. At this apparently calm stage in the day, BBC News interviews former Metropolitan Police officer Peter Power, who featured in the 'London under attack' simulation-documentary-premediation a year before the 7/7 London bombings. He describes the 'new normal':

PRESENTER: Peter. If I said to you ten years ago it would be perfectly normal to see police and NBC [nuclear, biological, chemical] suits on streets in East London and it barely raises an eyebrow, what would your reaction have been?

POWER: It means that when we go to Heathrow or Gatwick airports, we're now thoroughly used to seeing heavily armed officers walking around ... Well that preceded seventh of July. The fact is now, when I talked about crossing that Rubicon, that officers have to wear this level of protection if they're going to succeed in their task in the front end ... and it is going to be more frequent. It isn't an everyday occurrence, let's not get carried away with that. But when you say people don't bat an eyelid, that's largely true, that's the way it's going.

So it means that when we get stopped by police in [the] future and if they're wearing that sort of protective clothing and carrying guns now we do what the police officer says for fear of being shot. In the old days we stopped when a police officer asked us because we recognised his legitimate authority to stop us. So there are subtle changers here and the police are very aware of them. And frankly, what choice have they got?

Powers presents this as an imperfect situation, but an unavoidable one; police officers would prefer to be recognised because of their authority, not because of mortal fear, but if one accepts the diagnosis of a diffuse terrorist threat then 'what choice have they got' but to carry guns?

As the day proceeds, Channel 4 News begins to note 'pockets of anger … fears of a backlash *from* the Muslim population' who felt victimised. The Vice-Chair of Forest Gate Mosque, Mohammed Zaki Ahmed, told a reporter, 'There is no radical in this Newham borough. It's very clean and peace-loving people'. Sky News interviews a teenage boy who describes hearing smashed glass, screams, then looking out of his window to see police with 'gas masks'. A head teacher adds, 'I think the community at large is quite nervous'. In the Channel 4 News studio, Azad Ali of the Muslim Safety Forum is interviewed and directly addresses the comments of the young female Muslim interviewed earlier who claimed to have gone to school with the brothers. Ali said:

> Well, one of the shocking statements that was made by one of the persons that were interviewed was that they described [the brothers] as normal before and weird later on, and that's blatant Islamophobia. It just goes to show the perception of the Muslim community that's been created by different sectors of the community, media included.

Television news does not report what is hidden, and it possible that many people stayed indoors after the police raid. Previous research indicates the individuals from marginalised or stigmatised communities retreat from public spaces (Gillespie and O'Loughlin, forthcoming). Unhappiness at the police action became evident in the aftermath. On 18 June, following the brothers' release and appearances in news media, nearly 5,000 people from across different local communities protested at Forest Gate Police Station at the violent nature of the police actions (BBC News 2006e).

In sum, in the absence of official information, journalists interview local people who report signs of radicalisation. These alleged signs included a turn to religious appearance and behaviour, not signs of involvement in terrorist activities. This does not help inform audiences about what is happening, and perpetuates a stereotype about the appearance and behaviour of 'dangerous' people. This model of radicalisation is contested by one TV interviewee, who protests at the logic of inference: 'If you grow a beard, you're a terrorist'. There is much attention on the counterterrorism response, and whether such incidents are part of a new normal. The event is interpreted through a schema connecting Forest Gate with 7/7 and the mistaken shooting of Jean Charles de Menezes. Ultimately the police actions are contested, on screen and in the coming weeks. There is no discussion of al-Qaeda or connection of the brothers to terrorist networks, only that police acted on suspicion of 'international terrorism'.

The transatlantic bomb plot: 'it's precautionary rather than based on any intelligence'

On 10 August 2006 police arrested a number of men in connection with an alleged plot to blow up a number of airlines flying from Heathrow airport in London to a number of airports in Canada and the US. Here we analyse news coverage on the day of the arrests from BBC in the UK and Fox News in the US. The focus of the day was Heathrow. As 'BREAKING NEWS: TERROR PLOT' rolled across the BBC news screen, cameras lingered on planes idle on runways and crowds of passengers standing talking to each other in the departure areas. The voiceover adds, 'these pictures say it all, people waiting, waiting for information, knowing they won't be travelling anywhere anytime soon'. It is reported that flights are delayed or cancelled because police had uncovered a plot to smuggle liquids in handbags onto planes to assemble and detonate bombs mid-flight, and that 18 people had been arrested in London and the Thames Valley region. However, the journalist voiceover notes the absence of further information. Home Secretary John Reid announces 'police believe the alleged plot [would have threatened] a considerable amount of life'. Like the reporting of the Forest Gate raids, as a breaking news story about security, the Heathrow bomb plot story is dependent on official sources for concrete information since officials are the actors determining the course of events by making the arrests.

Speculation fills the empty space of the rolling news: journalists begin to interview each other. The BBC presenter in the studio exchanges vague statements with BBC Security Correspondent Gordon Corera. First, just as the first question in the Forest Gate coverage concerned 'how serious' the events were, they seek to offer a measure of the significance of the story. The presenter says, 'This seems to have been a very ambitious plot', to which Corera replies, 'Very ambitious indeed. It seems to be one of the biggest we've seen'. He adds, 'It is important to understand the scale of this plot and how close it was to being carried out'. However, without concrete information made public about the scale of the plot or how close it was to being carried out, these judgements lack meaning.

However, Corera then acknowledges this lack of information and what this might imply: 'The question is will they find any evidence … this is very important after Forest Gate'. This connection is important. It suggests that after the false alarm of the Forest Gate raid, then the default assumption now may be until there is evidence made public, the journalist and viewers cannot be sure evidence will emerge. Moreover, it links the event to the precautionary principle that is part of the response to global risks; if there is a one per cent chance of an event happening, authorities must presume it will happen and act to stop it, even if the danger never arises. A few minutes later Peter Power, the former Metropolitan Police officer who appeared in the original 'London under attack' simulation and who is now appearing live as an expert to analyse this real, unfolding event, said:

> unlike the IRA where we used to wait and wait until the bomber put the explosives in the car to make your arrest so you'd have tremendous evidence

to convict, in this case I'm pretty sure the police erred on the side of caution. *There may not be strong evidence* to associate all those people arrested so far with the crime. *But had they* committed it and carried it out, the risk was so great that they had to trigger some [police response] right now. The threat was very real. (Italics added)

The relationship between *knowledge of* the risk or threat in question and *communication about* the risk or threat in question is in tension throughout the coverage. Early in the coverage, the BBC's correspondent in Washington, DC, John Kay, reports that the US has 'announced that all flights coming from the UK go up to the highest security threat level, which is known as severe or red ... this will have a big impact.' This impact is illustrated visually by continual footage of people standing around, in particular a woman who is holding a child, and interviews with airlines consultants who warn about a dire economic impact for the airport owner BAA. Later in the day, the Shadow Foreign Secretary William Hague is interviewed by the BBC and announces, 'I think the government is right to have taken precautionary measures'. He is challenged by the reporter, who asks whether this 'alarms people unnecessarily'. What this tension points to is the emotional or 'neurotic' governance Isin pointed to (Chapter 1, this volume): that government sometimes (and increasingly) addresses citizens in emotional terms, offering reassurance and support rather than facts or information. Security Correspondent Gordon Corera acknowledges this. Following a joint press conference between Home Secretary John Reid, the Deputy Commissioner of the Metropolitan Police, the Transport Secretary and the Chief Executive of BAA, Corera reports:

> I picked up a few messages. One was reassurance saying security measures have taken place, as a precautionary step, saying they believe they caught the major players involved in this plot. Of course they can't be sure of that and thus they feel they have to raise the security and threat level, but making sure it's *precautionary rather than based on any intelligence* that they know someone is out there planning to attack.

The message is the mood. Government is signalling to citizens – at home and abroad – that it is aware there are threats out there and that it is willing to act to keep citizens secure. Returning to the 'London under attack' simulation, the experts advising government presume citizens would be looking for reassurance and the impression of leadership under the circumstances now happening.

A second dilemma reflecting assumptions of the global risk discourse concerns the status of al-Qaeda and its relation to the planned attacks. Live coverage of the events provided by UK news coverage and Fox News in the US contain frequent references to al-Qaeda from its own journalists and, particularly in the US, from politicians. Taking a lead from the UK government, the BBC and Sky News do not seek to label the alleged attackers as part of any *religious* group, presumably so as not to antagonise British Muslim viewers anxious about casual connections being made in media between Islam and terrorism. But the first public response on the day from President Bush, covered on all channels, is to remind American people that, 'this nation is at war with Islamic fascists who will use any means to destroy our love of freedom'. When this is broadcast on BBC News, the presenter reminds the audience twice that Bush used the term 'Islamic fascists' (not the BBC). Bush immediately connects the (at this stage) alleged plot to a global threat. Later, on Fox News, US Congressman Peter Hoekstra notes the role of teamwork between US, UK and Pakistani intelligence agencies and argues the arrests show 'the benefit of international coordination and cooperation in the global war on terror'. But what is the nature of this apparently global threat? The BBC report that the plot 'follows warning from al-Qaeda that involvement in Iraq and Afghanistan as well as recent developments in Lebanon were likely to bring further attacks to Britain and the United States'. But in the Sky News studio, security analyst Michael Goodman suggests those arrested are 'likely to be a *self-radicalising* group … this is unlikely to be an al-Qaeda related event.'

If it is the case that the viewer is presented with an *un*co-ordinated global risk of terrorism, is this more threatening than the notion of an al-Qaeda hierarchy that is tangible and could potentially be destroyed? Self-radicalising individuals would be hard to detect. The very possibility of self-radicalising individuals could be used to justify universal precautions, since anybody could be a risk! The Sky News presenter asks, 'Muslim extremists, home grown … is this the new wave of the future?'

Like the Forest Gate coverage, rolling news on 10 August 2006 offered little information about the arrested men. Journalists sought neighbours to interview. Again, it was not clear the neighbours knew the men involved, but their impressions were reported anyway. Around one area cordoned off by police, one said, 'there was always people coming and going in there, sort of changing hands all the time … [I was] never actually knowing who was there'. Some local people added, 'large lorries would pull up every couple of days and load some crates and take them round the back … certainly there was lots of activity around here'. These vague descriptions could apply to many neighbourhoods, presenting nothing unusual or exceptional. Officials were keen not to connect the arrests to Islam or Muslims, and Metropolitan Police Deputy Commissioner Paul Stephenson made a statement concluding, 'I wish to stress that this is not about communities. It's about criminals and murderers … This is about people who might masquerade within a community behind certain faiths'. However, this simply implies that murderers or criminals might be masquerading among certain faith communities, from which is could be implied that these communities might help identity them to the authorities. Indeed, Stephenson confirmed there had been 'extensive dialogue with community leaders'. So while Stephenson managed to avoid mentioning Islam or Muslims, we might expect viewers to infer he was referring to Muslim communities in which murderers were hiding.

Despite greater attempt to offer restrained reporting, news from both the US and UK on the day of transatlantic air plot arrests is characterised by uncertain and indefinite spatial and temporal boundaries to the threat; and the possibility of 'home-grown' radicalised bombers undermines the relevance of boundaries anyway. Live news coverage again offers an 'extended present' promising a future featuring self-radicalising individuals, more 'Forest Gate-style' raids on Muslim homes, and reassurance from government. This future is brought into the present, but does it create fear among the audiences who watch it? 'The future *is*', writes Nowotny (2008: 2), and '[i]ts content, its shape, and its fullness – the images we construct of it – always have significance only in the here and now'. An analysis solely of the mediation of the future alone cannot tell us its significance, so we turn in Chapter 6 to examine audience understandings of radicalisation, terrorism events and the discourses of risk, fear and resilience.

Conclusion

Broadcast media like television and radio contribute to an extended present, a representation of unfolding events as a singular series of ongoing crises within a global war on terror of indefinite and unknowable duration. This continuity-of-the-moment was reinforced by premediations in which broadcasters joined with state and unofficial 'experts' to simulate and anticipate – rather accurately it transpired – actual attacks to come. Such coverage inadvertently sustains discourses of global fear and risk which may contribute not only to the legitimate government counterterrorism strategies predicated on the global war on terror, but not necessarily help constitute the 'reality' of al-Qaeda as a meaningful entity. This discursive reinforcement depends on two factors. First, there is a lack of verifiable information journalists can report about the suspected perpetrators and nature of the incident, which creates a vacuum filled by speculation by unreliable neighbour testimonies, expert analyses and by security correspondents themselves. Second, concepts of global fear and risk are sustained by the lack of a clear understanding of what 'radicalisation' might be, how the presumed radicalisation process operates, or how al-Qaeda may be connected to these specific incidents. This absence enables the broader condition of 'hypersecurity' in the post-9/11 period, the sense of uncertain, contingent but generalised threat. Yet, even without naming al-Qaeda or individual suspects, reference to the need to engage Muslim communities in the aftermath of these breaking security events offers an identity to the threat if only by implication.

Mainstream television becomes the primary news source at times of catastrophic security events, but media literate audiences and policymakers are reflexive about how such events are constructed, staged or contested for political ends. Nevertheless, the features we find central to the form taken by television coverage of security events adds considerable nuance to the basic questions of legitimation of Jihadists or counterterrorism strategies. Media representations of normality, temporality, social identities and resilience, and the role of the Internet will, we suggest, contribute to how audiences make sense of radicalisation as a real, credible, verifiable phenomenon; how audiences *then* confer legitimacy can only be ascertained once these basic or underlying understandings of the media-security nexus are identified.

5   The mainstream nexus of radicalisation

The 2008–2009 Gaza conflict

In our opening chapter we set out the context for our investigation into the relationship between media and radicalisation, namely the new media ecology. It would be misleading to think the development of this mediatised environment as a shift from so-called 'old' to 'new' media. These categories do not serve an understanding of the dynamics of our new media ecology but rather serve to obfuscate the connectivities through which media content and forms are 'remediated' (Bolter and Grusin 1999) through both established and emergent media, and through what Hoskins and O'Loughlin (2007) conceive of as a 'renewal' of mainstream media. Indeed, that which Dan Gillmor (2006) calls 'Big Media' such as the BBC, CNN, *New York Times* or *Le Monde*, remain dominant and all have invested significantly in their digital and online presence. Instead, the new media ecology involves a struggle between the established and relatively ordered regime of mainstream news – particularly television news – and an 'ordered disorder' of information that is potentially much more diffused.

Part of the new equilibrium of this ecology is the ways in which the Internet and other digital media are both conceived of and inhabited by increasingly entrenched 'mainstream' news cultures. Entrenched, that is, as they are often demarcated and defined in contradistinction with that which is 'outside' or beyond the mainstream, the alternative, the unregulated and limitless domains of the Internet. And it is precisely the uninhabited (by those in the mainstream) zones of the new media ecology that are often represented (in mainstream news discourses) as the central incubator and harbinger of the evils of the digital: radicalisation, terrorism, and paedophilia, for example. Moreover, across our projects exploring radicalisation and language of extremism, consumers of mainstream news consistently saw themselves as exempt from or immune to the influences or 'effects' of such evils, whether more 'directly' consumed via unofficial, amateur or 'radical' sources or as mediated through and translated by Big Media. In terms of the potential of any media to radicalise or to promote extremist views and violence, we found a clear disjuncture between a perception of the vulnerability to persuasion of 'other' individuals and groups, against a sense that the individual self being interviewed is impervious.

In this way, we can map a mainstream/non-mainstream distinction as one of the critical characteristics of the new media ecology, operating in at least two key dimensions. The first is the multiple ways in which mainstream news media represent, translate and remediate that which it takes or constructs as inhabiting media-in-the-wild: all that which is amateur, unofficial, unregulated, and especially that which it self-censors as not being appropriate for its imagined mainstream audience (too explicit, graphic or violent, for example). For the purposes of this chapter, we will mostly refer to this dimension in terms of 'translation' and also take it at its literal meaning in relation to the extraction and translation of online extremist texts in Arabic into Western English mainstream news. The second dimension is the distinction routinely made by mainstream news consumers that they individually possess a particular reflexive awareness (as noted above), such that they are not vulnerable to mainstream or non-mainstream media influences. This awareness extends to a capacity to identify mainstream or non-mainstream audience 'types' that were vulnerable. We call this the 'othering' of the mainstream. Both of these mainstream/non-mainstream distinctions, developed partly in response to the rapid emergence of the Internet, have been vehicles for the comprehension or otherwise of the discourses of radicalisation in our new media ecology. In this chapter we use some examples of translation and othering drawn from different contexts to illuminate the significance of the mainstream in the mediatisation of radicalisation.

The mainstream nexus of radicalisation

One of the characteristics said to be distinctive of the contemporary thoroughly mediatised era is that of saturation, of the pervasiveness or ubiquity of media and digital technologies. If one then takes media as the life blood of terrorists in terms of the velocity and penetration of the terrorist message and threat, then as we set out in our introductory chapter, the media themselves have become weaponised. In this way the potential threat posed by those who advocate and undertake violence has taken on a persistent co-presence through the very 'informational infrastructure' through which everyday life in the developed world is experienced. The condition of connectivity – the connective turn – has facilitated a shift from when nodal conflicts and threats to civilisation punctuated the twentieth century to today's seemingly perpetual connection with wars and the threat of terrorism (cf. Shaw 2005). Of course, there are important qualifications that can be made to this statement in terms of the 'chicken-and-egg' constitution of this relationship, as well as a need to avoid technological determinism. But it is not just an infrastructure of media that has ushered in this sense of a continuity and pervasiveness of threat, it is also a mainstream news culture of insecurity, that which we identified as hypersecurity in our opening chapter, that has accelerated as a response to the 11 September 2001 terrorist attacks on the United States. Richard Grusin identifies one of the key dynamics of this news culture as 'premediation' (see also Chapter 4). This he defines as 'a form of medial pre-emption' and he argues: 'Premediation works to prevent citizens of the global mediasphere from experiencing again the kind of systemic or traumatic shock produced by the events of 9/11 by perpetuating an almost constant, low level of fear or anxiety about another terrorist attack' (2010: 2). So, in the wake of 9/11 (but also amplified by the seeming succession of terrorist attacks over the past decade including in London, Madrid and Mumbai) mainstream news generates continual speculation as to the possibility, nature and timing of another terrorist attack, so that there is a consistent level of preparedness to mitigate the effectiveness in terms of surprise, shock and related trauma, if and when such an attack takes place. This is more than simply the premeditative simulations such as the BBC's 'London under attack' broadcast before London was actually attacked; Grusin is referring to a broader social orientation to the future which cuts across any issue, not just security.

Furthermore, the constancy of the premediated news discourse on terrorism functions to diminish journalists' responsibility (and the responsibility of other public agents of speculation in their contributions to these discourses) for the impact of such events should they occur in the future. In contrast, 9/11 was seen as effective terrorist attack partly because of the unhindered and paradoxically *un*mediated means through which the shock and trauma was delivered live and direct into the homes and lives of mass audiences, in other words an exemplar of the weaponisation of the media. The frames, vernaculars and formats through which news is routinely packaged and that constitute news mediation *broke down*; viewers were presented simply with footage, as journalists did not know what to say; thus the *containing* function of news mediation failed. In this way some culpability for the immediate but also the extended impact of the 9/11 attacks was attached to or felt by the principal conveyors of the mediatised experience, namely journalists and other news workers, hence their subsequent strategy of premediation. And it is this strategy of premediation that is both responsive to the apparent pervasiveness and continuity of the new media ecology connectivity of terrorist threat, but also that perpetuates it. This kind of double bind parallels the 'radical ambiguity' that we set out in Chapter 1, namely that 'western societies themselves governed by terror in the process of trying to bring terror within the orbit of their political rationalities and governmental technologies' (Dillon 2007: 8). In other words, mainstream news media are entangled in and spin further the very same web of hypersecurity through the very strategic speculation and premediation they undertake which functions to contain such future events and to render them 'reportable'. This contrasts with the mainstream news media's default but latent containment of terrorist and other catastrophic events through repetition as a key mechanism of amelioration, as was so readily evident in the hours, weeks and months following 9/11 (cf. Silverstone 2002; Hoskins and O'Loughlin 2010b).

In terms of the cross-cutting dimensions of the mainstream identified above, a fundamental paradox, and thus problematic for any inquiry into contemporary discourses of and about radicalisation, is the fact that the mainstream is often conceived of as a relatively benign node in the new media ecology. So, emergent discourses on and responses to the nature of the threat(s) posed by the rapid establishment of the Internet, for example, are distracted from a focused consideration of the significance of the role or potential role of the mainstream in amplifying and/or assuaging such threats of violent extremism or terrorism. Put differently, the consequences of the discursive 'translation' of terror messages, their (re)presentation in and through so-called mainstream media (including on the Internet) and their interpretation by audiences and 'users', is significantly overlooked by those who are charged with the very study of radicalisation. For instance, the Change Institute's comprehensive *Studies into Violent Radicalisation*, commissioned by the European Commission, aimed to explore 'the beliefs, narratives and ideologies that underpin violent radicalism with a view to developing a much deeper understanding of the causes and remedies for violent radicalisation as part of an ideological response to the main terrorist threat facing Europe' (2008: 4). However, despite the considerable resources invested in the organisation and the undertaking of '145 stakeholder and primary fieldwork interviews in four Member States' (ibid.) and also in an extensive 'analysis of the content and imagery of terrorist rhetoric and propaganda found on the internet' (op. cit.: 8) this research excluded consideration of other mainstream news media and the role of its agents (i.e. commentators, journalists, 'experts') in translating and remediating 'the beliefs, narratives and ideologies' that it sought to understand. In what follows, we will illuminate some of these components of the mainstream, seemingly disregarded or not assumed as significant in such studies.

To begin with, a significant proportion of extremist discourses that circulate online, for instance from the group seen as the most prominent of which the 'war on terror' was being waged against, al-Qaeda, is at least originally in Arabic. A critical question interrogated through our New Security Challenges and CPNI research projects was: what is the means by which extremist 'messages' are translated from Arabic, for instance from online postings, videos, and discussion groups, into a version available to and/or by the English news mainstream? It is the systemic and institutionalised nature of the dynamics of translation that appear to be overlooked in terms of an understanding of the iterations and penetration of extremist messages in our new media ecology. We found that there are two dominant sources or modes of translation. The first are the terrorist groups themselves. So, to take al-Qaeda as an example, this organisation became more active over the period 2008–2010 than previously in providing translations for the main 'productions' from their media wing within days of their release. Many videos, such as *as-Sahab* productions, are released with English subtitles and there appears to be a continuing improvement in the quality of these translations. The main translation providers include *as-Sahab*, the Global Islamic Media Front (GIMF), and the Jihad Media Battalion.

Whilst the communication wings of terrorist groups are becoming more mainstream-savvy in their attempts to maximise the reach of their outputs, over the same period the number of 'terrorism monitoring groups' has increased. These monitoring organisations tend to provide translations for statements by senior al-Qaeda figures, rather than regular Jihadist propaganda, and their services are often not freely available but are paid for by those in or representing the mainstream (news, security services, academics). These groups include: the SITE Intelligence Group (analysts/academics), LauraMansfield.com, and The Nine/Eleven Finding Answers (NEFA) Foundation (which provides full access without subscription). It is these 'translation gatekeepers' then who are potentially one of the principal determinants of the meaning of extremist messages for Western audiences, journalists and policymakers. Our investigation of how these translations enter into and are remediated through mainstream discourses found a simple, consistent but significant disjuncture: those producing and shaping mainstream security discourses are often not working with the original terrorist texts, but with translations. These translations often obfuscate or lose altogether what is significant to much of the meaning conveyed in the original texts, since they only translate one figure's words within a whole multimedia production. One significant consequence of this is a potentially pervasive and diminished understanding of why terrorist discourses might have resonance with those individuals and groups who can consume the original text with a full command of the complete richness of various songs, poems and other modes of attunement to the mood of the text, which are routinely and often entirely omitted from Western mainstream news reporting. So, in sum, mainstream security journalism reports on terrorism in a way that retards public understanding of al-Qaeda and its sympathisers (see Hoskins and O'Loughlin 2010b) and much more work is required to reveal the differential consumption of extremist messages by mainstream news publics.

We now turn to provide an example of mainstream news translation or rather speculative remediation of the threat posed by terrorism, and British government responses to it. The example is a discussion on BBC Radio 4's *Today* programme between the news programme's anchor, Sarah Montague, and her studio guests. These are Ed Husain who is a self-declared 'former radical' and co-founder of one of the mainstream translation organisations, the anti-extremism think-tank the Quilliam Foundation, and an academic, Dr John Gearson from King's College, London. In Box 5.1, we have set out our transcription of this exchange broadcast live on the morning of the 8 September 2009.

Husain, as an expert on the subject of radicalisation given his claims to have 'travelled a journey' of radicalisation and then de-radicalisation, might be expected to possess a readily demarcated and well-honed account of this phenomenon. Yet, his lengthy opening response is notable for the extensive scope he affords radicalisation and the range of its constituents including extremist websites and the 'digital ghetto' of satellite television channels. The media he indicts here appear as relatively obvious and direct radicalising influences and there is a fast-emergent history of the use of niche digital channels or programmes both as tools of extremist propaganda as well as counterterrorism. Whereas, our position is that it is precisely the ways in which messages and texts are routinely translated, conceived of and diffused across the mainstream media (including in this very same *Today* programme) that demands greater attention in understanding the trajectories and the reception of the discourses of radicalisation.

Box 5.1 *Today* **programme BBC R4 broadcast Tuesday, 8 September 2009**

SARAH MONTAGUE [M, BELOW]: It's clear from the details of the trans-Atlantic bomb plot that a huge terrorist attack was averted by police back in August 2006. So does it suggest that our counterterrorism approach is working? Ed Husain [H, below] is a former radical who co-founded an anti-extremism think-tank, the Quilliam Foundation. He joins us from Westminster and we're also joined by Dr John Gearson [G, below] who's reader in terrorism studies at King's College London and Director for the Centre for Defence Studies. Good morning to you both.

H: =Good morning

G: =Good morning

Ed Husain, do you think this shows that we've got it right?

H: Mm well, yes and no, um it shows that we've got this one particular operation right, thank God. But um I can just sit here and refer you to much of our research but also my own thoughts on the fact that we have you know lots, I don't want to say millions, but tens of thousands of Muslims who live in Britain physically but psychologically were connected to Pakistan or other Muslim-majority societies. Evidence of that is the fact that we've got a huge radicalisation problem in in in the prison service, ten thousand Muslims in prison, a disproportionate number to any other minority community, erm sharing space with a huge number of terrorism convicts, s- private seminaries erm. That's the second point, private seminaries that have literalist rigid mind-set from the Deabandi?? School, y'know the school that produced the Taleban-run h- – several institutions across the north produce huge amounts of imams that will be taking over mosques in years to come. A third issue will be websites which provide virtual communities for extremists to reject the kind of news that came out yesterday as news from unreliable sources and continuing to plan the kinds of things they plan. Fourth would be the displaced Somalians that don't feel part of the British Muslim community nor part of Somalia nor part of Britain and what we saw with the al-Shabab movement recently in Somalia gives every rise for concern there. A fifth concern would be the satellite television channels that we've got on on what one might one might call the digital ghetto

M: OK…

H: I mean I could go on,

M: yea-

H: the problem is ubiquitous an- and it remains with us.

M: Dr John Gearson and the fact that Ed Husain could go on, suh- would suggest that the problem's got *worse* in the last few years

G: Yes, I think in intelligence and policing terms we can be quietly satisfied so far that we've averted major attacks erm in many cases and and only one significant attack, 7/7, has been successful. But that said I think even people within the government would accept that the PREVENT strand of their counter-terrorism strategy that is to to undermine radicalisation has not made as much progress and the problem here is that we still have not managed to, I believe, coherently link our domestic counterterrorism struggle with what we're doing overseas to prevent terrorism getting a foot-hold in countries like Afghanistan. We have not articulated other than saying it's linked properly how these these two strands go together, but more importantly we haven't co-ordinated the two strategies in reality. We've got a police and intelligence service protecting us and we have frankly a military campaign and mostly American-led which is not always in synch with our domestic measures.

M: How do you link them?

G: Well you you start trying to identify the linkage between counterinsurgency and counterterrorism to try to understand rather better than we have to date how the activities that you undertake in Pakistan and in Afghanistan may have an effect. But that's not to say that you will not re- continue to have a residual rump of people who are already radicalised and and recruiters trying to take more people into that. What we need to do is target the majority of Muslims who have got grievances which perhaps can be undermined by better explanations. But that- that's not to say that there will not be people who will be continue to be radicalised.

M: Right. Ed Husain, the government always tells us that the reason we're in Afghanistan is to prevent terrorism here, there's almost an argument from listening to what both of you say, that actually you're more likely to prevent terrorism here by not being in Afghanistan.

H: That's a valid criticism and that's a valid argument but but your point and Dr John Gearson's point both refer to foreign policy a-a- in response I would only say that we have, y'know, in excess of about four million Muslims living in America and America is quote unquote at war in Afghanistan, in occupation in Iraq. And yet we don't have that kind of radicalisation among American Muslims that want to blow up fellow Americans. The question is why. My answer is that there's a greater sense of belonging, integration, shared participation between Muslims in America and wider society. We don't have that here yet. And therefore this is just a centre-

M: But there- but there's talk of that and that talk of the PREVENT element which Dr John Gearson says hasn't made as much progress, is it making any progress?

H: It's making progress, but Dr Gearson is right, it's not making a- as much progress as it should because we've got Muslim leaders and community groups that are in denial about the nature of the problem much rather blame foreign policy and government than admit that we've got an infrastructural institutional ideological problem in our midst.

M: Dr John Gearson would you also point the finger towards Muslim groups rather than erm the host community shall we say and the government?

G: Well I don't think it's about pointing fingers. I think it's more about identifying how the enemies of this country exploit grievances, not to attack those grievances necessarily but to under- undermine that ideology as best you can. But also let's let's be a little bit honest about what we face. Er the British had tremendous intelligence about the threat from

M: Just briefly

G: the the IRA for twenty-five years and it didn't stop all attacks because [y-something]

M: Dr John Gearson and Ed Husain we must leave it there, thank you.

The apparent imprecision as to the relative weight, order of priority, or relationship between the elements of radicalisation listed by Husain supports our argument as to the sheer scope of the term having increasingly 'gone wild' as we set out in Chapter 1. Furthermore, the sense of a pervasive condition of hypersecurity (also introduced in our opening chapter) is reflected in the programme anchor's intervention, halting Husain's list from growing longer, and he then reflects 'I mean I could go on ... the problem is ubiquitous and it remains with us'. This oft-stated yet ill-defined sense of the pervasiveness of radicalisation serves to enhance its unquantifiable character and thus the uncertainty of the threat it poses, in terms of timing, place, frequency or other scalable attributes. This in turn makes the prospects for its neutralisation difficult to grasp: if 'radicalisation' is not understood, not even understandable, how can 'de-radicalisation' policies be effective?

It is only at the time of the identification of suspects of planned or actual terrorist attacks or, as with the example of this radio extract, when bomb plotters are prosecuted, that news discourse or indeed policymakers are available to sidestep the significant unknowns and unknowables of radicalisation. This may seem initially an obvious point to make, but it is precisely because the process of radicalisation in this context can only be successfully defined in relation to a violent act or attempted violent act. In this way, the ultimate and only definitive measure of someone having been radicalised – actual attempts at violence – sets a very high threshold for its attainment and labelling. So, in the context of pervasive speculation and premediation, these few moments of clarity and fact are necessarily a *retrospective* action.

Mainstream news media are very effective in assembling these stories. Television and radio news and documentaries have a commanding capacity to digitally stitch together biographical details of the radicalised with 'choices' they were faced with at different stages in relation to radicalising influences (people, places and events), interspersed with 'witness' commentaries, 'warning signs' (and security services' apparent failure to notice or to act sufficiently in response to those signs) to produce and package a chronological process which retrospectively accounts for the violence or attempted violence of an individual or group as the end consequence of their 'radicalisation'. And it is this assemblage of radicalisation that can be seen as a process of 'retrospective premediation' (Hoskins and O'Loughlin 2009), a retrospective coherence afforded to various signifiers of radicalisation that can only be illuminated through a working back from the final act, but which can then enable a narrative arc that suggests those concerned were 'always going to' be vulnerable to radicalisation. It is in this way that the vagaries of the ubiquity of the 'huge radicalisation problem' (Husain, above) and its tangible manifestation create a discursive disjuncture or even credibility gap that policymakers have found increasingly difficult to fill.

The 2008–2009 Gaza conflict: the perfect storm

However, where Western mainstream news could be seen to have the greatest potential for impact, or for being 'weaponised', in the translating and amplifying of the discourses of radicalisation, is in 'event time' (Gitlin 1980; Hoskins 2001, 2004a, 2004b). This is the time during which the news reporting on an ongoing event has the potential to feed, or is increasingly represented as feeding into affect or shape the event itself. There is a wide spectrum of intensities to this 'effect' depending upon the nature and duration of the event and also the scale of the coverage. Typically, television has been seen as the pre-eminent medium in shaping events which it depicts, and increasingly so over the past 20 years as news channels have become much more competitive and promotional in positioning their own correspondents 'into' the stories being covered. This construction of an authorial relationship to events involves a televisual news discursive shift from 'here is the world' to 'we bring you the world', and even to 'we shape the world' (cf. Hoskins and O'Loughlin 2007). In the context of translation by mainstream news discourses in event time, this can be characterised not as retrospective pre-mediation but 'speculative remediation', which refers to how news content from numerous sources – professional and amateur, factual and entertainment – are stitched together in real-time to establish meanings of an ongoing event which television itself is bringing us, the viewers. We now turn to explore a key example of speculative remediation to assess the relationship between online (non-mainstream) discourses of radicalisation and their articulation (and non-articulation) in the mainstream relating to an ongoing event. This event is the Israeli military assault on Gaza launched on 27 December 2008 and which continued for 22 days.

Here, we focus on this conflict as an exemplar of *potential* radicalisation. This was due to the nature and extensiveness of news reporting around the globe of the humanitarian catastrophe unfolding in Gaza, particularly in relation to the availability of a steady stream of images of Gazan civilian suffering, and especially of children. In addition, reporting focused on a sense of an absence of a response from Western governments and other organisations proportionate to the media coverage. As we find in the analysis below, these two aspects were expected to raise anger among Muslim audiences, even to 'radicalise' some. First, we give an overview of some of the controversies of the British broadcast media reporting of the conflict to provide an insight into the nature and intensities of the debate in its Western mainstream context. Second, we explore online extremist discourses using the plight of Gazans (and the also absence of intervention by the West) to legitimise a call for global Jihad. And, finally, we focus on how a mainstream news programme in the UK – BBC2's *Newsnight* – represented the relationship between images of apparently unchecked Israeli destruction of Gaza and its people on the one hand, and a process of radicalisation in UK communities and online on the other; in other words, a case of speculative remediation.

The Israelis claimed their offensive was in response to rocket attacks from Hamas in Gaza on their population. At the end of the almost three-week long assault, the death toll had reached over 1,300 Palestinians and 13 Israelis, with a great deal of the Gaza strip left in ruins and tens of thousands made homeless. The Israeli government prevented access to most foreign journalists wishing to enter the conflict zone. As a result, most had to report from the Israeli-Gaza border in the absence of individual journalistic co-verification of accounts. Nevertheless, there was a steady stream of images and video of injury, death, and destruction, available for their reports and played out across news media around the globe and online.

UK mainstream broadcast news became embroiled in a series of controversies over their coverage of the Gaza conflict. Notable of these was Channel 4 News film reports of alleged attacks on or near (and that distinction became just one point of controversy) UN-run schools in Gaza. The incident that dominated some of the reporting – and continued to with post-conflict recriminations and accusations and Israeli, UN and journalistic investigations – was the killing of 43 people (initially reported as 30 people) by an Israel Defence Force (IDF) mortar on 6 January 2009 just outside the UN-run al-Fakhura primary school at the Jabalya refugee camp. On Channel 4 News that evening Alex Thompson, reporting live from Jerusalem, introduced a report by their foreign affairs correspondent Jonathan Rugman on the Gaza border: 'Much of the footage of the carnage of the school is far too graphic to show on British television at this hour in the evening. But his report does contain distressing images from the start'. The video footage includes scenes of the panic and destruction following the incident at Jabalya, including the carrying away of bloodied civilian wounded and dead, including children. Thompson states in his introduction, and also repeated twice more in the recorded report, that the UN gave the GPS co-ordinates of its schools and other buildings to the Israelis, and hence these are locations where Palestinians had sought shelter. According to the IDF these are also where Hamas fighters seek cover, from where they launch mortar shells into Israel. Channel 4's reporting of the IDF's use of a variety of weapons, especially white phosphorous, provoked the Israeli government into taking to the airwaves to fiercely challenge the channel's reporting of the conflict and accusing the programme's reporter, Jonathan Miller, of being 'strong-armed' by Hamas.[1]

This was just one example of Israel's attempts to learn lessons from its public relations failure after its attacks against Lebanon in 2006. This time, initially at least, Israel was much more effective in mounting a real-time global news presence by providing official spokespeople to as many international broadcasters as possible (Gowing 2009: 58). However, for Gowing (ibid.) it was the 'information doers' that significantly shifted the balance of support away from Israel in terms of the media messages of the conflict. He argues:

Despite all the detailed planning to counter the new information transparency, Israel had largely failed. Too much digital data and imagery flowed from Gaza on multiple platforms in a host of ways that defied all Israel's control measures. None of what emerged helped the Israeli case to justify its operation to smash Hamas's military capability. Instead it undermined their claims, especially because of the way the IDF's official statements appeared to be tailored more for propaganda purposes than to make a realistic representation of what took place, including on apparent targeting errors.

(Gowing 2009: 59)

Whilst the Israeli cause appeared to be suffering via digital information flows and their seemingly propagandistic responses, in the UK it was not only Channel 4 News that was caught up in the fierce mediatised climate over the legitimacy of the Israeli offensive in Gaza and the politics of news coverage. For example, the BBC was subject to intense public and political pressure, receiving more than 10,000 complaints following its decision not to air an appeal by the Disasters Emergence Committee (DEC) to raise emergence funds for humanitarian aid for Gaza. This pressure also manifested itself in a widely reported mass placard-waving rally of protestors outside the BBC's Broadcasting House. A BBC spokesman explained the Corporation's rationale for their decision not to air the DEC appeal, as owing to: 'question marks about the delivery of aid in a volatile situation and also to avoid any risk of compromising public confidence in the BBC's impartiality in the context of [a] news story.'[2] Meanwhile, ITV, Channel 4 and Channel 5 all broadcast the appeal, and Sky News did not. In a message to all Sky news staff, John Ryley, Head of Sky News, explained:

> the nature of an appeal is that it sets out to provoke a specific response from the viewer. We don't believe that broadcasting such an appeal on Sky News can be combined with the balance and context that impartial journalism aims to bring to the highly charged and continuing conflict in Gaza.[3]

In sum, the intensifying disjuncture between the global news mainstream's often graphic depiction of the suffering of Palestinian civilians at the hands of the IDF and the apparent lack of a meaningful response or intent to intervene from Western governments in full sight of this humanitarian disaster fed a crisis of military, political and journalistic legitimacy at a number of intersecting levels in the new media ecology. For instance, the BBC's claims as to 'impartiality' in deciding not to broadcast the DEC Gaza appeal attracted more of a conspiratorial clamour than would other broadcasters who made the same decision (such as Sky) who do not have similar historical, political or institutional status, nor comparable global reputation and reach. In this way, the Gaza conflict was a perfect storm in its event-time connectivity of various sets of grievances that could manifest in a powerful legitimising of a global Jihad (against Israel and her allies). We now turn to explore evidence of attempts to harness this perfect storm in online extremist discourses, before concluding this chapter with our examination of the *Newsnight* speculative remediation of these discourses.

The 2008–2009 Gaza conflict: legitimisation of global Jihad

Following the launch of the Israeli offensive on Gaza on 27 December 2008, postings to and discussions on Jihadi online forums quickly became almost entirely focused on the conflict, and the actual volume of traffic also significantly increased. For example, compared with an average of 8–13 postings per day on the al-Faloja forum, the Gaza crisis triggered an increase to an average of 60–65 postings per day and a ten-fold increase in the number of pages of content. Jihadi forums placed large banners across their home pages with declarations of support for Gazans and images of civilian casualties. For example, one such banner on the al-Faloja home page read, 'There is no good in a life in which honour is violated and men's dignities trodden on by the enemies of Allah. Don't the images of your sisters [reference to female Palestinians] crying out for help move you?!'[4] Most of these messages were attributed directly to senior Jihadi figures, including from al-Qaeda. Messages urged violent attacks against Jews, 'crusaders', and those countries seen to be allied to them, particularly the US. The calls for and postings seeking to legitimise a global Jihad on Jihadi forums following the opening of the Israeli assault on Gaza were comparable in their intensity and extent to those that followed the invasion and occupation of Iraq in 2003.

As early in the conflict as 29 December, al-Faloja member Jundallah posted some points explicitly detailing acts on '*How to Support Gaza*'[5]:

1   Target all Jews on Muslim land [This provides religious legitimacy for such attacks];
2   If you don't have weapons, buy them or get them through targeting police or security forces [This provides legitimacy: them being 'apostates' and 'serving tyrant rulers to crush Muslims'];
3   Fight individually or in groups, kill [them] individually or in groups [This echoes Abu Musab al-Suri's teachings];
4   If you decide to publicise the operations/attacks you carry out, make sure to accompany the news with pictures … Only report/publish *suitable* news. For example, do not report the targeting of apostates and their soldiers [i.e. Muslim police/security] but only that of Jews and Christians. [This is significant in the jihadists' efforts to legitimise their acts and avoid publishing material that could incriminate them. However, the writer contradicts himself. First he explains, resorting to Sharia, why it is legitimate to target Muslim governments and their soldiers. He then asks jihadists to keep private news or images on the targeting of these 'apostates'.]
5   Do not say:

    a   I am not prepared [for jihad];
    b   I am not sure of the legitimacy of this matter;
    c   Do it [jihad] yourself rather than preaching about it [which the author himself seems to be doing].

Following the legitimacy crisis al-Qaeda faced at the time (see Chapters 2 and 3) advocates of the Salafi-Jihadi ideology in general focused on 'defensive Jihad', or Jihad in conflict zones, to avoid accusations of wrongful killing of civilians. Explicit calls for Jihad in peaceful countries in general and in Western ones in particular had been relatively absent in Jihadist media. However, the Gaza offensive transformed their approach. For example, proponents of the Salafi-Jihadi ideology no longer shied away from calling for an all-open Jihad against not only aggressors but those who support them (or are perceived to do so) or who do nothing to stop them. By early 2009, vague calls for Jihad had been replaced by strong and daring calls for Jihad against Israelis, Westerners, Arab rulers and their militaries.

Several Jihadi media major productions were released on forums explicitly legitimising as well as promising attacks against the West. On 22 January, *as-Sahab* released a video statement by top al-Qaeda ideologue Sheikh Abu Yahya al-Libbi in relation to Gaza. In his speech, al-Libbi named Britain as the main reason behind the misery and sufferings of Palestinians, thus seeking to legitimise attacks, and even promising such attacks 'soon'. He mocked political efforts being made by Britain to secure a cease to hostilities over Gaza: 'a wolf is a wolf even if dressed as a lamb'.[6] On 18 January, *as-Sahab* released a video, in German, of a 'mujahid' German-Muslim who promises a great attack in Germany soon, saying that Germany did not heed the lesson in the July 2005 bombings in London.[7] On the same day,[8] al-Fajr circulated an article written by one of al-Qaeda's top writers Sheikh Attiyatallah (appeared in one *as-Sahab* video alongside al-Zawahiri) in which he strongly justifies the killing of Western civilians, 'just as our civilians are being killed. An eye for an eye'.[9]

After an absence of nine months, al-Qaeda leader Osama bin Laden released a statement on 13 January 2009 entitled *A Call for Jihad to Stop Aggression Against Gaza*.[10] Bin Laden began his statement by showing how political efforts by Arab states and groups, even those claiming to want to liberate Palestine, have all failed from 1948 onward. Such failures, he explains, have led to the past and present 'massacres' of Palestinians at the hands of Israelis and humiliation and subjugation of Muslims. The futility of past political or semi-political efforts serves to justify the call for *Jihad as the only solution*, a slogan that Muslim masses in the Arab world would themselves recognise and raise. 'Our duty today is to incite the Muslim youth to engage in Jihad and enrol in Jihadi brigades to fight the Zio-Crusade alliance and its agents', he said, 'rather than having them [youth] exhaust their energy in *unarmed* demonstrations and protests.' A good proportion of his statement stressed that present Western democracies did not obtain their rights through 'peaceful means, as they wish to preach us to follow today,' but through armed struggle, hence legitimising Jihad. The part of Bin Laden's statement that members on Jihadi forums found intriguing and discussed was his hinting to the opening of new Jihad fronts. Members speculated about where these fronts might be located. Guesses included Eastern and Western countries.

On 6 January, Ayman al-Zawahiri, second in command of al-Qaeda, released a statement titled, *Gaza Massacre and Siege of Traitors*.[11] Al-Zawahiri's words were more indicative of global Jihad rather than a defensive Jihad restricted to Palestine. In his statement, which was divided into three parts, each addressing a different audience, al-Zawahiri repeatedly urged Muslims to target 'the Crusader–Zionist alliance wherever and through whatever means possible and available'. The Amir of the Islamic State of Iraq (ISI, or al-Qaeda in Iraq) Abu Umar al-Baghdadi issued a statement dated 9 January titled, *[All] Believers are Brothers*.[12] To incite Muslims to fight, he started his speech with the following words:

The brothers of apes and pigs[13] are pouring lava on our people in Gaza. They have killed women, the elderly, and destroyed houses over their occupants. They became more extravagant in their tyranny and went further to blow up homes of Allah, the mosques. All this they did before the whole world through the media. And what have you done in response O Muslim *ummah*?

He goes on to stress that Jihad today has become '*fard ayn*' (obligatory) and that Muslims who do not partake in it today to defend Gazans will be complicit in their killings and held responsible for them 'in this life and the one after'. Unlike Bin Laden and al-Zawahiri, al-Baghdadi, who allegedly leads a group of militants himself, offered practical advice on how to go about this crisis:

1   wise men should lead the angry masses in neighbouring countries towards Gaza, cross the borders by force and join the Gazans in their Jihad;
2   soldiers and officers in Muslim armies must help by at least smuggling weapons outside their units or providing information to allow others to do so [to support Jihad in Gaza];
3   all those fighting for Allah's sake today in Gaza must unite under one umbrella and forget differences;
4   Palestinians all over the world, and you are many in every country, you have the duty of supporting your people. You are known for your military and technical savviness and therefore you have the duty to strike Jewish and American interests wherever in the world.

In the early days of the Israeli attacks, al-Qaeda supporters eagerly awaited a strong al-Qaeda response to set an example for 'true Jihad'. Days passed and al-Qaeda released no statement. This embarrassed supporters, especially given that strong condemnations of the attack and calls for support of Gazans came from all over the world. For Jihadists, the greatest fear was that a strong response, especially an act, would come from their rivals, the Shiites, namely Hizbollah or Iran. Ironically, while al-Qaeda and supporters did nothing to support Gaza, on forums they constantly attacked Hizbollah for its 'cowardice' and 'impotence' and considered its inaction to 'reveal its agency'.

On Jihadist forums, members rushed to justify the absence of an al-Qaeda response (a topic repeatedly raised in moderate forums such as Aljazeeratalk). Some of the main excuses included: al-Qaeda was plotting something big, logistical difficulties, security constraints on al-Qaeda senior figures and thus difficulty in preparing and disseminating messages, and neighbouring countries and groups had the main responsibility given their geographical advantage. Later, al-Qaeda's presence returned, issuing several strong statements, all calling for Jihad, as supporters had hoped. However, it was not different from the many helpless or autonomous groups around the world who had all called for Jihad as well. Despite its inciting Jihad, al-Qaeda itself was physically absent from the conflict zone and showed no signs of having any leverage there. This sparked a lot of debates on moderate forums such as Aljazeeratalk where many accused al-Qaeda of being full of empty words.

Given the recent legitimacy crisis of al-Qaeda in the Muslim world, members of Jihadi forums believed this was the best opportunity for al-Qaeda to clear its name. Faris Dawlet al-Islam, a member of al-Faloja, posted an article on 5 January in which he stressed that this was a golden opportunity for al-Qaeda because 'the whole world is watching' and whatever operation al-Qaeda will carry out against the Israelis, it will be considered legitimate and carry people to publically cheer and support al-Qaeda.[14] But al-Qaeda has been and continues to be absent from the most important Muslim front, Palestine, and this absence could be seen as costing it much of its popularity in the Arab world.

To summarise, the Israeli assault on Gaza and the apparent failure of any political (or other) pressure from Israel's allies or enemies to slow, pause or stop the IDF's 22-day military offensive, and the mass mainstream and non-mainstream remediation of the images of suffering, injured and dead Palestinians, did not result in a wholesale radicalisation, despite attempts by Jihadists and their supporters in the calling for violent responses. The fact that no such response was forthcoming was very much inflected in the frustrations played out in the online forums our projects examined, which, in turn, could be seen as increasing the pressure for such a response. Yet, this unfolding scenario – a military assault on Gaza, a failure of so-called democratic governments to respond in a significant way, and key Western and Arabic news medias whilst documenting this conflict at the same time perceived also to be legitimising its continued waging – was also reflexively played out in the mainstream through the speculative remediation of news discourses, and we now turn to consider this mainstream holding up a mirror to this crisis and to itself as inextricable instruments of this perfect storm.

The 2008–2009 Gaza conflict: speculative remediation on *Newsnight*

Newsnight is a 45-minute current affairs programme broadcast at 10.30 p.m. on weekdays on BBC2 in the UK. It has a reputation for 'quality' rather than 'tabloid' coverage, providing more in-depth and investigative analyses of issues than other UK free-to-air news and current affairs programmes, and it does not always follow their headlines or prioritisation of stories. On 12 January 2009 at around the peak of the intensity of the global attention attracted by the Gaza conflict, 'peak' in terms of both mainstream news and extremist discourses we have set out so far in this chapter, *Newsnight* devoted their headline piece to this story. The channel's continuity announcer warned viewers of 'some graphic scenes from the start of the programme' and the programme opened with video of blood being hosed away from a Gazan street and a casualty being hurriedly carried to an ambulance. *Newsnight*'s anchor Kirsty Wark introduces the headline story over the opening VT: 'The bloodshed in Gaza is being used by extremist Islamist groups in the UK to radicalise British Muslims. How dangerous is this?' Following the programme ID Wark continues:

KW: Tonight here in Britain fears of the radicalising impact of the conflict in Gaza. *Newsnight* has uncovered evidence of propaganda and recruitment efforts. The Communities Secretary tells us of her fears.

HAZEL BLEARS (Communities Secretary): I am very concerned indeed that the events in Gaza could well be used by those people who want to peddle pernicious extremist views to draw particularly vulnerable young people into that kind of extremism.

KW: Good evening: United Nations is reporting that more than 900 people have died in Gaza as a result of the fighting, almost 300 of them children. It's statistics like this which the British Justice Minister Shahid Malik says is having a profoundly acute and unhealthy effect on British Muslims. Today the Communities Secretary and the Foreign Secretary met Muslim leaders to discuss their fears that Gaza is having a radicalising impact here in the UK. Tim Whewell today discovered that these fears are well-founded.

WHEWELL: For two weeks now they have been seeing images like this on their TV screens [visual stills from the Gazan conflict shown include a bloodied child being held by an adult] and now protestors at London University are outraged that the death toll in Gaza is still rising.

Whewell's report is a compressed package of speculative premediation. It combines a series of statements from or interviews with politicians, the security services, Muslim community leaders, London university student protestors and a survivor of the July 2005 London bombings, with an assortment of events including noisy and aggressive crowds protesting against Gaza and confronting police on the streets of London and 'extremist Islamic websites'. It is these contributions from that which we are calling a 'consortium of witnesses' that offer a powerful example of speculative remediation. We will focus on two of Whewell's interviews to develop this point. First, Usama Hasan, an Imam of Masjid al-Tawhid as one of a group of 'British Muslim representatives', was invited to meet the Foreign Secretary to discuss concerns about the risks the continuation of the war in Gaza posed for Britain. He is introduced by Whewell as 'he understands the psychology that leads young people into violent Jihad. Years ago he himself went to fight in Afghanistan and he's seen renewed attempts to promote Jihad here in recent days'.

UH: We thought we were winning the battle actually against violent extremism. But if there's anything which will inflame people's emotions and anger and actions more it's perceived ... it's the perception that the British government is siding with Israel in this conflict. So, for example, in my local area, posters went up over the weekend saying 'Jihad – the only solution for Palestine', and by that they mean terrorism or armed conflict forever rather than peaceful negotiations.

The contributions by the consortium of witnesses are woven together to provide an authoritative and compelling narrative of a connected set of external conditions and events shaping an inexorable trajectory of radicalisation – of young British

Muslims – to a point where 'Jihad' or 'terrorism' is likely. But again the precise factors or events required in terms of a threshold for Jihad to take place, as with the general mainstream discourses of radicalisation we have examined, remain undefined. Instead, the Whewell report and the broader *Newsnight* programme is an example of the routine but effective compression of speculations into a vague but nonetheless hypersecuritising narrative on the prospects of radicalisation.

At the same time, Whewell's introduction to the contribution by Hasan ('he understands the psychology that leads young people into violent Jihad') reflects the widely mediated idea that for an individual to be radicalised, they must possess some predisposition – a particular mindset for instance. It is this notion that feeds (and is fed by) the demand for 'former radicals' to appear as experts in the British mainstream media. For example, regular contributors to British news and documentary programmes have included Ed Husain (see the BBC Radio 4 *Today* extract, above), a self-declared 'former radical', and Maajid Nawaz who became a leading member of Hizb ut-Tahrir – a political organisation whose goal is a pan-Islamic state or caliphate – before undertaking a 'journey' to eventually contest the theological foundation of 'radical' interpretations of Islam (see Hoskins and O'Loughlin 2009).

The affordances of 'expertise' to media commentators and other contributors employed as security 'experts' sometimes functions to construct or bolster narratives of radicalisation connecting terrorist events and the prospects of future events from occurring. This is particularly the case when the contributor is directly associated with the terrorist event, for example as a member of the security services charged with preventing or responding to terrorism or as a bystander/witness or survivor of a terrorist atrocity. In this respect, the second interviewee of Whewell's *Newsnight* report we want to focus upon is Rachel North, who survived the July 2005 London bombings (at Kings Cross). In the recorded report North speaks in a considered fashion, choosing her words carefully. Box 5.2 below presents an extract from this report.

Box 5.2 Extract of Tim Whewell report incorporating interview with Rachel North, *Newsnight* broadcast 12 June 2009, BBC2

[shot of North (sitting next to Whewell) looking at computer screen beginning with page open at 'Hizb ut-Tahir' site with headline: 'UK government guilty of aiding the preparation and commission of Israeli terrorism']

TW: Rachel North is a survivor of the 7/7 terror attacks in London. Now in her spare time she monitors Islamist websites.

RN: The anger is widespread and intense. The anger is legitimate I think but it provides cover. It's a sea in which people who bring their anger to the point of violence swim.

[shot of extremist message posting on screen]

TW: And in some recent messages posted on the Web on other sites she finds chilling echoes of the sentiments of the London bombers.

RN: When I look at the Internet now when I look at what's been written. I see phrases like [video cuts to head-and-shoulders shot of North speaking seated in studio] 'we must rise up', 'they are murdering us', 'they are raping our women', 'they are killing us, they are killing our children'. And it reminds me. Exactly. Of what Mohammed Sidique Khan said in his last video when he said 'This is a war and-

TW: The ringleader of 7/7.

RN: The ringleader of 7/7.

TW: He said 'This is a war and I am a soldier, and until you stop the bombing, raping, gassing, and torturing and imprisonment of my people, you will know no rest'.

TW narrative continues over Gaza conflict video images of: a small child's body wrapped in white being carried by an adult, an injured baby being attended to by medics, and another injured child being hurriedly carried to presumably receive treatment.

The use of the London bombings as an interpretative news frame is an example of a 'media template' (Kitzinger 2000; Hoskins 2004a, 2004b; Hoskins and O'Loughlin 2007, 2010a), notably, 'a crucial site of media power, acting to provide context for new events, serving as a foci for demands for policy change and helping to shape the ways in which we make sense of the world' (Kitzinger 2000: 81). However, the deployment of Rachel North as a 'memory arbiter' of 7/7 and thus the status invested in her as a co-present witness and survivor of the London Bombings affords her a particular kind of authenticity and authority to speak. This attributes a powerful resonance to the template comparison being applied to the online radicalising discourses in response to the conflict in Gaza. North is, in effect, inextricably bound up in the media template.

Less convincing in this piece of speculative remediation is the mainstream commentary, provided here by North, and the expertise that is at least inferred upon her role as a 'monitor' of 'Islamist websites' that she undertakes in her 'spare time'. Her reading of 'recent messages posted on the Web' and the credibility she attaches to them – and the emphasis this report affords them (orally and visually) – does not appear to be based on any evidence presented or referred to in the programme. In other words, the particular expertise and systematic examination of online Jihadist discourses one would expect to be required to substantiate the comparative claims being made through this media template appear absent, with the evidence base for these claims instead being wholly reliant on the survivor/eyewitness status of North. This is not to undermine the terrible experiences of North or show anything other than complete admiration for her ability to cope and to acknowledge her media-defined role as a kind of unofficial spokesperson for the bereaved and survivors of 7/7. Rather, it is the rapid mediatisation of her experience of and since 7/7 that involves an 'external media logic' (Brown and Hoskins 2010) insinuating itself in the processes of speculative remediation shaping the contemporary condition of hypersecurity.

North's contribution to the *Newsnight* programme is also noteworthy in her articulation of the critical distinction in defining radicalisation in delineating the actual 'tipping point' from the process of radicalisation to the violent act. North (above) describes the online responses to Gaza she has monitored: 'The anger is legitimate I think but it provides cover. It's a sea in which people who bring their anger to the point of violence swim'. This is an interesting identification of a significant body of people inhabiting online spaces who are seen to articulate extremist and violent views but who nonetheless do not appear to translate their anger into actual violence.

It is the programme's articulation of the co-present crowd, the extremists posting threatening and inciting violence messages to various websites, message boards and social networking sites, and various 'communities' (represented here by 'Muslim leaders', for example) that constitute that which Hoskins and O'Loughlin (forthcoming) call the 'new mass'. This is the 'mass' conceived of and represented through an emergent set of iterations connected through the new media ecology, including how the times and spaces of the Internet are constituted by and incorporated into the mainstream. The multiple layers of the new mass: the local and the global, the proximate and distant, the real and the virtual are radically connected through the radicalisation narrative weaved through the programme. And it is through connecting the new mass that provides the basis for the perfect storm of the diffused but also variously concentrated (in various time and spaces) powerful radicalising effects as synchronised by *Newsnight* in the here-and-now of event time. We can thus conceive of this example as a *nexus* of radicalisation that is powerfully assembled and connected around unfolding events and which serves as a powerful legitimising force, despite and even partly because of, the ambiguities of the term radicalisation documented above.

Conclusion

In this chapter we have set out some of the complex iterations of the discourses of radicalisation as shaped and connected – and also not connected – by and across mainstream news cultures in the UK. We have highlighted the importance of the ways in which the mainstream routinely conceives of and translates from the non-mainstream, that seen as inhabiting media-in-the-wild (the amateur, unofficial, explicit, illegal and unregulated). We have argued that radicalisation is a construct and a threat that is easily subject to mainstream speculative remediation, partly owing to the way that its inherent unpredictability sits easily with the amorphousness of the medium seen as its key harbinger – the Internet.

However, the extent to which mainstream news audiences are actually convinced by the mainstream assemblage of the threat posed by radicalisation and also the legitimacy of the advocating of violent extremism (if not actually the undertaking of violent acts) is difficult to discern although we have indicated some scepticism from our limited audience findings. For example, across our projects and at workshops, symposia and in focus groups consisting of academics, journalists, Home Office personnel and lay people, we have shown edited and full versions of the *Newsnight* programme on radicalisation and the Gaza conflict. We found a clear consensus from participants that the programme does not provide a balanced view of either the Israel–Palestine conflict nor of the nature of Islam, though we are not suggesting possessing either systematic data or thus having a systematic assessment of these viewings and responses. There was significant criticism from our focus group and workshop members of the quality of the journalism, partly owing to its limited critical analysis of the UK government's position concerning the conflict and the alleged consequences of the conflict on domestic politics, but also, as we have suggested, the affordance of particular expertise and authority to the contribution made by Rachel North.

The mainstream translation and presentation of the discourses of radicalisation demand much more attention for an accurate and comprehensive understanding of the ways in which violent acts and the calling for such acts are legitimised in the context of the new media ecology. This requires an interrogation of the dynamically configured 'nexus' of radicalisation through the undertaking of a 'nexus analysis' (Scollon and Scollon 2004) approach, as set out in our opening chapter. Having explored the connectivities between Jihadist and mainstream media cultures, in the next chapter we investigate how audiences make sense of this nexus.

6 Audience uncertainties
Imagining the mainstream and extremes

How do ordinary citizens understand radicalisation? Our concern is not simply with whether or not citizens are scared of terrorism or trust government counter-terrorism policies. More important is the way citizens think about issues like radicalisation – issues where there is little concrete reliable data in the public domain, issues that may involve thinking about a complex set of further problems (immigration, religion, multiculturalism, policing), and issues where should a problem be established, then any response would involve trade-offs of political values like liberty, equality and security. Climate change is another such issue: the science is (said to be) contested, any solution would involve domains of energy, economy, and science and technology, and such responses would entail difficult normative trade-offs based on what values we prioritise over others. By asking not just *what* citizens think but *how* they think about radicalisation, we open up the processes of deliberation and negotiation – with themselves, and with others – through which citizens engage with complex political problems. Indeed, explaining these processes has been identified as one of the key challenges for political analysis today (Stoker 2010: 60). If one aim of this book is to understand why different groups in different cultural contexts connect with discourses of radicalisation, then such an approach is absolutely essential.

Finding out how citizens think about issues like radicalisation is much more difficult than finding out simply what they think. Opinion polls and surveys offer regular updates on 'the public mood'. These snapshots offer timely guides to general sentiments, but can easily obscure as much as they reveal. For instance, public opinion polls in the UK in recent years have offered many seemingly contradictory views held. In August 2006, a Yougov/Spectator poll[1] indicated that 53 per cent of British citizens wanted the Blair government be 'tougher and more aggressive' in its foreign policy approach to 'the terrorist threat'. A month later, a Yougov/Sky News poll[2] showed that 77 per cent of the same population thought 'Tony Blair's policies towards the Middle East have made Britain more of a target for terrorists'. Would a tougher foreign policy have made Britain less of a target? Similarly, in the August poll, a majority supported 90-day detention of those only suspected, not charged, with terrorist offences, tougher controls at airports, and increased police profiling. These were the very policies that were making British Muslims feel insecure and alienated from Britain (Gillespie and

O'Loughlin, forthcoming). Did the public offer support for further alienating the very community from which 'the threat' is considered to emanate? The approach taken in this chapter begins to open up how such apparently contradictory positions can be held.

Connectivity, certainty (or lack of), and contradiction are the three characteristics of citizen understandings of security in Britain, according to recent analysis by Gillespie and O'Loughlin (2009). *Connectivity*: different discursive 'realities' from personal experience, religious beliefs, media consumption and the statements of political leaders can inter-lock and mutually reinforce one another to produce an understanding more determined than if supported only by one; *Certainty*: uncertainty is a problem for citizens as well as policy-makers, trying to piece together information about risks and threats; such uncertainty including learning how to 'modulate' and deal with the very fact of uncertainty itself; and *Contradiction*: in this context it is perhaps unsurprising that some individuals come to hold ambivalent and often contradictory perceptions of threats and the role of state and media in representing and responding to threats.

Jarvis and Lister followed with a briefer study[3] of whether people in the UK feel more secure as a result of counter-terrorism policy. Based on a series of focus groups in London, Oxford and Swansea, they found participants held a range of views on what security means, from simple human survival to contentment, hospitality, equality and freedom. This range was also reflected in variation in how people thought about security. Those who equated security with survival presumed others held the same narrow view as them; it was just common sense. Others held more complex and multi-layered ways of understanding security, especially those individuals who could hold several understandings of security together at once. They were more inclined to think how others might reflect on different forms of security too. In addition, a person's conception of security shaped their evaluation of recent counter-terrorism policy. Hence, there is policy value as well as scholarly interest in addressing not just what but how people think about security.

Gillespie and O'Loughlin's analysis used collaborative audience ethnography as a research method to find out how ordinary people understand security (Gillespie 2006, 2007). The Legitimising project developed and extended this method, conducted audience ethnography in four countries, the UK, France, Denmark and Australia. A total of 67 interviews were conducted. Eight ethnographers were recruited to conduct, transcribe and pre-analyse the interviews. Five of them conducted interviews in the UK. The population of research participants was broad, with news audiences of different generation, gender and faith (see Appendix I). Participants initially recruited were part of the social networks of the ethnographers, with further participants recruited through snowballing. In addition to the interviews, two focus groups were conducted: one focused on a specific episode of BBC's *Newsnight* on the Gaza crisis, another on citizens' anxieties around media technologies. The analysis of the interviews was first organised through their coding into *Nvivo8*. Categories for coding were designed in relation to this strand of the *Legitimising* project and to other strands, to achieve integrated analysis across the project of key themes such as legitimacy, violence and visuality. Concrete examples were mobilised in the interviews in order to elicit reactions as to whether or not they can meaningfully be described as instances of radicalisation. In this approach, what is constituted as *not* being related to radicalisation is as important as what is construed as being related to it. Close ethnomethodological analysis of the transcripts was then undertaken (for a full explanation of our methodological approach to the audience analysis, see Appendix II).

A key objective of the *Legitimising the Discourses of Radicalisation* project was to identify, map and evaluate mainstream news public under-standings and interpretations of political violence and the term 'radicalisation' and its associated terms, contexts and discourses. Hence, our interviews were designed to create a space in which radicalisation is made sense of. How, if at all, do audience members who constitute mainstream news publics understand the term radicalisation? If they felt comfortable using the term, did they use it to refer to the same processes or individuals that official or media discourses refer to? In a context of disconnection between the understandings of political leaders and citizens in the UK (Couldry *et al.* 2007; Gillespie 2006; Moss and O'Loughlin 2008) we sought to explore whether the introduction of the new radicalisation concept would create a further distance between official and public understandings of security, and to investigate the role media played in this relationship. If government was using a discourse to describe security concerns that made little sense to citizens, achieving legitimacy for policy would be difficult. In this article we analyse data from interviews in France and the UK.

The central idea underpinning the audience research is that the meaning of radicalisation, like the meaning of any other word, is ordinary. Minimally, this means that there is no need for a specialised language, academic or else, for radi-calisation to mean anything; it is an expression belonging to the ordinary lan-guage and hence that makes sense within this ordinary language. It does not have a meaning outside its practical uses, for instance, when 'talking about the news', or 'talking to the academics'. The interviews were not organised so as to decide what 'radicalisation' ultimately means but to elicit the 'way' people talk about radicalisation and media. Such an approach is informed by ethnomethodology but is not properly speaking ethnomethodological. For instance, we do not analyse the grammar of ordinary language in this article. Additionally, our treat-ment of interview talk as ordinary language differs from recent discourse and interpretive work in security analysis (Altheide 2007; Campbell 2007; Debrix 2008; Giroux 2006; Hansen 2006; Hoskins and O'Loughlin 2007; Jarvis 2009; Mirzoeff 2005) by demonstrating the understandings held by individuals not by identifying the terms or concepts they use but by analysing *the way they talk* about these issues.

The analysis that follows concentrates on the relationship between radicalisa-tion and the media from the point of view of the interviewees.

'You hear it on the news': the ambience of official and media discourses of radicalisation

Our starting point is to ask where individuals say they have heard the term radicalisation mentioned. Individuals' responses to this question offered insights to their implicit understandings of presumed or imagined news publics that they might include themselves within and other groups they exclude themselves from, such as 'the media' or 'elites' or 'Muslim youth' (O'Loughlin *et al.* forthcoming). It must first be stated that a minority of interviewees appear to have been acquainted with radicalisation independently of media; that is, independently of media coverage of the radicalisation of Muslims or of terrorism more generally. These interviewees seem to share characteristics as to their political outlook: they all refer to (and inscribe themselves into) a tradition of political radicalism. For them, not only is radicalisation a question of radicalism but it is also something that is not found in media.

However, a majority of interviewees had heard about radicalisation through news media. This was witnessed both by responding to the question 'Have you heard of the term radicalisation' with answers such as 'On the news, newspapers',[4] but also by the way some interviewees talk about radicalisation. RF[5] illustrates this point:[6]

JK: In what context have you heard of it [*the term radicalisation*]?
RF: It was more in a political context. In terms of Kurdish question. There are talks that Kurdish people became radicalised over the years because of ethnic discrimination towards Kurds and ethnic conflict in Turkey. Plus in Turkey also Islamic radicalism. We heard that extreme Islamism groups became powerful in Turkey. In the world stage we heard after 9/11 Islamic radicalism.
JK: In the context of the UK when did you hear the term of radicalisation and in which context?
RF: In the UK, after September 11 attack. This attack happened a year after I arrived to the UK. I heard in that context that Muslim youths are getting more radicalised. Not the Muslim society, but Muslim youth they were saying. Muslim youths there were born and bred here getting radicalised. I heard it in this context. This is their understanding of certain incidents: July the seven bombing or some suspects arrested in the UK linked with Islamic extreme and armed groups in the Middle East.

In his first answer, he cites a number of contexts in which he has encountered the term 'radicalisation'. He introduces these contexts in a peculiar way, by prefacing them with 'there are talks' and 'we heard that'. Whatever his positions regarding the links between these contexts and radicalisation, this way of introducing them indicates that he refers to some debate and discussions that exist beyond and independently of his judgements about them. This is manifested in part by the reference to 'we': it is not only him as an individual who has heard of these contexts being connected to 'radicalisation' but also and primarily a larger group of people. With 'we' he includes himself in such a group. 'We heard', of course, has a loose connection to the media as the sites in which political questions are discussed and shared with an audience; 'we hear' things in the news. So, *his acquaintance with 'radicalisation' was mediated through the news.* In addition, his description of himself and the audience group which he presumes he belongs to parallels Scannell's conception of media as 'for-anyone-as-someone structures' (2000).

The interviewee's second answer extends this point. Whilst he switches to 'I heard', the reference to the media as the place in which the radicalisation of Muslims was mentioned is still present. This is because the interviewee also refers to an unknown 'they': 'Muslim youth they were saying' and 'this is their understanding of certain incidents'. This reference to 'they' is important in that it shows that the association between radicalisation and Muslim youth in Britain is not something that he *himself* created but instead that he is reporting it as having been created *elsewhere and by others.* Whilst 'they' remains non-specific, elements to identify them are nevertheless provided: 'their understanding' and 'what they were saying' has been 'heard' by the interviewee. Again, the fact that it has been 'heard' makes a connection to media. So, these views about Muslim youth and radicalisation that he reports were heard in the news. For a public to be constituted, for members to consider themselves a public and for members and those outside it to address it as a public, a *series* of communications is required (Barnett 2003; Warner 2002). So, we might also speculate that the interviewee has heard this more than once. There can be no public of a single address or text, so the interviewee must be familiar with hearing this expressed. However, this series conception blurs the specificity of when he 'heard' the term radicalisation in the UK; our data indicates the term was almost unused in UK media before 2005, suggesting he is re-constructing his memory of his familiarity with the term.

This way of talking about radicalisation – as something everyone must be aware of, where everyone is a general mass of people cohered by ambient media – is also evident in an interview with FB[7]:

MD: What comes to mind when you hear about radicalisation, any kind of events or people or images or anything like that?

FB: Radicalisation is used most commonly with regards to Islam. That's the most common context in which you hear it. It is hard to dissociate. That is its primary association and it is hard to break that and see that applicable to anywhere else. But of course that is going on elsewhere, people become radicalised. It is a media issue and I am sure there are struggles going on all over the world that aren't reported on and yet that is the same polarisation of ideology that is going on.[8]

Let us focus on the first two sentences in FB's answer, which illustrate further how interviewees establish their distance from the context in which they hear about radicalisation. The first interesting feature of the beginning of his answer is the use of the passive voice: 'Radicalisation *is used* most commonly with regards to Islam'. Here, the passive voice entails the deletion of the acting subject: we are not told who uses radicalisation in relation to Islam. Nevertheless, the sentence is perfectly intelligible as it is. In fact, the very deletion of the subject in this sentence indicates that it would be redundant to identify it in so many words. Moreover, the generality that it conveys is exactly what is characteristic of the use of radicalisation in this way: it is an obvious and common thing to do. Thus, the use of the passive in this sentence without any specification about the subject of the action not only does not pose any problem of intelligibility (there is no urge to ask 'who?') but in addition, and in fact, *it constitutes this subject as so general and pervasive that there is no need to clarify the 'who'.* Moreover, this sentence is the beginning of the answer about what the interviewee thinks of when he hears about radicalisation. Both the question and the first sentence of the answer imply that 'radicalisation' appears in some *public, or publicly available,* locations. The fact that FB does not find it necessary to specify not only who uses radicalisation in this way but also *where* it is used constitutes this location as obvious and as *commonly shared.* Specifically, as this answer occurs in the context of the interview, it is shared by the interviewee and the interviewer, but the common or shared nature of this location extends beyond these two people. The generality and pervasiveness of the use of radicalisation in relation to Islam, conveyed by the use of the passive voice, suggests that it is not just FB or even the interviewer who can find this connection but *anyone* sharing their experience of hearing this connection.

The second sentence of FB's answer buttresses and adds further properties to the context specified in the first sentence through the expression 'you hear it' ('that's the most common context in which you hear it'). This expression unproblematically and immediately refers to the news. This is unproblematical and immediate in the sense that one thinks of the news as one reads or hears this expression. In English the news is something that one hears which everyday sentences such as the following illustrate: 'have you heard the news?'; 'I've heard in the news that an Air France aircraft disappeared off the Brazilian coast'; 'I've heard that General Motors has gone bankrupt'. Whether one finds one's news on the radio, on television, in newspapers, online, on one's mobile phone or elsewhere does not matter: in English it is a common way of talking about the news that one 'hears' it. The expression FB uses (i.e. 'you hear it') shares some common properties with the passive voice in the first sentence. Thus, it creates a similar sense of generality about the origin of where the thing is heard. Again, in English the pronoun 'you' can be used not only to refer to an interlocutor (or interlocutors) but also to speak in a generic way about everyone's experience. (Indeed, used in this way it constitutes a form of membership and shared intersubjective world and experience.) So when 'you' hear it, in fact *everyone* does as well. Finally, an expression such as 'you hear it' also removes the origin of what has been heard (just like the passive voice does), which also conveys a sense of generality.

This is indicative of the dynamics of media consumption in, but also a significant methodological challenge in researching and making claims about, the new media ecology. Whereas, when the disciplines of Media and Communication Studies grew at the pace of the television programming and audiences they sought to understand in the 1970s, the 'mass media' was relatively containable as a corpus (numbers of channels on television, rigid schedules of news programming, and the lack of alternative sources). More recently news has been characterised as 'ambient'. Ian Hargreaves and James Thomas (2002: 44), for instance, suggest that it is 'like the air we breathe, taken for granted rather than struggled for'. Moreover, media and news today is increasingly diffused, hybridised with other genres of media, and 'remediated' 24/7. Radicalisation as a term and as a phenomenon is understood and misunderstood through its radical diffusion, if you will. Our approach identifies and interrogates the meaning of radicalisation as fundamentally ongoing, constantly negotiated and renegotiated in *re*newed times and spaces. As with the news media's modulation back-and-forth, seeking past contexts to impose old frameworks of meaning on emergent events, consumers of these discourses operate in a similar way; piecing the fragments, images, and narratives of mediated pasts together to shape their understanding of radicalisation today (for RF, above, from Turkey and the UK). Moreover they do so even and especially when denying that they are a constituent consumer of the very same 'media' that affords them much of the content as well as the context of being able to speak about 'radicalisation'.

What does radicalisation mean to people?

We have established how ordinary people talk about radicalisation, and that awareness of such news issues gives people a sense of being part of a news public. We asked interviewees next what radicalisation meant to them. They were asked in particular if they know personally anyone who has gone through a process of radicalisation. Twenty of them answered positively and gave some details concerning these people. To be sure, radicalisation in this question was interpreted differently according to the interviewees and therefore the twenty examples of personal knowledge of radicalisation are as eclectic as is the list of examples that the interviewees gave to illustrate their conception of radicalisation.

Here are the 20 examples:

1 Activist friend
2 Anarchist friend
3 Animal rights activists
4 Best Muslim female friend
5 Converted friend (to Islam)
6 Feminist cousin
7 Feminist women
8 Friends in Iran in gay, women, left rights movements
9 Gay rights activists
10 Jewish friends

11 Maajid Nawaz
12 Muslim friend
13 Muslim kids he works with
14 (French) New Anti-capitalist Party activists
15 Orthodox Jews
16 priest brother
17 (French) Socialist Party activists
18 Someone in the US
19 Song writer Muslim friend
20 Wahabist friends

This list exhaustively compiles the 20 cases mentioned in the interviews. In this shape, it does not seek to organise the specific examples into general categories. Of course this does not mean that a systematic ordering of these cases cannot be accomplished, but in showing these examples in their brute and concrete characters the point of this list is to bring attention to their uniqueness and exemplarity. As a second step, it is nevertheless possible to classify these cases into overarching categories. The following is such an attempt:

1   Islam

    1   Best Muslim female friend
    2   Converted friend (to Islam)
    3   Friend in the US
    4   Maajid Nawaz
    5   Muslim friend
    6   Muslim kids he works with
    7   Song writer Muslim friend
    8   Wahabist friends

2   Rights movements

    1   Animal rights activists
    2   Feminist cousin
    3   Feminist women
    4   Friends in Iran in gay, women, left rights movements
    5   Gay rights activists

3   Left-wing politics

    1   Activist friend
    2   Anarchist friend
    3   (French) New Anti-capitalist Party activists
    4   (French) Socialist Party activists

4   Other religions

    1   Jewish friends
    2   Orthodox Jews
    3   priest brother

Seen in this way, the instances of personal knowledge of radicalisation show that Islam is the category that generates the most cases. Islam is a category distinct of other faiths. If they are collapsed together, however, religion in general accounts for the majority of cases of radicalisation (11 out of 20). All the same, given the emphasis on Islam in official and media discourses of radicalisation it is important to keep it separate from other religions in assessing its relative presence in these examples. Rights movements and left-wing politics also generate a number of cases; thus supporting a claim made previously concerning the omnipresence of political interpretations of radicalisation. There would be a valid basis for bringing categories 2 and 3 together as all the cited examples of rights movements pertain to left-wing politics. However, they are kept distinct from one another because rights movements are not always politically connoted or associated with the left.

In order to make sense of all these examples, it is important to delve into the details that the interviewees give about them. In doing so, it is possible to bring together some of the cases in each categories on the basis of their similarities. Table 6.1 accounts for them.

First, three of the eight cases of Islamic radicalisation refer to the sudden adherence to strict religious views and practices: people who use to enjoy a

Table 6.1 Summary of experience of radicalisation

Categories	Examples	Meanings
Islam	Best Muslim female friend Muslim kids he works with Converted friend (to Islam) Friend in the US Maajid Nawaz Muslim friend Muslim songwriter friend Wahabist acquaintances	Strict Islamic views and practices Understanding Islamic violence Radicalised and deradicalised Sudden hatred of Jews Justify retaliation against racism
Rights movements	Animal rights activists Feminist cousin Feminist women Friends in Iran in gay, women, left rights movements Gay rights activists	Use of bombs Radical feminist, etc., views
Left-wing politics	Activist friend Anarchist friend (French) New Anti-capitalist Party activists (French) Socialist Party activists	Contestation and delegitimation of world order Step further to the left
Other religions	Jewish friends Orthodox Jews Priest brother	Turn to violence against Muslims 'Wacky beliefs' but not violent Transformation of one's life

range of activities all of sudden stopped them and began to condemn them on religious grounds. One of them refers to the fact that a Muslim began to understand and legitimate violence committed by other Muslims. Another one began to develop hatred towards Jews, including towards his close Jewish friend. Two cases are rather unusual. The first one is the reference to the song-writer. The interviewee who brings it up explains that a Muslim friend of his had written a song in which he justified violent retaliation against those who had been racist towards him. This song was found in a library and consequently he was interviewed by the police to account for it. The second one is a reference to the current head of the Quilliam foundation, Maajid Nawaz, a government anti-radicalisation think-tank. The interviewee, who met Nawaz whilst a student at SOAS, suggests that Nawaz was first radicalised and was a member of Hizb ut-Tahrir for a decade. After spending time in prison in Egypt, he was de-radicalised which led him to his current post.

Second, four of the five examples share similar features whilst the last one stands apart from them. The examples of feminist acquaintances and gay rights activists all share the basis that people are radical because they advocate views which, according to the norms of a society, can be seen as progressive. The meaning of the last example, animal rights activists, departs from these four in that the interviewee insists on the turn to violence within the movement in order to describe its radical turn. This makes his view partly in line with official and media discourses of radicalisation that insist on violence that some Muslims are led to embrace and seek out.

Third, the examples under left-wing politics all share similar features despite referring to diverse fractions within the political left. In three instances, reference is made to specific political parties or movements: the liberal, parliamentary left; the French Socialist Party (a centre-left party); the French New Anti-capitalist Party (a revolutionary left party); and anarchism. In all these cases, the interviewees indicate that the persons they know radicalised their views and practices by moving from one position within left-wing politics to a more radical one. So, the Socialist Party activists moved from voting for this party to joining it and campaigning for it; the New Anti-capitalist Party activists became militants for this party; the anarchist friend moved from holding liberal, parliamentary views to anti-parliamentary and libertarian views. In addition, common to these examples is the insistence on the fact that these people are radical in that they contest the established order (whether it be social, cultural, political, economical) and that they carry out certain activities in order to make their contestation known and to help its diffusion.

Fourth, in all three cases of religious radicalisation (other than Islam) the interviewees insist on the transformations that occurred in their acquaintances, transformations which are grounded in their religious beliefs. So, one of them saw his French Jewish childhood friends express violent ideas against Muslims (it is legitimate to engage in acts of violence against them in order to protect Israel); another one knows several Orthodox Jews who have radical ideas about their religion and Israel but who do not engage in violence; and finally the last one saw her brother dropping his studies in order to join the seminary to become a priest.

To summarise, radicalisation was understood to mean political action against the presumed mainstream society and established political order. The statements analysed so far indicate that ordinary people identify certain social logics. Even when discussing different contexts, these logics are still present. But what is particularly interesting is that "the mainstream" or "established order" is not just liberal democracy, because some aspects of liberal democratic politics fall within the social logics with which radicalisation is associated.

This was reinforced in discussions in which some interviewees were asked if they thought that calls for violence could ever been legitimate. Twelve of them thought such calls could never be legitimate whilst twenty-four think that there is room for legitimacy in inciting to violence. Those believing calls for violence could never be legitimate felt little need to offer reasons. They expressed a sense that in democratic societies violence should not exist either because it is not useful or because other means of expressing views should be preferred, such as discussion and via parliamentary means. In other words, refusing to grant any form of legitimacy to violence is a way to protect the values and properties of democracies. At the same time, this refusal shows that these interviewees think about calls for violence only in the context of Islamic terrorism: attacks like 7/7 – i.e. by British citizens against other British citizens – cannot be justified because the perpetrators should have used other means to express their disagreement with the government.

On the other hand, twenty four interviewees thought that calls for violence – and violence itself – can be legitimate. When saying so, it is important to stress 'can': for all of them it is not a matter of saying that calls for violence are always and everywhere justified but that there may be circumstances under which it can become so. In all cases, these circumstances have to do with contexts broader than the British society. So, two interviewees use the argument expressed above that violence cannot be accepted in democratic societies, but instead in advancing a purely negative answer to the question they mitigate theirs by referring to situations – i.e. non-democratic societies – in which this can be. Indeed, the reference to dictatorships and any forms of oppression is what motivate most of the interviewees to say that violence can be legitimate. Nazi Germany and the Apartheid regime in South Africa are the two prime examples of what such circumstances might be. For example:

DL: Can calls for violence be ever legitimate?
TH: I mean history has shown us that the calls for violence ... can be legitimate. The call for violence against the Nazis was legitimate. Nobody wanted a Nazi regime in Europe. People would have liked to achieve that aim, at not having a dominant or prevalent Nazi force in Europe, by means other than violence, but that was not possible. So, that's a clear example when violence was legitimate.

And:

JK: Can calls for violence ever been legitimate?

FD: As I said, as I was saying, it depends on what type of violence, if it's not against people, I am only thinking about little bit of history I know, I am thinking again about South Africa, so if they were ... I don't know like damaging electric ... but you know without damaging, without actually killing people or things like that, yes I can understand that sometimes all like, the way Zimbabwe now, I think you need to use some, you know, not, maybe, if not violent force, you know but, I don't know if violence it depends what you mean, you know if you mean killing people

Necessarily, to argue that calls for violence and violence can be justified in some circumstances requires presenting these circumstances as essentially violating human life and as demanding violence in last recourse. In other less extreme circumstances, it is not so easy to find an answer to this question. Hence, calls for violence in democratic societies such as the UK, France, Denmark or Australia were considered illegitimate.

Should we feel concerned by radicalisation?

Whether or not interviewees thought radicalisation was something to be afraid of depended on the relationship they had to official and media discourses of radicalisation.

Amongst the 49 interviewees who have answered the question 'Is radicalisation a phenomenon that concerns you or are you largely indifferent to it? Why?', 16 say that they are not concerned by this phenomenon and 23 say that they are. Within the 16 who give a negative answer, five give a definite 'no' and the remaining 11 indicate that they are 'not really' concerned by the phenomenon.

Not surprisingly, whether the interviewees advance a positive or negative answer to the question their answer partly follows from their conception of radicalisation more generally. Thus those who tend to view radicalisation as a positive thing are not necessarily concerned about it, and in fact welcome it. However, some of those for whom radicalisation is a positive, progressive thing then answer subsequent questions indicating they are concerned about radicalisation. This *contradiction* arises because the interviewees appear to answer question about being 'concerned' in terms of the media and official conception of radicalisation, that is, as being a phenomenon that affects Muslims and that is made sense of in relation to contemporary issues of Islamic terrorism. Accordingly, these instances are just one manifestation of the difficulties that some of those who offer alternative conceptions of radicalisation have to sustain their views against the (powerful) assumptions about this notion that our own interview schedule conveyed.

First, for five interviewees radicalisation is not a phenomenon of concern. The reasons advanced are very disparate. Two of them simply state that they tend not

to be worried about things like that; the world is full of events that could potentially be a source of concern and it is best to avoid pondering on them too much.
Another interviewee thinks that Islam ought to be considered as a peaceful religion first and foremost and hence issues of radicalisation cannot be a source of
concern. In other words, the reality of Islam and its overwhelming practices and
manifestations should not be overshadowed by a few cases of violence and
killing; one must not let the forest be hidden by the tree. The other two interviewees justify their position in relation to the meaning they give to radicalisation. For one of them, the radicalisation of Muslims (in France) means that some
Muslims are in the process of defining their identities, strong religious identities.
According to this interviewee this process is only normal, indeed all the more
normal in a society and world where strong identities are lacking. For him, it is
an important and essential aspect of being human to define one's identity. For
the last interviewee, radicalisation is not a source of concern because she sees it
as an inherently positive thing in that it brings social and political change, in that
it is associated with people's rights and liberation's movements. There is, consequently, no reason to fear radicalisation; instead it should be actively
cultivated.

Second, 11 interviewees indicate that radicalisation is not really a source of
concern for them. At one level they relate to those of the preceding category in
that they formulate a negative answer to the question. However it is important
to keep them separate because the degree of negativity is not the same. In
saying 'not really', they introduce an element of *uncertainty*. Two of them do
not justify their position and another one says that he does not know enough
about the phenomenon in order to formulate a more definite judgement. One
reason shared by four interviewees is that they do not feel concerned about
radicalisation on a daily basis. Thus, when a terrorist attack happens some-
where in the world, and especially in London or closer to home, they may
reflect on them and feel worried about Islamic terrorism. However, outside
these circumscribed moments they do not think or worry about the radicalisation of Muslims that could lead to other such attacks. Two extracts can illustrate this way of thinking:

MD: Are you concerned about issues of radicalisation?
   JDB: I'd say no.
JE: Not on a day-to-day basis. It's not something that I worry about massively.
MD: Why aren't you hugely concerned about radicalisation?
JDB: Well literally my own life keeps me occupied.
JE: It just doesn't affect your daily life.
JDB: Yeah.
JE: Only when there is a big news story on and you hear it, you're being bom-
   barded with stuff about it, you start to think about it more. But then, once
   it's not in the news as much, it just goes to the back of your mind. Unless
   someone brings it up and then you start thinking about it again.

And:

MD: Is it something that concerns you at all or are you generally indifferent to it?

VP: It concerns me is so far as I live in London, I travel on the tube and periodically I think once upon a time there was somebody on the tube just like me and look what happened to them. However, it wouldn't stop me travelling on the tube. At the time when the IRA bombs were much more common that didn't stop me going into the West End and travelling. So, I obviously can't be that concerned, because there are people and there were people then who wouldn't. On the other hand I did work in a school and the head-teacher said I've just had a phone-call and someone has said there is a bomb in school and he said I think we can safely assume that's a hoax. I said I'm not prepared to assume that's a hoax, there's a thousand kids here. So, I would take it seriously at that level. Someone said about the IRA, they have to be lucky once and the police have to be lucky all the time. Therefore, that means there is always a risk that you or someone you know or that you are close to will be hurt. So at that level it's a concern.

What these three interviewees express in their diverse terms is that the phenomenon of radicalisation and the bomb attacks that it is tied to are a source of worry only when they explicitly think about them. However, everyday life is organised in such a way that these issues do not intervene or interfere; therefore they cannot be treated as real source of concern. For two other interviewees, the fact that they are not overwhelmingly concerned about radicalisation comes from what they see as an issue being hyped by the media and therefore they refuse to succumb to this media-led ambient paranoia. Like the previous interviewees, they can nevertheless express worries – if they think about the issue – because they are either aware of the lack of state's resources to prevent radicalisation or aware of the potential domestic consequences of international events (e.g. the war in Afghanistan). Finally, a last interviewee insists on the fact that he is not afraid of radicalism – because he sees it as a positive and good thing – but that he is afraid of Islamic radicalism when it takes the form of calling for violence and perpetrating bomb attacks.

Third, twenty-three interviewees express their concerns about radicalisation. Twelve of them either do not provide any justification for their view or refers to their distaste for violence in general. One of them makes his view more specific when he suggests that since bomb attacks have already been perpetrated recently in London there is a chance that similar ones could happen again. For people who live in London, according to him, it is difficult to ignore this possibility. In the same vein, another interviewee insists on the fact that bomb attacks are perpetrated by mad people, in which case radicalisation is a source of concern because their actions can never be predicted. Another interviewee suggests that any form of radicalisation is dangerous, not just the Islamic one. Thus Animal Front Liberation activists are also a source of concern to him in that they also go on to perpetrate violent actions. In a similar, albeit different, fashion another interviewee indicates that he feels concern by all forms of religious fundamentalism; again, Islamic fundamentalism is not singled out but is instead made sense of amongst other forms of religious extremism. Finally, two more reasons that depart from the previous ones are advanced to support the view that radicalisation is a source of concern. On the one hand one interviewee expresses his concerns not in the phenomenon itself but rather in the detrimental consequences of the focus on this phenomenon on the Muslim community as a whole:

DL: It is a phenomenon that concerns you or are you largely indifferent to it? Why?

OL: It concerns me because of the danger that the media and non-Muslims living in the west will be unable to draw distinctions between radicals who do use violence against civilians and simply ordinary Muslims. And because now I cannot walk into a room without individuals suspecting me, because I cannot get on the subway without individuals suspecting something if I had a backpack on ... or got onto a plane that people might think twice about sitting next to me ... being seated next to me. That is why the word radical is so important because unfortunately it has become associated with all Muslims. And I should say that I grew up in the UK ... I was born here ... you know in the 70s and the 80s discrimination was more based on the fact that I was brown. It wasn't based on the fact that I was Muslim. It was because I was brown ... I wasn't White. Okay and ... discrimination took place. Now it has become something else ... Islamophobia. It is a fear of a particular group. But the thinking is that brown people are usually Muslims or can be Muslims so ... now is this growing fear of brown people and of Muslims in particular. Which is different from the prejudice and the discrimination of the 70s and the 80s ... that was dislike, that was prejudice, that was discrimination, now its fear ... that's a different emotion altogether. And that's much more worrying.

On the other hand two interviewees think that radicalisation is a source of concern because it manifests itself in state terrorism including in England. This is perhaps the most unexpected answers. Here are the relevant extracts from the two interviewees:

DL: Is it a phenomenon that concerns you, or are you largely indifferent into it ... why so?

GA: No, it concerns me. I think it affects me in a very, very, very deep level. If you look at states that live with terrorism, Israel for instance, England ... It's come back to England now, I mean police armed to their teeth standing around with big guns. You can't walk into a bank without worrying about things that are on your head ... certain freedoms get washed away. I mean Look at the de Menezes case, it's unthinkable a few years ago, that you can walk into the tube and get shot by a policeman without being asked for your hands up first. Without at least running for the door, but that's exactly what happened, and that is an erosion of all of our liberties. We have Britain acting in a very small way, like a very, very undemocratic tin pot country, that the justification of protecting ourselves against radicalism, and that's erosion of our liberties.

And:

DL: Is it a phenomenon that concerns you, or are you largely indifferent into it ... why so?
VB: I am definitely concerned by it, I ... and the reason I am concerned by it is that ... in one, I happen to be an ethnic group is targeted by the state terror, which is, the state itself is funded by ... other governments that could control the world ...

Like OL, the fact that both GA and VB are of Islamic culture and of ethnic minority background is highlighted as one of the sources of their concerns: they feel that Islamophobic, and more generally xenophobic, sentiments are directly threatening them. Both interviewees refer to state terrorism, but GA is more detailed about its manifestations in England. The police, according to him, play a central role in the organisation of such terror given the way they have developed over the decades as a heavily armed force and as consequently carrying violent actions. Thus, violence associated with radicalisation is first and foremost encapsulated by the organisation and activities of the police forces.

In sum, whether interviewees are concerned by radicalisation depends on their conception of radicalisation more generally. Even those concerned about radicalisation are thinking about a range of issues together, rather than al-Qaeda inspired terrorism. Several interviewees were uncertain about the nature of their concerns, and did not offer justifications. Others managed their own concerns by only thinking about radicalisation when large-scale media events grabbed their attention. This again highlights the importance not simply of what people think, but *how* they choose to think about an issue.

This connections to our argument, earlier, about the way in which audiences speak about radicalisation as a concept *anyone* would hear, but also speak as *someone*, as not-your-typical-viewer, as more cynical or independent-minded than others in the presumed news public they position themselves within. Interviewees contested or dismissed official and media discursive connection of the concept radicalisation and the sole context of Jihadist-inspired terrorism. We have suggested that such understandings may serve various *functions* for individuals, such as establishing or maintaining a political identity or membership of a news public. It may also allow them to achieve a measure of certainty and ontological security amid conditions of hypersecurity (O'Loughlin *et al.* forthcoming).

Should we be afraid of calls for violence?

Interviewees were also asked whether they felt personally threatened by calls for violence. If radicalisation is to be seen as negative and as something to avoid, as official and media discourses would have it, then statements that incite violence and that value terrorist attacks may be found as being not only dangerous but also threatening.

Thirty-six interviewees answered this question: seven of them say that 'do not' feel threatened by calls for violence; seven that they 'do not really' feel threatened or that they do to a certain extent only; and an overwhelming majority, 22, 'do' feel threatened by such calls. The seven interviewees who do not feel under threat by calls for violence tend to answer the question by substituting 'threatening' by something else, for instance 'stupid' or 'unnerving', as in the following extracts:

YP: All right. Do you find this call for violence threatening?
EW: Uhm.
YP: Or the actual acts, the call for violence?
EW: I find them offensive, but I don't know that I feel threatened as such.

And:

MD: Do you find calls for violence threatening?
JR: I don't find them threatening, I just find them sad and stupid and unnecessary.

What these examples show is that 'threatening' does not appear to be the adequate way to frame the issue. For these interviewees, the question of threat is not the most relevant one and others are in fact more important. The seven interviewees who do not feel that these calls pose a threat share some views similar to the previous seven, but they also tend to emphasise the fact that they do not feel under any particular *personal* threat. That is to say, unlike those who do not feel threatened at all by calls for violence because they do not see them as threatening in themselves, these seven interviewees recognise that the calls can be threatening in themselves but they do not personally identify with such threats. This is the way in which to interpret the following remarks:

MD: Do you find these calls for violence threatening at all?
IB: Personally, I don't find them threatening personally. Post 7/7 it kind of can be, but when people make these comments, they make that comment but then nothing is going to happen for a while. But then there is a police seizure on a house and they've found x amount of weapons and something was about to go off in a nightclub, Tiger, Tiger or something in London. So yes it was quite shocking – there was a car park outside with a 50 lb bomb in it. It can be.

Finally, 22 interviewees claim that they do feel calls for violence threatening. For many of them, the reason is that they know that many of these calls will not materialise into acts but some will do and the actualisation of these calls always possesses an element of randomness, unpredictability. What is interesting about these 22 interviewees is that they almost all answer the question as if it were an odd one. This is manifested in the following examples:

CS: Do you consider calls for violence to be threatening?
JP: Of course I do.

And:

CS: Do you find calls for violence to be threatening?
ME: Doesn't everyone?

In these two extracts, both JP and ME make it sound like the answer 'yes' to the question is the most obvious, natural and hence the only possible one to exist. In the first instance the surprising and odd character of the question is made clear with the use of 'of course'. There is a difference between answering 'yes, I do' and 'of course I do': the latter produces a judgement about the question itself and it creates a generality about the sentiment of threat. With this second point, in answering the question in such a way, JP renders his answer not only valid for his own personal experience but for *anyone* living in this society. 'Of course' conveys a sense of obviousness and naturalness and these characteristics are such only if they are shared by an ensemble of people, by people considered as being members of a same group (in this case British society). Both these points are also present in the second extract, and the second one more explicitly. Again, the fact that ME answers the question by asking another one 'Doesn't everyone?' suggests that he thinks his answer should be obvious on the very basis that it is the answer that *everyone* in *this* society should make to such a question.

Conclusion: the mainstream

This chapter has illuminated how ordinary people understand radicalisation, its representation in media, and its relationship to their feelings of security. We find that

1   awareness of news about radicalisation gives people a sense of being part of a news public, and that radicalisation is assumed to be something 'everyone hears about' even if its precise meaning is not clear;
2   that although radicalisation has a very diverse range of meanings – interviewees give twenty in our study – these meanings all express an understanding of a relationship between a mainstream democratic society and marginal or extreme figures who contest that society, in some cases through calls for, or use of, violence. In other words, to talk about radicalisation is to talk about social logics that transcend particular cases or contexts, including al-Qaeda inspired terrorism;

3   even those concerned about radicalisation are thinking about a range of issues together, rather than solely al-Qaeda inspired terrorism. Several interviewees were uncertain about the nature of their concerns, and did not offer justifications. Others managed their own concerns by only thinking about radicalisation when large-scale media events grabbed their attention. This again highlights the importance not simply of what people think, but *how* they choose to think about an issue;

4   finally, a majority of interviewees said they felt threatened by calls for violence. They assumed everyone must feel threatened, just as 'everyone hears' about these threats, and that this was a natural reaction. A minority rejected the framing of 'threatening' in the first place, saying radicalisation was more stupid or sad than threatening.

7 Conclusion
The new media ecology model

Our empirical research has allowed us develop a model of a new media ecology, represented vis-à-vis radicalisation in Figure 7.1 below. Through variants of this model, we can understand how phenomena such as radicalisation, war (Hoskins and O'Loughlin 2010a) and memory (Brown and Hoskins 2010; Hoskins 2011) operate.

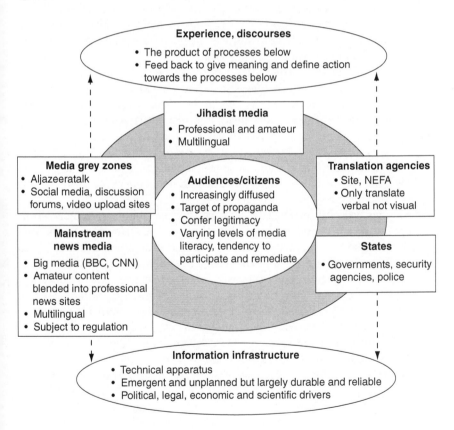

Figure 7.1 The new media ecology vis-à-vis radicalisation.

The new media ecology is dependent first and foremost on the classification, circulation and organisation of 'information', which together forge an 'information infrastructure'. Bowker and Star, for instance argue that this infrastructure involves an increasing convergence of 'standards, categories, technologies, and phenomenology' (1999: 47). In terms of radicalisation, the information infrastructure affords not just a framework through which actors, institutions, and the practices of these groups and the relationships between them can be mapped out, but rather a more dynamic configuration of the nodes and networks ushered in through the connective turn. The 'structure' is in multiple ways self- (as well as institutionally or 'externally') configured through the connections or linkages individuals and groups make between and across the infrastructure already travelled. For more on this aspect of the new media ecology model we can draw on the development of the phenomenon of 'emergence'. For instance, Hoskins and O'Loughlin (2010a) develop this idea in relation to work on complexity (see Urry 2005: 5) with emergence defined as: 'the processes whereby the global behaviour of a system results from the actions and interactions of agents' (Sawyer 2005: 2), or put differently as 'collective phenomena that are collaboratively created by individuals, yet are not reducible to individual action' (op. cit.: 5). Emergence then is one of the key ways in which the information infrastructure is continually 'renewable' through its relations with the other elements of the new media ecology mapped out above.

In Figure 7.1, the key actors in respect of radicalisation are Jihadist media, mainstream news media, states, translation agencies, and audiences/citizens who can confer legitimacy on the others and hence are the target of appeals in the form of propaganda or public diplomacy from the others. Through the interactions of this set of agents a number of discourses (on and of radicalisation) and a range of experiences (fear, anxiety, mistrust, uncertainty) emerge via a diffused information infrastructure. These discourses 'modulate' in intensity and extensity, for instance around key events as we demonstrated in our nexus analysis (in Chapter 5) of the mediatisations of the Gaza conflict.

Nexus analysis has allowed us to trace the constitution of a new media ecology around the phenomenon of radicalisation. The creators of nexus analysis, Scollon and Scollon (2004), suggested an important aspect of the approach is mapping the scale and scope of any nexus, what they called *circumferencing*. This refers to the identification of the past origins of action; its future direction; its expanding circles of engagement with others near and far; the timescales on which the action depends and the layers of geopolitical discourses in which it is embedded. Using this approach, the temporal trajectories and trends of radicalising discourses and discourses *about* radicalisation were identified, as well as their spatial connectivities, and local and global influences.

We have theorised the interactions of agents in this model in terms of mediatisation, the process whereby social relationships are subsumed within, or dependent on, the media and their logics. The particular media logics that drive interactions examined in this book have included premediation (the anticipation of a range of potential future scenarios to prevent traumatic surprises), retrospective premediation (media reports which represent individuals' life trajectories depicting incidents in their youth as signifying that they were always bound to be radicalised), and speculative remediation (translation of extremist discourses through mainstream news discourses in event time). These media logics operate along the dynamic axis of chaos versus control (cf. McNair 2006) through which the tension between professional and amateur media has unfolded in both Jihadist and mainstream media.

It must be noted that the sets of actors represented in the diagram are by no means discrete. Some private terrorist monitoring agencies and translation agencies are funded by states, others by individuals who feel it is their civic duty. There have always been suspicions that some Jihadist media were organised by intelligence agencies in order to monitor Jihadist communication, and we now know that al-Hesba was actually run by the CIA. Audience members may have shifting engagements with news about radicalisation, for instance if a terrorist attack occurs or they have a personal experience connected to what they feel is radicalisation. We have also included a category, 'grey zones', to indicate where discourses of radicalisation are present but not necessarily in ways planned by Jihadists or in spaces where such ideas are subject to contestation and debate.

In this concluding chapter, we review the findings of this book and their implications for security, terrorism and media.

The uncertain connectivities of media and terror

'Radicalisation' is a phenomenon that has emerged in the early twenty-first century because the new media ecology enables patterns of connectivity that *can* be harnessed by individuals and groups for practices of persuasion, organisation and the enactment of violence. The very possibility of this happening but uncertainty about how it happens created a conceptual vacuum which 'radicalisation' filled. The case of Jihadist radicalisation has depended on these conditions. Often, however, this feared connectivity does not happen, or happens in ways not predictable and controllable by those seeking to incite, direct or carry out violence. Hence, Jihadist networks have seen shifts in the organisations' form, practices of legitimation and relation of ideology to action, shifts which have often challenged and defied Jihadist leaders. Yet the spectre of successful connectivity by Jihadists – a spectre given material form by a string of attacks around the world since the 1990s – has allowed the formation of discourses of global fear, risk and hypersecurity, created, perpetuated or adapted by Western security agencies, political leaders and mainstream news media.

While the development and proliferation of digital media is the condition for these processes, they have not determined the emergence of Jihadists per se or war on terror responses. The political interests, grievances and ambitions driving these forms of response would require studies of regional politics, religious debates and the changing character of war that are beyond our scope of explanation here. Our focus in this book has been on how digital media have enabled connectivities that amplify or contain the dispersion of radicalising discourses and discourses *about* radicalisation. What marks these connectivities is a profound and intrinsic contingency. As a result, we have witnessed a series of attempts to conceptualise political actors such as al-Qaeda in the last decade, for instance the horizontal 'leaderless Jihad' proposed by Marc Sageman (2006) or the religious-ethical entity that 'acts without being an actor' described by Faisal Devji (2008). In the context of the contingent connectivity our study has documented, Knorr Cetina's conception of 'global microstructures' seems helpful. She writes that the 'world of Al Qaeda appears to be fluid, processual and aterritorial':

> As the flow of events into which Al Qaeda members are plugged is continuously reiterated, updated and extended, the various temporal and other coordinates of this world are continuously articulated and changed as operational goals are adopted, religious commentary and messages are interpreted, new decrees are issued, and the activities of various 'enemies' are observed and decoded. The very accoutrements of this non-institutional timeworld change as new events take place and become food for imagined new scenarios and works.
>
> (2005: 222)

The fluid networks Knorr Cetina labels 'global microstructures' are unified by members sharing a meaning of time; a long-term outlook based around historical narratives such as a battle between the three monotheisms. The Jihadists' success (or survival) has depended on harnessing mediatised, translocal socialities and continuously adapting as the new media ecology develops, always finding new supporters or members who will create interpretations of new events to fit the longer narratives. While we have seen that this adaptation has not necessarily been planned, and is rather the outcome of competition between putative leaders of 'the Jihad', the effect has been to take advantage of the 'contingent openness' that characterises the new media ecology.

We have been able to explain this by applying a methodology that integrates a number of strands of research. We have followed media content or stories (like the Gaza conflict) across a number of cultures operating simultaneously: multilingual Jihadist media, mainstream news and audience cultures. Since the sheer volume of media sources and content makes it impossible to systematically code and analyse any 'comprehensive' measure of Jihadist or mainstream media, instead of choosing a practical but restrictive corpus of material to analyse, we have turned conventional media-security analysis upside down by *following the story*. This 'nexus analysis' parallels a model of the 'circulation of commodities' offered some years ago by Arjun Appadurai (1986). By circulation, he was concerned with the production and consumption of commodities and what drives the demand for them; not simply the market dynamics of modern economics, but the *meaning* certain objects have in certain *cultural* contexts. His model resonates with our exploration of the demand for, and patterns of circulation of, Jihadist materials. He wrote:

we have to follow the things themselves, for their meanings are inscribed in their forms, their uses, their trajectories. It is only through the analysis of these trajectories that we can interpret human transactions and calculations that enliven things. Thus, even though from a *theoretical* point of view human actors encode things with significance, from a *methodological* point of view it is the things-in-motion that illuminate their human and social context.

(Appadurai 1986: 5)

Tracing the movement and proliferation of items of Jihadist media content is a means to the ends of establishing, among other things:

• what connectivity exists between Jihadist and mainstream cultures;
• what responses such connectivity engenders from mainstream publics, whether fear of terrorism or bemusement or hilarity at Jihadist culture; and
• whether mainstream news media inadvertently legitimise Jihadist ideas and cultures, and create fear in news audiences.

For Appadurai, as for contemporary media theorists (e.g. McNair 2006) circulation can be explained by a dialectic between control and chaos. Political and social elites in most societies try to ensure that exchange relations keep to a certain order – that the movement of goods, people and information is stable, predictable and structured in a way that prevents the emergence of any challenge to the elites themselves. However, such control is never total or permanent, and a certain *breaching* will occur:

What is political about [circulation] is the constant tension between the existing frameworks (of price, bargaining, and so forth) and the tendency of commodities to breach these frameworks.

(Appadurai 1986: 57)

The point Appadurai made, and that nexus analysis puts into practice, is that it is by following the content – looking from the content's point of view, even – that we can gain a perspective on those whose hands the content passes through, and their goals and beliefs at the time. Appadurai looks at the kula system of exchange in the Western Pacific, 'the best documented example of a non-Western, preindustrial, nonmonetized, translocal exchange system' (op. cit.: 18). The kula, he writes, 'is an extremely complex regional system for the circulation of particular kinds of valuables, usually between men of substance, in the Massim group of islands' (ibid.). Two types of objects are usually exchanged: necklaces go round the islands in one direction, while armshells go the other way. As these objects move, they gain a biography and a reputation of sorts. Equally, it is through this circulation that the reputations are established of the men who take hold of the necklaces and shells and later pass them on. Moreover, the ritual as a whole creates a larger meaning in the society and political arrangements of these islands. Memories, hierarchies and partnerships are enacted.

Jihadist leaders constructed a media system through which digital content was produced, disseminated and discussed. In Chapter 2 we found that the Jihadists, despite having a relatively coherent narrative which was reinforced by the Global War on Terror discourse offered by political leaders in the US and else-where, failed to mobilise mass popular support among Muslims; al-Zawahiri lamented 'the extent of the gap in understanding between the Jihad movement and the common people'. The circulation of images signifying Muslim suffering, Western hypocrisy, Jihadist heroism and so on was intended to create effects: to legitimise violence and recruit and mobilise supporters. The new media ecology facilitated the circulation and dispersion of the Jihadists' narrative and hence the opportunity to legitimate their violent actions. However, the very openness of that ecology resulted in a loss of control of the 'core message' as alternative interpretations and versions of the narrative emerged and charismatic figures explicitly challenged the positions of al-Zawahiri and others. We explained in Chapter 3 how this system was breached by autonomous Jihadists themselves, who contested core messages and produced their own content and disseminated it independently of the official Jihadist media system. It was in the interests of these Jihadist supporters to do so. The system was also breached by agencies which simply obliterated the official Jihadist media system by taking down their websites. The control-chaos dialectic is driven by competing interests, particularly among elites:

> [I]t is possible to witness the following common paradox. It is in the inter-ests of those in power to completely freeze the flow of commodities, by cre-ating a closed universe of commodities and a rigid set of regulations about how they are to move. Yet the very nature of contests between those in power (or those who aspire to greater power) tends to invite a loosening of these rules and an expansion of the pool of commodities. This aspect of elite politics is generally the Trojan horse of value shifts.
>
> (Appadurai 1986: 57)

Identifying a closed, failing elite, new actors emerged who cultivated legitimacy by deeds rather than words, and a new mix of on- and offline behaviour took hold. To be a Jihadist leader was as much about actions in the field of kinetic war as about clerical expertise.

The missing connection between Jihadists and mainstream news and audiences

How did this Jihadist culture connect to mainstream news content or audience understandings of 'radicalisation'? The unavoidable fact is that for the two years of our study, the only explicit moment of connection identified in our integrated study was the 2008–2009 Gaza crisis, when British news media reported on the presumed radicalising effect of Israel's actions (and Britain's lack of opposition to those actions), to the extent that news reports briefly addressed online Jihadist media propaganda being disseminated in those weeks. Jihadism was an implied *presence*, becoming materialised in the form about police raids on Muslim homes, attempted and actual attacks, and the implication that young, 'vulnerable' individuals must have been radicalised to some extent by extremist 'materials' or 'through the Internet'. But despite the 'existential' threat posed by Jihadist 'global terrorism', mainstream news and audience understandings were both characterised by an absence of the shifting characters, ideology, network form, and successes and failures of Jihadism. Instead, uncertainty about the nature and form of this threat enabled unverifiable discourses about radicalisation to run wild. And as was clear in Chapter 6 (and see below) this correlated with anxieties about terrorism threats even among those sceptical about the concept or policies they associated with 'radicalisation'. Hence, discourses about radicalisation may have in themselves generated terror.

Our study has offered evidence of the ways in which television in particular functions to reproduce these discourses about radicalisation, while offering very little information about Jihadist culture. In contrast to the millennial time frame of Jihadists, Western news media coverage of 'radicalisation'-related events in the years following 9/11 saw the likes of Sky News, CNN and the BBC in particular deliver to viewers a particular temporality, the extended present. In the extended present, unfolding events are represented as a known and possibly unavoidable series of ongoing crises within a global war on terror of indefinite and unknowable duration. The extended present is fortified by the manner in which mainstream television offers simulations or premediations of terrorist attacks, featuring in the BBC's case many of the very journalists, political advisors and unofficial 'experts' who featured in the coverage of the actual 7/7 attacks. This blurring of fact and fiction, official and unofficial, may sustain, legitimate or even normalise discourses of global fear and risk whose relation to the actual activities and capacities of Jihadists is unknowable.

Security journalism around radicalisation-related events is an awkward vocation, given the absence of verifiable information and the need to fill the 24-hour news schedule. Nor can we blame journalists for offering vague notions of 'radicalisation' when security services admit any model is impossible (Githens-Mazer and Lambert 2010) and politicians continue to use this 'useful fiction' in their public statements. Nevertheless, regardless of good intentions and challenges faced, the actual product of security journalism in the period studied perpetuated stereotypes and global fear discourses. For instance, although British media were reluctant to even mention al-Qaeda or give details on individual suspects, reference to the need to engage Muslim communities in the aftermath of these breaking security events offers an identity to the threat if only by implication. Nowhere were these problems more evident than in BBC *Newsnight*'s episode on the Gaza crisis broadcast on 12 January 2009.

In Chapter 5 we identified the *Newsnight* programme as an exemplar of speculative remediation. This was evident in its multiple connecting of the images and other media modalities (around the new media ecology) of apparently unchecked Israeli destruction of Gaza and its people, to a process of radicalisation in UK communities and online. In this way the Gaza conflict was a 'perfect storm' in the potential weaponisation of Western mainstream news through its translation and amplification of the discourses of radicalisation within the intense highly reflexive period of 'event time' of the conflict. We juxtaposed the *Newsnight* reporting with our analysis of the actual attempted legitimisation of Global Jihad that was taking place online within the same event timeframe. Through this we demonstrated how the new media ecology is both 'imagined' and traversed through the multiple representations of the mainstream in the non-mainstream and vice-versa as the discourses on the conflict modulated between chaos and order, amplification and containment. The larger and complex iterations of these discourses across all or even many mainstream news platforms and the wider new media ecology would be impossible to systematically code and analyse.

However, in our selection and analysis of a practical but restrictive corpus of material we illuminated a nexus of radicalisation that developed through the connectivities of the information infrastructure, but also despite them. In other words, this nexus is not just about the direct linkages made between a set of agents but about a particular kind of speculation (speculative remediation) that involves assumptions as to the nature of the formation and extent of the discourses being represented on the Internet. One can therefore conclude that it is the mediality of the Internet that affords the medium an impact beyond simply the ways in which it is represented (in this case on television). Its impact is related to an implicitly shared sense of how the medium is 'consumed' and accessed and used by the various agents connected to this particular nexus including by journalists representing or 'imagining' the Internet as a medium in and through which radicalisation emerges.

How then do ordinary citizens understand radicalisation? Previous studies have shown that although people often have contradictory or unclear understandings of security and their own relation to threats 'out there', these understandings are (a) explicable, and (b) affect their attitude to government security policy and whether they believe such policy is legitimate. It was important, then, to explore how people have been living with and making sense of the security context of the period, and 'radicalisation' in particular. Through comparative ethnographic analysis, we found that audiences-cum-citizens do not simply believe or not believe what they are being told about radicalisation by journalists and politicians. Rather, the practice of consuming news about radicalisation is one of several ways in which people come to understand the nature of their society, their own position in it, and the boundaries of the mainstream and margins or extremes. This includes the emergent role of mediality in shaping such mediatised understandings. Hence, not only is a study of everyday understandings of radicalisation instructive for security studies in itself, but it opens up more long-standing sociological questions about the logics of identity and difference through which contemporary societies are being constituted. The social function of the term 'radicalise' was implicit in Raymond Williams' entry on 'radical' in his *Keywords* (1983):

Radical has been used as an adjective in English from C14, and as a noun from C17, from fw *radicalis*, lL, rw *radix*, L – root. Its early uses were mostly physical, to express an inherent and fundamental quality, and this was extended to more general descriptions from C16. The important extension to political matters, always latent in this general use, belongs specifically to lC18, especially in the phrase **Radical Reform**. **Radical** as a noun to describe a proponent of **radical reform** was common from eC19: 'Radical is a word in very bad odour here, being used to denote a set of blackguards...' (Scott, 1819); 'Love is a great leveler; a perfect Radical' (Cobbett, 1822); 'the term Radical once employed as a name of low reproach, has found its way into high places, and is gone forth as the title of a class, who glory in their designation' (1830); 'the radical mob' (Emerson, 1856). **Radicalism** was formed from this use, in eC19, and was followed by **radicalize**. The words then have a curious subsequent history. **Radical**, especially with a capital letter, was by the second half of C19 almost as respectable as *liberal*, and Radicalism generally followed. But **radical** was still available, in some uses, in the sharper eC19 sense. Where in 1852 we find 'incipient radicalism, chartist tendencies, or socialist symptoms', there was by lC19 a clear distinction between Radicals and Socialists, and in the course of time most Radical parties, in other countries, were found considerably to the right of the political spectrum.

Whether 'radical' denotes left, right, respectable or violent, the term will continue to be used in relation to a social mainstream, and hence uses of the term 'radical' and 'radicalise' are indicators of social and political imaginaries in any period. We found, for instance, that consuming news about radicalisation gives people a sense of being part of a news public, since radicalisation is assumed to be something 'everyone hears about' even if its precise meaning is not clear or often politicised. While research participants offered a very diverse range of meanings when asked what 'radicalisation' means, their understandings all expressed some notion of a relationship between a mainstream democratic society and marginal or extreme figures who contest that society, in some cases through calls for, or use of, violence.

Even those concerned about radicalisation are thinking about a range of issues together, rather than the Jihadist terrorism so central to contemporary security policies. Some were unsure what they thought about radicalisation, others only gave it attention when large-scale media events broke. But it is striking that a majority of interviewees said they felt threatened by calls for violence. Moreover, they assumed everyone must feel threatened, just as 'everyone hears' about radicalisation, and hence theirs was a natural reaction. That a fairly critical sample of interviewees still largely felt a sense of threat perhaps demonstrates the effect of living in conditions of hypersecurity; uncertainty may be the condition to believe the worst, despite one's self-identity as critical or 'not-your-typical-viewer'. We are only just beginning to understand the relation between uncertainty (including types of uncertainty), media, and responses to security policy.

Appendix I
Demographic information

Appendix I Demographic information (total: 51 respondents)

	Frequency	*Percentage*
Gender		
Female	22	43
Male	29	57
Age		
20–29	20	39
30–39	20	39
40–49	9	18
50–59	2	4
Country		
England	37	72
France	10	20
Denmark	3	6
Australia	1	2
Religion		
Christian	4	8
Muslim	3	6
Jewish	3	6
No religion	27	53
Not disclosed	14	27

Appendix II

Phenomena interviewees associate with 'radicalisation'

The following list of items refers to the range of phenomena that audience interviewees spoke about when asked what 'radicalisation' meant to them. It is not quite an A–Z.

1968
Abu Hamza
Afghan women protesting
Anarchists
Animal rights
Anti-capitalist movement
Anti-EU views
Black power salute 1968 Olympics
Blockage of universities
Born again Christians
Boss snapping
Capitalism
Catholic church
Choreology
Communists
Crusades
Darwin
Dictatorships
Dieudonné
Early Labour Party
Ecological activists
English civil war – Cromwell
Extreme left
Extreme right
Fathers 4 Justice
Feminism
Fundamentalist Christians
Gandhi
Government

Hippies
Homophobia
Hooligans
Hoyerswerda
Human rights
Ian Paisley
Irish Republican Army
Islamic radicalism
Israel–Palestine relations
It doesn't exist
Jihad
Ku Klux Klan
Kurdish question
Martin Luther King
Marxist groups in Kerala
Media propaganda
Militant Jews
Minority groups in Iran
Mongols
Movements against segregation
Nail bomber
National Society for the Prevention of Cruelty to Children
Native Americans
Nazis
North/South Korea
Nouveau Parti Anticapitaliste
Omagh bombing
Opposition movements in Iran
Opposition to the Vietnam war in the US
Organisations against Animal Cruelty
Osama bin Laden
Parti Radical de Gauche
Parti Socaliste
Protests in Thailand
Radical sexual politics
Right wing groups
Right wing groups in Russia
Riots in Greece (November–December 2008)
Roman Empire
Sarkozy
September 11, 2001 attacks
Skinhead
Société Nationale des Chemin de fer français
Social movements in Latin America
Socialists

Sociological concept
Sri Lanka cricket team
Stopping taking showers
Tarnac people
Terrorism
The police
The Pope on contraception
The Socialist Workers Party
Tibet
Tiananmen square protestors
Tony Blair
Women's right movements
Yugoslavia

Notes

1 Media and radicalisation: grappling uncertainties in the new media ecology radicalisation gone wild

1 The Iraq Inquiry (see www.iraqinquiry.org.uk) launched on 30 July 2009 aimed to 'identify lessons that can be learned from the Iraq conflict'. Witnesses that appeared in person before the committee members included the most senior members of the UK political elite including the former Prime Minister Tony Blair and (at the time of his appearance) the sitting Prime Minister Gordon Brown. Baroness Manningham-Buller's comments should be seen in the context of her giving evidence to the Inquiry following its break for the 2010 UK general election. In other words, the ensuing change of government may come to be seen as a marker which enabled a more public critical reflection on policy and practice in terms of a rationale for the 2003 invasion of Iraq, especially by those who were members of the government/security services over that period.
2 Oxford English Dictionary entry available at: http://dictionary.oed.com/cgi/entry/50297778 [accessed 11 April 2010].
3 Oxford English Dictionary entry available at: http://dictionary.oed.com/cgi/entry/50196101 [accessed 11 April 2010].
4 'Studies into violent radicalisation; Lot 2 The beliefs ideologies and narratives', Change Institute for the European Commission (Directorate General Justice, Freedom and Security), February 2008, note 3, p. 7, online, available at: http://ec.europa.eu/home-affairs/doc_centre/terrorism/docs/ec_radicalisation_study_on_ideology_and_narrative_en.pdf [accessed July 2008].
5 The research project is: 'Legitimising the discourses of radicalisation: political violence in the new media ecology', Award Number: RES-181-25-0041, led by this book's authors. See www.newmediaecology.net/radicalisation/index.html and www2.warwick.ac.uk/fac/soc/pais/research/nsc.
6 We are indebted to Paul Eedle, a member of the ESRC Programme Advisory Board and Managing Director of Out There News for making available this material to us.
7 We are indebted to Carole Boudeau for these observations and analysis.

2 Legitimising Jihadist ideology

1 This chapter is developed from an earlier article: Awan, A.N. (2009) 'Success of the Meta-Narrative: How Jihadists Maintain Legitimacy', in *CTC Sentinel*, 2(11): 6–9.
2 The phrase 'hearts and minds' is most famously associated with the British counter-insurgency campaign in Malaya (1948–1960), and President Lyndon B. Johnson's employment of it during the Vietnam War. However, the phrase has been increasingly invoked by politicians, commentators, security services and governmental organisations in the current conflict with radical Islamism. See for example the 2007 report from the UK Dept. for Communities and Local Government entitled *Preventing*

Violent Extremism – Winning hearts and minds www.communities.gov.uk/publications/communities/preventingviolentextremism.

3 Letter from Ayman al-Zawahiri to Abu Musab al-Zarqawi, 9 July 2005, The Office of the Director of National Security, online, available at: www.globalsecurity.org/security/library/report/2005/zawahiri-zarqawi-letter_9jul2005.htm.

4 Letter from Osama bin Laden to Mullah Omar, 5 June 2002, US Military Academy Counterterrorism Center, Document AFGP-2002–600321.

5 Al-Zawahiri, Ayman (2001) *Fursan Taht Rayah Al-Nabi (Knights Under the Prophet's Banner)*, Part 11, section 1.A, online, available at: www.scribd.com/doc/6759609/Knights-Under-the-Prophet-Banner.

6 Whilst Osama bin Laden had released other statements prior to the 1996 'fatwa', these earlier messages are considered to have been addressed to more local Saudi audiences such as the *Ulama* (scholars) or wider appeals to Arab or Muslim constituencies.

7 Online, available at: www.mideastweb.org/osamabinladen1.htm.

8 In a speech given on 16 September 2001, President George W Bush stated, 'This is a new kind of – a new kind of evil. And we understand. And the American people are beginning to understand. This crusade, this war on terrorism is going to take a while.' Online, available at: www.georgewbush-whitehouse.archives.gov and navigate to News, 2001, September, 16.

9 From the sermon 'Among a Band of Knights', 14 February 2003, cited in Lawrence (2005).

10 'Bounty set over Prophet cartoon', BBC News, 15 September 2007, online, available at: http://news.bbc.co.uk/2/hi/middle_east/6996553.stm [accessed 15 September 2007].

11 The Global Jihadists have consistently appealed to anachronistic medieval categories of this nature in order to frame the current conflict.

12 From a speech given by George W. Bush on 6 November 2001, online, available at: http://archives.cnn.com/2001/US/11/06/gen.attack.on.terror.

13 Transcript online, available at: http://english.aljazeera.net/archive/2004/11/200849163336457223.html.

14 See Tim Reid, 'Al-Qaeda supporters back John McCain for president', *The Times*, 23 October 2008.

15 Online, available at: www.alhesbah.org [accessed 21 October 2008].

16 See Haroon Siddique 'McCain adviser says terrorist attack would boost campaign', *The Guardian*, 24 June 2008.

17 Letter from Ayman al-Zawahiri to Abu Musab al-Zarqawi (2005), online, available at: www.cfr.org/publication/9862/letter_from_ayman_alzawahiri_to_abu_musab_alzarqawi.html.

18 The literal meaning of the commonly used phrase *Jihad fee sabeelillah.*

19 These include *The Caliphate Voice Channel* (http://cvc-online.blogspot.com) and the previous incarnation, *The Mujahideen Shura Council* (http://albayanat.blogspot.com).

20 In this case being the 'criterion for demarcating right from wrong'. See for example *Surah* 25 of the Quran.

21 Prior to the 'downing of the Jihadist forums', these were considered to be the most important Jihadist new media spaces available; see Awan and al-Lami (2009).

22 This term was coined by Kepel (2004) to describe Salafi Muslims who began developing an interest in violent Jihad during the mid-1990s.

23 Letter from Ayman al-Zawahiri to Abu Musab al-Zarqawi, 2005.

24 For a detailed discussion of the legitimate parameters of war in the Islamic tradition see Kelsay (2008).

25 See McCants (2006).

26 Reinforcing our reciprocal legitimation thesis, this tactic is a employed by a number of Islamophobic commentators and organisations too.

27 For a discussion of some of the arguments put forward by radicals in order to justify the killing of civilians, see Wiktorowicz (2005).

28 It is now widely recognised that a significant proportion of Jihadist forum members include a motley crew of counterterrorism officials, anti-Jihadist activists, journalists, and academics. Indeed there is growing evidence that al-Hesbah, the most secure and respected of the Jihadist forums was in fact a CIA vehicle – of course this does not mean that the forum was not used by real Jihadists as the case of Abu Dujanah proved (see Chapter 3).

29 This is not to imply that these traditional ideologues may not also be immersed in the new media environments; al-Maqdisi has a number of websites and has engaged in debates directly on Jihadist forums.

30 The Lesser Jihad refers to conventional warfare against an external enemy (predominantly defensive in nature), whereas the Greater Jihad entails every Muslim's internal spiritual struggle; see Firestone (1999).

31 The Lesser Jihad in the classical tradition is recognised not as an individual duty (*fard 'ayn*), but rather as a collective or communal duty (*fard kifaya*).

32 For more on Faraj, see Jansen (1986).

33 Khan, Muhammad Siddique (2005) *Martyrdom Testament*, online, available at: http:// news.bbc.co.uk/1/hi/uk/4206800.stm.

34 Bin Laden, Osama (1998) *World Islamic Front Statement for Jihad Against Jews and Crusaders*, online, available at: http://fas.org/irp/world/para/docs/980223-fatwa.htm.

35 Ibid.

36 Literally meaning Seceder, the Kharijites were an early heretical Islamic sect.

37 Osama bin Laden, al-Jazeera TV Channel Interview, 1991.

38 As is now well known, the vast majority of victims of Jihadist violence have been Muslims; i.e. only 15 per cent of the fatalities resulting from al-Qaeda attacks between 2004 and 2008 were Westerners. During the most recent period studied the numbers skew even further. From 2006 to 2008, only 2 per cent are from the West, and the remaining 98 per cent are inhabitants of countries with Muslim majorities. See Helfstein *et al.* (2009).

39 Such as using Down's Syndrome sufferers (Howard 2008), or women raped by Jihadists as suicide bombers (Haynes 2009).

40 Cf. Bennett *et al.* (2007).

41 Juba is the *nom de guerre* of one (possibly more) highly trained sniper involved in the Iraqi insurgency, who claims to have killed hundreds of US soldiers; see www.baghdadsniper.net.

42 Alali and Eke (1991) first used this term in suggesting that journalists act as 'rhetorical amplifiers' for either terrorists or government officials when reporting on a news story on terrorism.

43 See Chapter 3 for more on the control exerted.

44 Both figures have impeccable Jihadist credentials and were arguably present at the founding of al-Qaeda in 1988 in Peshawar.

45 The prohibition on *takfir* was one of the three principle points endorsed by *The Amman Message* in 2005, which brought together 200 of the world's leading Islamic scholars from 50 countries. See www.ammanmessage.com.

46 Ibid.

47 Letter from Ayman al-Zawahiri to Abu Musab al-Zarqawi.

48 Al-Zawahiri has attempted to engage his critics through his text *The Exoneration* (2008) and through the 2008 virtual open meeting facilitated by *as-Sahab*, however, his response has focused principally on the critics' inability to comprehend the *true* state of the situation due to their absence from the Jihad fronts.

3 Media Jihad

1 Parts of this chapter are based upon an earlier article: Awan, A.N. (2010) 'Jihadist Ideology in the New Media Environment', in Deol, J. and Kazmi, Z. (eds) *Contextualising Jihadi Ideology*. London: C. Hurst & Co.

2 Indeed some commentators have even suggested it is a distinctly modern *Western* phenomenon; a product of globalisation and modernisation that is far removed from traditional Muslim societies, and in many ways reminiscent of the Protestant Reformation; see Roy (2004).
3 Quoted in Ulph, S. (2005).
4 The term 'counterculture' is a variant of the subculture theme first popularised by Roszak (1968).
5 Abdullah Yusuf Azzam was a highly influential Palestinian scholar and advocate for defensive Jihad, particularly during the Soviet invasion of Afghanistan. He also served as an early mentor for Osama bin Laden in Afghanistan.
6 Abu Huthayfa, Memo to the Honorable Sheikh Abu Abdullah, 20 June 2000, pp. 9–11. Harmony database, AFGP-2002–003251.
7 O'Loughlin, B. (2010) 'Images as weapons of war? Representation, mediation and interpretation', *Review of International Studies*, doi: 10.1017/ S0260210510000811.
8 See for example Fisk's (1996) eyewitness account at the time and his later book *Pity the Nation: Lebanon at War* (2001), particularly chapter 18.
9 Historically the regions that demarcated *dar al-Islam* from *dar al-harb*, and therefore the realm that animates bin Laden and his ilk most strongly.
10 This is the most widely accepted definition of Web 2.0; see www.oreillynet.com/pub/a/oreilly/tim/news/2005/09/30/what-is-web-20.html.
11 Al-Ansari, Abu al-Harith (2008) *Irshad al-Sa'ul ila Hurub al-Rasul*, online, available at: http://pdfdatabase.com/download/abu-al-harith-al-ansari-irshad-al-saul-ila-hurub-al-rasul-d8a5d8b1d8b4d8a7d8af-d8a7d984d8b3d8a4d988d984-d8a5d984d989-d8add8b-1d988d8a8-d8a7d984d8b1d8b3-doc-4571909.html.
12 Al-Salim, Muhammad bin Ahmad (2003) *39 Ways to Serve and Participate in Jihad*, online, available at: www.archive.org/details/39WaysToServeAnd Participate.
13 Al-Awlaki's work is in fact based upon al-Salim's (2003) text, with large portions of the text having been plagiarised outright without any sort of acknowledgement or attribution.
14 Al-Awlaki, Anwar (2009) *44 Ways to Support Jihad*, online, available at: http://ibnab-dullah.blogspot.com/2009/05/44-ways-to-supoort-jihad.html.
15 Al-Suri is perhaps best known for this theory decentralised 'leaderless terrorism' which he describes as *nizam la tanzim* (system, not organisation), and which has informed the modus operandi of most Jihadist terrorists attacks in the post-9/11 milieu.
16 Al-Suri, Abu Musab (2005) 'Theory of Media and Incitement in the Call to Global Islamic Resistance' in *Call to Global Islamic Resistance*, online, available at: www.archive.org/details/TheGlobalIslamicResistanceCall.
17 Cited in Black (2007).
18 Cited in Homeland Security Policy Institute and Critical Incident Analysis Group Task Force on Internet-facilitated Radicalisation (2007).
19 See *Economist* (2007).
20 Ibid.
21 See www.almasry-alyoum.com/printerfriendly.aspx?ArticleID=217021.
22 Quoted in *The Economist* (2007).
23 Online, available at: www.opsi.gov.uk/acts/acts2006/pdf/ukpga_20060011_en. pdf.
24 See *Telegraph* (2009).
25 See *The Economist* (2007).
26 Online, available at: www.religioscope.com/info/doc/jihad/azzam_defence_3_chap1. htm.
27 Online, available at: www.worldofislam.info/ebooks/joincaravan.pdf.
28 Al-Zarqawi 'Ilhaq bi-al-Qafila', online, available at: www.youtube.com/watch?v=1rIq Yt21FWA.
29 See AIVD (2008).
30 Al-Suri (2005) 'Theory of Media and Incitement in the Call to Global Islamic Resistance' in *Call to Global Islamic Resistance*.

31 Ibid.
32 Formerly available at: www.alm2sda.net.
33 Cited in Weimann (2006).
34 See Labi (2006).
35 'Three jailed for inciting terror', *BBC News*, 5 July 2007, online, available at: http:// news.bbc.co.uk/2/hi/uk_news/6273732.stm.
36 Demir, Adem and Dickey, Christopher 'The Bomber's Wife', *Newsweek.com*. 7 January 2010, online, available at: www.newsweek.com/id/229792.
37 Ibid.
38 Online, available at: www.shamikh1.net/vb/showthread.php?t=59653.
39 Demir and Dickey 2010.
40 Site at www.al-faloja.info/vb is now lapsed.
41 See Awan and al-Lami (2009).
42 See http://shamikh1.net/vb/.
43 See McLuhan (1964).

4 Media events: televisual connections 2004–2006

1 This is a consistent finding across three interlinked studies: Afterseptember11.tv, Shifting Securities, and Legitimising the Discourses of Radicalisation.
2 Shifting Securities, Strand A, Interview Z2.1, lines 156–163, italics added.
3 Shifting Securities, Strand A, Interview Z2.1, lines 164–168.
4 See http://news.bbc.co.uk/2/hi/programmes/the_day_britain_stopped/default.stm.
5 See www.bbc.co.uk/drama/smallpox2002.

5 The mainstream nexus of radicalisation: the 2008–2009 Gaza conflict

1 See for example, Jonathan Miller, 'Phosphorous controversy in Gaza' www.channel4.com/news/articles/politics/international_politics/phosphorous%2bcontroversy%2bin%2bgaza%2b%2b/2909012.html, updated 22 January 2009.
2 Nicholas Watt, 'ITV and Channel 4 to air Gaza appeal as pressure mounts in BBC', *The Guardian*, 24 January 2009, available at: www.guardian.co.uk/media/2009/jan/24/bbc-gaza-aid-appeal-dec.
3 Paul Bromley, 'Gaza Appeal – Sky's decision explained', blog available at: http://blogs.news.sky.com/editorsblog/ then navigate Older Blogs/ to 26 January 2009.
4 Translated from the original Arabic.
5 See: Shumookh Al-Islam forum www.shamikh1.net/vb/showthread.php? t=30650 and Ana Muslim Islamist forum http://muslm.org/vb/showthread.php?t=324347 [both accessed 25 October 2010].
6 Formerly available at: www.msnbc.msn.com/id/28790359/.
7 Site at www.al-faloja.info/vb/showthread.php?p=224623 is now lapsed.
8 The date on the article reads 8 November 2008 but was only released on 18 January by al-Fajr. The only reason we can think of for this delayed release, or perhaps recirculation and advertisement, was because it suited al-Qaeda's current campaign to legitimise the targeting of 'Jews and Crusaders wherever and however'. Also, producers may be hoping to achieve more credibility for Attiyatallah's arguments [on killing Westerners] following the killing of many civilians in Gaza.
9 Site at www.al-faloja.info/vb/showthread.php?p=224620 is now lapsed.
10 Site at www.al-faloja.info/vb/showthread.php?t=42210 is now lapsed.
11 Site at www.al-faloja.info/vb/showthread.php?t=41319 is now lapsed.
12 www.aljazeeratalk.net/forum/showthread.php?p=1988687.
13 Reference to Jews.
14 Site at www.al-faloja.info/vb/showthread.php?t=40866 is now lapsed.

6 Audience uncertainties: imagining the mainstream and extremes

1 Online, available at: http://today.yougov.co.uk/sites/today.yougov.co.uk/files/YG-Archives-pol-spectator-WarOnTerror-060817.pdf.

2 Online, available at: http://today.yougov.co.uk/sites/today.yougov.co.uk/files/YG-Archives-pol-skynews-WarOnTerror5years-060911.pdf.

3 'Anti-Terrorism, Citizenship and Security in the UK', Economic and Social Research Council, Award ref: RES-000–22–3765. See: www.esrcsocietytoday.ac.uk/ ESRCInfo-Centre/ViewAwardPage.aspx?ts=1&data=%2FFrXHTl993r3JquW%2FO3REmBC1H M8rUZ3TLl%2F8jkbSfAanMoCh9fMFy4xfWhxErZ2HgE2fB7I%2BX6SXJqvUW6h HoDHCgMRr%2F5R5vDjnFXvGaA7Jj6m3Iu9Pw%3D%3D.

4 *Legitimising*, Interview JE & JDB, line 80. All names have been anonymised.

5 RF is a 35 years old Kurdish male who has been living in London for nine years and who works for a human rights NGO. Politically, he is an anarchist and consequently holds no religious beliefs.

6 Legitimising, Interview RF, lines 114–21.

7 FB is a 42 years old Franco-English male who lives in London and who works as a fundraising manager for a children charity. Politically, he describes himself as a liberal and, religiously, as an atheist.

8 Legitimising, Interview FB, lines 153–6.

References

AIVD (2008) Annual Report AIVD 2007 (Dutch), 22 April 2008, online, available at: www.aivd.nl/contents/pages/92308/jaarverslagaivd2007.pdf.

Alali, A. Odasuo and Eke, Kenoye Kelvin (eds) (1991) *Media Coverage of Terrorism: Methods*, London: Sage Publications.

Al-Lami, Mina (2008) 'Studies of Radicalisation: State of the Field Report', No. 11 in *RHUL PIR Working Paper* series, online, available at: www.rhul.ac.uk/politics-and-IR/ Working-Papers/RHUL-PIR-NPCU_Working_Paper-11_Al_Lami_Radicalisation_and_ New_Media.pdf.

Alshech, E. (2008) 'The Emergence of the "Infallible Jihad Fighter" – The Salafi Jihadists' Quest for Religious Legitimacy', in *The Middle East Media Research Institute: Inquiry and Analysis,* No. 446, online, available at: www.memrijttm.org/ content/en/ report.htm?report=2685&param=AJT.

Altheide, D.L. (2007) 'The Mass Media and Terrorism', *Discourse and Communication*, 1(3): 287–308.

Al-Zawahiri, Ayman (2001) *Fursan Taht Rayah Al-Nabi (Knights Under the Prophet's Banner)*, Part 11, section 1.A, online, available at: www.scribd.com/doc/6759609/ Knights-Under-the-Prophet-Banner.

Appadurai, A. (1986) 'Introduction: Commodities and the Politics of Value' in Appadurai, A. (ed.) *The Social Life of Things: Commodities in Cultural Perspective*, Cambridge: Cambridge University Press.

Awan, Akil N. (2007a) 'Transitional Religiosity Experiences: Contextual Disjuncture and Islamic Political Radicalism', in T. Abbas (ed.) *Islamic Political Radicalism: A European comparative perspective*, Edinburgh: Edinburgh University Press.

Awan, Akil N. (2007b) 'Virtual Jihadist Media: Function, Legitimacy, and Radicalizing Efficacy', *European Journal of Cultural Studies* (Special Issue), 3(10): 389–408.

Awan, Akil N. (2007c) 'Radicalization on the Internet? The Virtual Propagation of Jihadist Media and its Effects', *Journal of the Royal United Services Institute*, 3(152): 76–81.

Awan, Akil N. (2008) 'Antecedents of Islamic Political Radicalism Among Muslim Communities in Europe', *Political Science & Politics*, 1(41): 13–17.

Awan, Akil N. (2009) 'Success of the Meta-Narrative: How Jihadists Maintain Legitimacy', *CTC Sentinel*, 2(11): 6–9.

Awan, Akil N. (2010) 'Jihadist Ideology in the New Media Environment', in Deol, J. and Kazmi, Z. (eds), *Contextualising Jihadi Ideology*, London: C. Hurst & Co.

Awan, Akil N. and al-Lami, Mina (2009) 'Al-Qaeda's Virtual Crisis', *Journal of the Royal United Services Institute*, 154(1): 56–64.

Barad, K. (2007) *Meeting the Universe Halfway*, London: Duke University Press.

Barker, Martin (2006) 'I Have Seen the Future and It Is Not Here Yet ...; or, On Being Ambitious for Audience Research', *The Communication Review*, 9(2): 123–41.

Barnett, Clive (2003) *Culture and Democracy: Media, Space and Representation*, Edinburgh: Edinburgh University Press.

Baudrillard, Jean (1983) *Simulations*, New York: Semiotext.

Bauman, Z. (2006) *Liquid Fear*, Cambridge: Polity Press.

BBC News (2006a) 'Raid Police Hunt Chemical Device', 3 June, online, available at: http://news.bbc.co.uk/1/hi/uk/5042724.stm.

BBC News (2006b) 'House Raid Police had "No Choice"', 6 June, online, available at: http://news.bbc.co.uk/1/hi/uk/5049800.stm.

BBC News (2006c) 'Blair Defends Police Terror Raid', 6 June, online, available at: http://news.bbc.co.uk/1/hi/uk_politics/5053618.stm.

BBC News (2006d) 'Raid Police Apologise for "Hurt"', 14 June, online, available at: http://news.bbc.co.uk/1/hi/uk/5077198.stm.

BBC News (2006e) 'Marchers Demand Apology over Raid', 18 June, online, available at: http://news.bbc.co.uk/1/hi/uk/5092452.stm.

Beck, Ulrich (2006) 'Living in the World Risk Society', Hobhouse Memorial Public Lecture, The London School of Economics and Political Science, 15 February, online, available at: www.libertysecurity.org/IMG/pdf_Beck-2006.pdf.

Bennett, W.L., Lawrence, R.G. and Livingston, S. (2007) *When the Press Fails: Political Power and the News Media from Iraq to Katrina*, Chicago, IL: University of Chicago Press.

Bergen, Peter (2006) *The Osama bin Laden I Know*, New York: Free Press.

Bergen, Peter and Footer, Lawrence (2008) 'Defeating the Attempted Global Jihadist Insurgency: Forty Steps for the Next President to Pursue against al Qaeda, Like-Minded Groups, Unhelpful State Actors, and Radicalized Sympathizers', in *The Annals of the American Academy of Political and Social Science*, 1(618): 232–47.

Bergin, Anthony, Osman, Sulastri Bte, Ungerer, Carl and Yasin, Nur Azlin Mohamed (2009) *Counte ring Internet Radicalization in Southeast Asia*, Special report 22 RSIS–ASPI, online, available at: www.aspi.org.au/publications/ publication_details. aspx?ContentID=202

Black, Andrew (2007) 'Jihadi Statement Extols Virtues of the Internet', *Terrorism Focus*, 18 September.

Bleiker, R. and Hutchinson, E. (2008) 'Fear No More: Emotion and World Politics', *Review of International Studies*, 34(S1): 115–35.

Bolt, N., Betz, D. and Azari, J. (2008) *Propaganda of the Deed 2008: Understanding the Phenomenon, Whitehall Report 3–08*, London: Royal United Services Institute.

Bolter, J.D. and Grusin, R. (1999) *Remediation: Understanding New Media*, London: The MIT Press.

Bonner, M.D. (2006) *Jihad in Islamic History*, Princeton, NJ: Princeton University Press.

Bowker, Geoffrey C. and Star, Susan Leigh (1999) *Sorting Things Out: Classification and its Consequences*, Cambridge, MA: MIT Press.

Bracewell, Michael (2002) *The Nineties: When Surface Was Depth*, London: Flamingo.

Brachman, Jarret (2008) *Global Jihadism: Theory and Practice*, New York: Routledge.

Brown, Steven D. and Hoskins, Andrew (2010) 'Terrorism in the New Memory Ecology: Mediating and Remembering the 2005 London Bombings', *Behavioral Sciences of Terrorism and Political Aggression*, 2(2): 87–107.

Bunt, Gary (2003) *Islam in the Digital Age: E-jihad, Online Fatwas and Cyber Islamic Environments*, London: Pluto Press.

Campbell, David (2007) 'Geopolitics and Visuality: Sighting the Darfur Conflict', *Political Geography*, 26(1): 357–82.

Castells, Manuel (2009) *Communication Power*, Oxford: Oxford University Press.

Change Institute for the European Commission (Directorate General Justice, Freedom and Security) (2008) 'Studies into Violent Radicalisation; Lot 2 The Beliefs, Ideologies and Narratives', February 2008, Note 3, p. 7, online, available at: http://ec.europa.eu/justice_home/fsj/terrorism/prevention/fsj_terrorism_prevention_prevent_en.htm [accessed July 2008].

Chyi, Hsiang Iris and McCombs, Maxwell (2004) 'Media Salience and the Process of Framing: Coverage of the Columbine School Shootings', *Journalism & Mass Communication Quarterly*, (81)1: 22–35.

Coll, Steven and Glassner, Susan B. (2005) 'Terrorists Turn to the Web as Base of Operations', *The Washington Post*, 7 August.

Cottle, Simon (2006) *Mediatized Conflict: Developments in Media and Conflict Studies*, Maidenhead: Open University Press.

Couldry, Nick (2008) 'Mediatization or Mediation? Alternative Understandings of the Emergent Space of Digital Storytelling', *New Media & Society*, 10(3): 373–91.

Couldry, N., Livingstone, S. and Markham, T. (2007) *Media Consumption and Public Engagement*, Basingstoke: Palgrave.

Coulter, J. (1979) *The Social Construction of Mind: Studies in Ethnomethodology and Linguistic Philosophy*, London: Macmillan.

Debrix, F. (2008) *Tabloid Terror: War, Culture and Geopolitics*, London: Routledge.

Devji, Faisal (2005) *Landscapes of the Jihad: Militancy, Morality and Modernity*, London: C. Hurst & Co.

Devji, Faisal (2008) *The Terrorist in Search of Humanity: Militant Islam and Global Politics*, London: C. Hurst & Co.

Dillon, Michael (2007) 'Governing Terror: The State of Emergency in Biopolitical Emergence', *International Political Sociology*, 1(1): 7–28.

Eco, Umberto (1987) *Travels in Hyperreality*, London: Picador.

Economist, The (2007) 'A World Wide Web of Terror', *The Economist*, 13 July.

Entman, Robert M. (1993) 'Framing: Toward Clarification of a Fractured Paradigm', *Journal of Communication*, 4(43): 51–8.

Entman, Robert M. (2004) *Projections of Power: Framing News, Public Opinion, and U.S. Foreign Policy*, Chicago, IL: University of Chicago Press.

Entman, Robert M. (2006) 'Framing Public Life: Perspectives on Media and our Understanding of the Social World', *Political Communication*, 1(23): 121–2.

Festinger, L. (1957) *A Theory of Cognitive Dissonance*, Evanston, IL: Row, Peterson.

Firestone, Rueven (1999) *Jihad: The Origin of Holy War in Islam*, Oxford: Oxford University Press.

Fisk, Robert (1996) 'Qana, Massacre in Sanctuary; Eyewitness', *The Independent*, 19 April.

Fisk, Robert (2001) *Pity the Nation: Lebanon at War*, London: Oxford University Press.

Fuller, M. (2007) *Media Ecologies: Materialist Energies in Art and Technoculture*, Cambridge, MA: MIT Press.

Furedi, Frank (2007) *Invitation to Terror: The Expanding Empire of the Unknown*, London: Continuum.

Furedi, Frank (2008) 'Fear and Security: A Vulnerability-led Policy Response', *Social Policy and Administration*, 24(6): 645–61.

Gillespie, Marie (2006) 'Security, Media, Legitimacy: Multi-Ethnic Media Publics and the Iraq War 2003', *International Relations*, 20(4): 467–86.

Gillespie, Marie (2007) 'Shifting Securities: News Cultures Before and Beyond the Iraq Crisis 2003: Full Research Report', ESRC End of Award Report, RES-223-25-0063, Swindon: ESRC.

Gillespie, Marie and O'Loughlin, Ben (2009) 'News Media, Threats and Insecurities: an Ethnographic Approach', *Cambridge Review of International Affairs*, 22(4): 667–85.

Gillespie, Marie and O'Loughlin, Ben (forthcoming) *Insecurity, Media and Multiculturalism*, Basingstoke: Palgrave.

Gillmor, Dan (2006) *We the Media: Grassroots Journalism By the People, for the People*, Sebastopol, CA: O'Reilly Media, Inc.

Gilroy, P. (2006) 'Multiculture in Times of War', Inaugural Lecture, London School of Economics and Political Science, 10 May, online, available at: http://www2. lse.ac.uk/publicEvents/pdf/20060510-PaulGilroy.pdf.

Giroux, Henry (2006) *Stormy Weather: Katrina and the Politics of Disposability*, Boulder, CO: Westview Press.

Githens-Mazer, J. and Lambert, R. (2010) 'Why Conventional Wisdom on Radicalization Fails: The Persistence of a Failed Discourse', *International Affairs*, 86(4): 889–902.

Gitlin, Todd (1980) *The Whole World is Watching – Mass Media in the Making and Unmaking of the New Left*, London: University of California Press.

Gottschalk, Peter and Greenberg, Gabriel (2008) *Islamophobia: Making Muslims the Enemy*, Lanham, MD: Rowman & Littlefield Publishers.

Gowing, Nik (2009) ' "Skyful of Lies" and Black Swans: The New Tyranny of Shifting Information Power in Crises', *Reuters Institute for the Study of Journalism working paper*, Oxford: University of Oxford.

Grusin, Richard (2010) *Premediation: Affect and Mediality After 9/11*, Basingstoke: Palgrave Macmillan.

Guardian (2010) 'Iraq Invasion Radicalised British Muslims and Raised Terror Threat, Says Ex-MI5 Chief', *Guardian*, 21 July, p. 7.

Hammond, Philip (2003) 'The Media War on Terrorism', *Journal for Crime, Conflict and the Media*, 1(1): 23–36.

Hansen, L. (2006) *Security as Practice: Discourse Analysis and the Bosnian War*, London: Routledge.

Hargreaves, Ian and Thomas, James (2002) *New News, Old News*, London: ITC/BSC.

Haynes, Deborah (2009) 'Female Suicide Bomb Recruiter Samira Ahmed Jassim Captured', *The Times*, 3 February.

Helfstein, Scott, Abdullah, Nassir and al-Obaidi, Muhammad, (2009) *Deadly Vanguards: A Study of al-Qa'ida's Violence Against Muslims* (*CTC Occasional Paper series*), West Point, VI: Combating Terrorism Center.

Hine, C. (ed.) (2005) *Virtual Methods: Issues in Social Research on the Internet*, Oxford: Berg Publishers.

Hjarvard, Stig (2008) 'The Mediatization of Society: A Theory of the Media as Agents of Social and Cultural Change', *Nordicom Review*, 29(2): 105–34.

Hobson, J.M. and Seabrooke, L. (eds) (2007) *Everyday Politics of the World Economy*, Cambridge: Cambridge University Press.

Hoffheinz, Albrecht (2007) 'Arab Internet Use: Popular Trends and Public Impact', in Sakr, N (ed.), *Arab Media and Political Renewal: Community, Legitimacy and Public Life*, London: I.B. Tauris.

Hoffman, Bruce (2006) *Inside Terrorism*, New York: Columbia University Press.

Homeland Security Policy Institute and Critical Incident Analysis Group Task Force on Internet-facilitated Radicalization, (2007) *NETworked Radicalization: A Counter-Strategy*, online, available at www.gwumc.gwu.edu/hspi/old/reports/NETworked Radicalization_A Counter Strategy.pdf.

Home Office (2006) *Report of the Official Account of the Bombings in London on 7th July 2005*, London: The Stationery Office (TSO), online, available at: www.official-documents.gov.uk/document/hc0506/hc10/1087/1087.pdf.

Hoskins, Andrew (2001) 'Mediating Time: The Temporal Mix of Television', *Time & Society*, 10 (2/3): 333–46.

Hoskins, Andrew (2004a) *Televising War: From Vietnam to Iraq*, London: Continuum.

Hoskins, Andrew (2004b) 'Television and the Collapse of Memory', *Time & Society*, 13(1): 109–27.

Hoskins, Andrew (2011) *The Mediatization of Memory: Media and the End of Collective Memory*, Cambridge, MA: MIT Press.

Hoskins, Andrew and O'Loughlin, Ben (2007) *Television and Terror: Conflicting Times and the Crisis of News Discourse*, Basingstoke: Palgrave.

Hoskins, Andrew and O'Loughlin, Ben (2009) 'Pre-Mediating Guilt: Radicalization and Mediality in British News', *Critical Terrorism Studies*, 2(1): 1–13.

Hoskins, Andrew and O'Loughlin, Ben (2010a) *War and Media: The Emergence of Diffused War*, Cambridge: Polity Press.

Hoskins, Andrew and O'Loughlin, Ben (2010b) 'Translating Terror: On "Gatekeeping" New Security Discourses', *International Affairs*, 86(4): 903–24

Hoskins, Andrew and O'Loughlin, Ben (forthcoming) *The New Mass*.

Howard, Michael (2008) 'Bombs Strapped to Down's Syndrome Women Kill Scores in Baghdad Markets', *Guardian*, 2 February.

Huntington, Samuel P. (1996) *The Clash of Civilizations and the Remaking of World Order*, New York: Simon & Schuster.

Isin, E.F. (2004) 'The Neurotic Citizen', *Citizenship Studies*, 8(3): 217–35.

Iyengar, Shanto and Kinder, Donald R., (1987) *News That Matters*, Chicago, IL: University of Chicago Press.

Jansen, Johannes J.G. (1986) *The Neglected Duty: The Creed of Sadat's Assassins and Islamic Resurgence in the Middle East*, New York: Macmillan.

Jarvis, L. (2009) *Times of Terror: Discourse, Temporality and the War on Terror*, Basingstoke: Palgrave Macmillan.

Juergensmeyer, Mark (2004) *Terror in the Mind of God: The Global Rise of Religious Violence*, Berkeley, CA: University of California Press.

Kagan, R. (2004) *Of Paradise and Power: America and Europe in the New World Order*, New York: Knopf.

Kelsay, John (2008) *Arguing the Just War in Islam*, Cambridge, MA: Harvard University Press.

Kepel, Gilles (2004) *Jihad: The Trail of Political Islam*, London: I.B. Tauris.

Kimmage, Daniel (2008) *The Al-Qaeda Media Nexus: The Virtual Network Behind the Global Message*, Washington: RFE/RL.

Kitzinger, Jenny (2000) 'Media Templates: Key Events and the (Re)construction of Meaning', *Media, Culture and Society*, 22(1): 61–84.

Knorr Cetina, K. (2005) 'Complex Global Microstructures: The New Terrorist Societies', *Theory, Culture and Society*, 22(5): 213–34.

Labi, Nadya (2006) 'Jihad 2.0', *The Atlantic Monthly*, 297(6), online, available at: http://www.theatlantic.com/magazine/archive/2006/07/jihad-20/4980.

Langley, P. (2008) *The Everyday Life of Global Finance: Saving and Borrowing in Anglo-America*, Oxford: Oxford University Press.

Lawrence, Bruce (ed.) (2005) *Messages to the World: The Statements of Osama Bin Laden*, London: Verso.

Lesch, David W. (ed.) (2003) *The Middle East and the United States: A Historical and Political Reassessment*, Boulder, CA: Westview Press.

Lia, Brynjar (2006) 'Al-Qaeda Online: Understanding Jihadist Internet Infrastructure', *Jane's Intelligence Review*, 1 January, online, available at; www.mil.no/multimedia/archive/00075/Al-Qaeda_online_und_75416a.pdf.

Livingstone, Sonia (2009) 'On the Mediation of Everything: ICA Presidential Address 2008', *Journal of Communication*, 59(1): 1–18.

Lynch, M (2006) 'Al-Qaeda's Media Strategies', *The National Interest*, Spring, online, available at: http://nationalinterest.org/article/al-qaedas-media-strategies-883.

McCants, Will (ed.) (2006) *CTC Militant Ideology Atlas*, West Point, NY: Combating Terrorism Center, US Military Academy, online, available at: www.ctc.usma.edu/atlas/Atlas-ResearchCompendium.pdf.

McLuhan, Marshall (1964) *Understanding Media*, London: Routledge.

McLuhan, Marshall (1978) Interview with the Italian newspaper *Il Tempo*, 19 February.

McNair, Brian (2006) *Cultural Chaos: Journalism, News and Power in a Globalised World*, London: Routledge.

Manovich, Lev (2001) *The Language of New Media*, Cambridge, MA: MIT.

Masco, Joseph (2006) *The Nuclear Borderlands: The Manhattan Project in Post Cold-War New Mexico*, Princeton, NJ: Princeton University Press.

Mirzoeff, Nicholas (2005) *Watching Babylon: The War in Iraq and Global Visual Culture*, London: Routledge.

Moss, Giles and O'Loughlin, Ben (2008) 'Convincing Claims: Representation and Democracy in Post-9/11 Britain', *Political Studies*, 56(3): 705–24.

National Coordinator for Counterterrorism (2007) *Jihadis and the Internet*, online, available at: www.investigativeproject.org/documents/testimony/226.pdf.

Nowotny, H. (1994) *Time: The Modern and Postmodern Experience*, Cambridge: Polity.

Nowotny, H. (2008) *Insatiable Curiosity: Innovation in a Fragile Future*, trans. Mitch Cohen, Cambridge, MA/London: The MIT Press.

O'Loughlin, Ben (2010) 'Images as Weapons of War? Representation, Mediation and Interpretation', *Review of International Studies*, doi: 10.1017/ S0260210510000811.

O'Loughlin, B. *et al.* (forthcoming) 'Keeping the Extraordinary at a Distance: Audience Understandings of Discourses of "Radicalisation"', *Continuum: Journal of Media and Cultural Studies*.

Oxford English Dictionary entry 'radicalization' available at: http://dictionary.oed.com/cgi/entry/50297778 [accessed 11 April 2010].

Oxford English Dictionary entry 'radical' available at: http://dictionary.oed.com/cgi/entry/50196101 [accessed 11 April 2010].

Pain, R. (2009a) 'Globalized Fear? Towards an Emotional Geopolitics', *Progress in Human Geography*, 33(4): 466–86.

Pain, R. (2009b) 'The New Geopolitics of Fear', *Geography Compass*, 4(3): 226–40.

Pew Research Center (2005) *Islamic Extremism: Common Concern for Muslim and Western Publics (Pew Global Attitudes project)*, Washington: Pew Research Center.

Pew Research Center (2009) *Confidence in Obama Lifts U.S. Image Around the World (Pew Global Attitudes project)*, Washington: Pew Research Center.

Postman, N. (1970) 'The Reformed English Curriculum', in A.C. Eurich (ed.), *High School 1980: The Shape of the Future in American Secondary Education*, New York: Pitman, pp.160–68.

Prensky, Marc (2001) 'Digital Natives, Digital Immigrants', *On the Horizon* 5(9): 1–6.

Poynting, Scott, Noble, Greg, Tabar, Paul and Collins, Jock (eds) (2004) *Bin Laden in the Suburbs: Criminalizing the Arab Other*, Sydney: Sydney Institute of Criminology.

Reid, J. (2006) 'Security, Freedom, and the Protection of our Values', speech to Demos, 9 August, online, available at: www.demos.co.uk/files/ johnreidsecurityandfreedom.pdf [accessed 18 November 2006].

Richardson, R. (ed.) (2004) *Islamophobia: Issues, Challenges and Action*, Commission on British Muslims and Islamophobia, Stoke-on-Trent: Trentham Books.

Roszak, Theodore (1968) *Making of a Counter Culture: Reflections on the Technocratic Society and Its Youthful Opposition*, Berkeley, CA: University of California Press.

Roy, Olivier (2004) *Globalized Islam: The Search for a New Ummah*, London: C. Hurst & Co.

Sageman, Marc (2004) *Understanding Terror Networks*, Philadelphia, PA: University of Pennsylvania Press.

Sageman, Marc (2008) *Leaderless Jihad: Terror Networks in the Twenty-First Century*, Philadelphia, PA: University of Pennsylvania Press.

Said, E. (1981) *Covering Islam: How the Media and the Experts Determine How We See the Rest of the World*, London: Routledge.

Sawyer, R. Keith (2005) *Social Emergence: Societies As Complex Systems*, Cambridge: Cambridge University Press.

Scannell, P. (2000) 'For-Anyone-as-Someone Structures', *Media, Culture and Society*, 22(1): 5–24.

Scheuer, Michael (2004) *Imperial Hubris*, Dulles, VA: Brasseys Inc.

Schlesinger, P. (1991) *Media, State and Nation: Political Violence and Collective Identities*, London: Sage Publications.

Schmid, Alex and De Graaf, Janny (1982) *Violence as Communication: Insurgent Terrorism and the Western News Media*, Beverly Hills, CA: Sage.

Scollon, R. and Scollon, S.W. (2004) *Nexus Analysis: Discourse and the Emerging Internet*, London: Routledge.

Shalev, A.H. and Errera, Y. (2008) 'Resilience is the Default: How Not to Miss It', in Blumenfield, M. And Ursano, R.J. (eds), *Intervention and Resilience After Mass Trauma*, Cambridge: Cambridge University Press, pp. 149–72.

Shaw, Martin (2005) *The New Western Way of War: Risk-Transfer War and its Crisis in Iraq*, Cambridge: Polity.

Silverstone, R. (2002) 'Mediating Catastrophe: September 11 and the Crisis of the Other', *Dossiers de L'Audiovisuel*, 105, online, available at: www.infoamerica.org/documentos_pdf/silverstone07.pdf.

Sonwalkar, Prasun (2004) 'New Imperialism: Contra View from the South', in Paterson, C. and Sreberny, A. (eds) *International News in the Twenty-first Century*, London: John Libbey.

Soriano, Manuel R. Torres (2008) 'Terrorism and the Mass Media after Al Qaeda: A Change of Course?', *Athena Intelligence Journal*, 1(3): 1–20.

Stevens, Tim and Neumann, Peter R. (2008) *Countering Online Radicalization: A Strategy for Action*, London: ICSR.

Stohl, Michael (1988) 'Demystifying Terrorism: The Myths and Realities of Contemporary Political Terrorism', in Stohl, M. (ed.), *The Politics of Terrorism*, New York: Marcel Dekker.

Stoker, G. (2010) 'The Rise of Political Disenchantment', in C. Hay (ed.), *New Directions in Political Science*, Basingstoke: Palgrave Macmillan, pp. 43–63.

Tatham, Steve (2006) *Losing Arab Hearts and Minds: The Coalition, Al Jazeera and Muslim Public Opinion*, London: C. Hurst & Co.

Taylor, Paul (2007) 'The Pornography of Violence and the Pornography of the Image', in Nossek, H., Sreberny, A. and Sonwalkar, P. (eds), *Media and Political Violence*, Cresskill, NJ: Hampton Press.

Telegraph, (2009) 'Terror Suspect Wins £60,000 Damages from Met Police over Assault', in The *Telegraph*, 19 March, online, available at: www.telegraph.co.uk/news/uknews/law-and-order/5012794/Terror-suspect-wins-60000-damages-from-Met-Police-over-assault.html.

Theobald, John (2004) *The Media and the Making of History*, Aldershot: Ashgate Publishing.

Ulph, S. (2005), 'A Guide to Jihad on the Web', in *Global Terrorism Analysis: Terrorism Focus*, 7(2): 5–7.

Urry, John (2005) 'The Complexity Turn', *Theory, Culture and Society*, 22(5): 1–14.

Warner, M. (2002) 'Publics and Counterpublics', *Public Culture*, 14(1): 49–90.

Weimann, Gabriel (2006) *Terror on the Internet: The New Arena, the New Challenges*, Washington, DC: United States Institute of Peace Press.

Wiktorowicz, Q. (2005) *Radical Islam Rising: Muslim Extremism in the West*, Lanham, MD: Rowman & Littlefield.

Williams, R. (1983) *Keywords: A Vocabulary of Culture and Society*, second edition, London: Fontana, pp. 251–252.

Wittgenstein, Ludwig (1967) *Philosophical Investigations*, Oxford: Blackwell.

Index